Reflecting on t
European Fran
Reference for Languages
and its *Companion Volume*

NEW PERSPECTIVES ON LANGUAGE AND EDUCATION
Founding Editor: Viv Edwards, *University of Reading, UK*
Series Editors: Phan Le Ha, *University of Hawaii at Manoa, USA* and
Joel Windle, *Monash University, Australia.*

Two decades of research and development in language and literacy
education have yielded a broad, multidisciplinary focus. Yet education
systems face constant economic and technological change, with attendant
issues of identity and power, community and culture. What are the
implications for language education of new 'semiotic economies' and
communications technologies? Of complex blendings of cultural and
linguistic diversity in communities and institutions? Of new cultural,
regional and national identities and practices? The New Perspectives
on Language and Education series will feature critical and interpretive,
disciplinary and multidisciplinary perspectives on teaching and learning,
language and literacy in new times. New proposals, particularly for edited
volumes, are expected to acknowledge and include perspectives from the
Global South. Contributions from scholars from the Global South will be
particularly sought out and welcomed, as well as those from marginalized
communities within the Global North.

All books in this series are externally peer-reviewed.

Full details of all the books in this series and of all our other publications
can be found on http://www.multilingual-matters.com, or by writing to
Multilingual Matters, St Nicholas House, 31-34 High Street, Bristol, BS1
2AW, UK.

NEW PERSPECTIVES ON LANGUAGE AND EDUCATION: 104

Reflecting on the *Common European Framework of Reference for Languages* and its *Companion Volume*

Edited by
David Little and Neus Figueras

MULTILINGUAL MATTERS
Bristol • Jackson

DOI https://doi.org/10.21832/LITTLE0190

Library of Congress Cataloging in Publication Data

A catalog record for this book is available from the Library of Congress.

Names: Little, D.G., editor. | Figueras, Neus, editor. | CEFR: Towards a
  Road Map for Future Research and Development (Conference) (2020:
  London, England)

Title: Reflecting on the Common European Framework of Reference for
  Languages and its Companion Volum/Edited by David Little and Neus
  Figueras.

Description: Bristol; Jackson: Multilingual Matters, [2022] | Series: New
  Perspectives on Language and Education: 104 | Based on conference The
  CEFR: Towards a Road Map for Future Research and Development which was
  held at St Martin-in-the-Fields, London on February 7–8, 2020. |
  Includes bibliographical references and index. | Summary: 'This book
  discusses the impact of the Common European Framework of Reference for
  Languages and its Companion Volume on curricula, teaching/learning and
  assessment in a wide range of educational contexts, identifies challenges posed by
  the Companion Volume and sheds light on areas that require further
  research and development' – Provided by publisher.

Identifiers: LCCN 2021052760 (print) | LCCN 2021052761 (ebook) | ISBN
  9781800410183 (paperback) | ISBN 9781800410190 (hardback) | ISBN
  9781800410206 (pdf) | ISBN 9781800410213 (epub)

Subjects: LCSH: Second language acquisition – Congresses. | Language and
  languages – Study and teaching – Congresses. | Common European Framework
  of Reference for Languages (Project) – Congresses | LCGFT: Conference
  papers and proceedings.

Classification: LCC P118.2 .R417 2022 (print) | LCC P118.2 (ebook) | DDC
  418.0071 – dc23/eng/20211208

LC record available at https://lccn.loc.gov/2021052760

LC ebook record available at https://lccn.loc.gov/2021052761

British Library Cataloguing in Publication Data

A catalogue entry for this book is available from the British Library.

ISBN-13: 978-1-80041-019-0 (hbk)
ISBN-13: 978-1-80041-018-3 (pbk)

Multilingual Matters
UK: St Nicholas House, 31-34 High Street, Bristol, BS1 2AW, UK.
USA: Ingram, Jackson, Tennessee, USA.

Website: www.multilingual-matters.com
Twitter: Multi_Ling_Mat
Facebook: https://www.facebook.com/multilingualmatters
Blog: www.channelviewpublications.wordpress.com

Typeset by Riverside Publishing Solutions.

Contents

Acknowledgements

The EALTA CEFR SIG is grateful to EALTA for providing financial support for the conference in which this book had its origin, to UKALTA for co-sponsoring the conference, and to the British Council for its generosity in hosting the conference.

The editors are grateful to the contributors for adhering strictly to tight deadlines in the unusual and challenging circumstances of the Covid-19 pandemic.

Contributors

Armin Berger is a Senior Lecturer and post-doctoral researcher at the Department of English and American Studies, University of Vienna, where he coordinates the English Language Competence Programme. He is also involved in teacher education and has acted as a consultant to a number of national and international language testing projects. His research on rating scale development and validation earned him the 2015 Christopher Brumfit thesis award (*Validating Analytic Rating Scales: A Multi-method Approach to Scaling Descriptors for Assessing Academic Speaking*, Peter Lang, 2015). He is currently engaged on an edited volume titled *Developing Advanced English Language Competence: A Research-informed Approach at Tertiary Level* (Springer, 2022).

Elaine Boyd has been involved in language teaching, teacher training and assessment design for a range of international organizations. She has developed courses for teacher educator training and assessment literacy and has published articles in the fields of assessment and intercultural communication as well as authoring several ELT coursebooks for various international publishers. These include *Look* (National Geographic Learning, 2019) and *Gold Experience* (Pearson, 2018). She is an associate tutor at University College London. Her research includes intercultural communication and pragmatics, and her PhD was an investigation of spoken language using corpus data. She is currently working with Lancaster University on the Trinity Lancaster Corpus of Spoken Language.

John H.A.L. de Jong is Professor Emeritus of Language Testing at VU University Amsterdam. He taught French for seven years before starting his career in language testing in 1977 at Cito. Since 2000 he has run the consultancy business Language Testing Services and has provided consultancy in language testing to national ministries of education, the World Bank, the OECD, the Council of Europe and the European Union. During his years at Pearson (2006–2016) he developed the Pearson Test of English Academic and the Global Scale of English and led Frameworks development for PISA 2015, 2018 and PISA for Development.

Bessie Dendrinos is Professor Emerita of the University of Athens (NKUA) and Director of the Research Centre for Language, Teaching, Testing and Assessment (RCeL), Department of English (www.rcel.enl. uoa.gr). She is Chair of the Board for KPG Multilingual Examination Suite (https://rcel2.enl.uoa.gr/kpg/en_index.htm) and President of the European Civil Society Platform for Multilingualism (http://ecspm.org). In 2003 she co-authored *The Hegemony of English* (Paradigm Publishers/ Routledge), which won the 2004 Critics Award of the American Educational Studies Association (AESA) and has since been translated into five languages. Her recent publications include *The Politics of Foreign Language Policies, Teaching and Testing* (Pedio Publishers, 2020), and a paper in Greek on the linguistic construction of our (anti)ecological ethos, contained in a Critical Discourse Analysis volume that appeared in 2020 (in Greek). Her current project is an edited collection entitled *Mediation in the Context of Plurilingual Education* (Routledge, 2022).

Neus Figueras coordinated the development of foreign language curricula and certificate examinations for adult language learners in the Catalan Ministry of Education in Spain for more than 20 years. She has been involved in international projects and has collaborated with the Council of Europe in the dissemination of the CEFR. She was one of the authors of the manual, *Relating Language Examinations to the Common European Framework of Reference for Languages* (Council of Europe, 2009). She is the author of 'Exploring the link between language awareness and assessment: A way forward?', in P. Garrett and J.M. Cots (eds) *Routledge Handbook of Language Awareness* (2017) and of 'Developing and using tasks for the assessment of speaking', which appeared in the Special Issue (ed. J. Grandfelt) of the *Journal of Applied Language Studies* on 'Learning, teaching and assessment of second foreign languages in school contexts' (13 (1), 2019: 133–149). Neus Figueras is currently coordinator of the EALTA CEFR SIG.

Elif Kantarcıoğlu is currently working at Bilkent University, Ankara, Turkey as Director of the English Preparatory Program. She completed her BSc and MA studies in English Language Teaching and her PhD on Language Testing. She has been involved in language assessment for more than 20 years and her areas of interest include test design, test validation, test analysis techniques, item response theory, many-facet Rasch measurement, and the CEFR. She has been the recipient of major research grants and has conducted projects for international examination bodies. She has worked as a consultant to the Turkish Ministry of Education and to the Centre for Assessment, Placement and Selection, Ankara.

Déirdre Kirwan was principal of a linguistically diverse primary school – Scoil Bhríde (Cailíní), Blanchardstown, Dublin, Ireland – from 1987 to

2015. She led the development of an integrated approach to language teaching and learning that supported the use of immigrant pupils' home languages in the classroom. She was awarded the European Language Label in 2008 and her PhD by Trinity College Dublin in 2009. She has contributed to the new Primary Language Curriculum (Ireland) and the Early Language Learning project of the European Centre for Modern Languages, Graz. She co-authored (with David Little) *Engaging with Linguistic Diversity: A Study of Educational Inclusion in an Irish Primary School* (Bloomsbury Academic, 2019).

Peter Lenz is currently working as Quality Development Officer for the Swiss Conference of Cantonal Ministers of Education, with a focus on large-scale assessments. Between 1990 and 2020 he worked as Lecturer and Senior Researcher at the University of Fribourg, Switzerland. He holds university degrees in philosophy, language and literature, and statistics. He has taught language courses and courses on linguistics, research methodology and language assessment at BA and MA level. He has been involved in a wide range of research and research-and-development projects and has commissioned evaluation studies in the fields of foreign language education and planning. He is currently President of EALTA (European Association of Language Testing and Assessment).

Constant Leung is Professor of Educational Linguistics in the School of Education, Communication and Society, King's College London. His research interests include academic literacies, additional/second language teaching and assessment, language policy, and multilingualism. He is co-editor of *Language Assessment Quarterly*, editor of research issues of *TESOL Quarterly*, and serves as a member of the editorial boards of *Language and Education* and the *Modern Language Journal*. He is a Fellow of the Academy of Social Sciences (UK). His work in developing the English as an Additional Language Assessment Framework for Schools (funded by the Bell Foundation) won the 2018 British Council ELTons International Award for Innovation.

Mark Levy is Head of English Programmes for the British Council in Spain, with responsibility for the British Council's support for the teaching and learning of English. This work is especially focused on multilingual/bilingual education programmes, and he manages the British Council's partnership with the Spanish Ministry of Education and regional governments on the national Bilingual Education Programme. He was previously an English teacher and teacher educator, working with Spanish teachers of English across Spain for many years. He has contributed articles to various journals and regularly speaks at conferences in Spain and beyond.

David Little is a Fellow Emeritus of Trinity College Dublin, Ireland. His principal research interests are the theory and practice of learner autonomy in language education, the management of linguistic diversity in schools and classrooms, and the use of the *Common European Framework of Reference for Languages* to support the design of second language curricula, teaching and assessment. He is co-author (with Leni Dam and Lienhard Legenhausen) of *Language Learner Autonomy: Theory, Practice and Research* (Multilingual Matters, 2017) and (with Déirdre Kirwan) of *Engaging with Linguistic Diversity: A Study of Educational Inclusion in an Irish Primary School* (Bloomsbury, 2019).

Margaret E. Malone is Director of the Assessment and Evaluation Language Resource Center (AELRC) and Research Professor at Georgetown University, Washington DC. She is also Director of the Center for Assessment, Research and Development at ACTFL (American Council on the Teaching of Foreign Languages). She has nearly three decades of experience in language test development; materials development; delivery of professional development and teacher training through both online and face-to-face methods; data collection and survey research; and programme evaluation. Her current research focuses on language assessment literacy, oral proficiency assessment, the influences of the Seal of Biliteracy on language teaching and learning, and the development of short-cut measures of proficiency.

Masashi Negishi is a Professor of Applied Linguistics at Tokyo University of Foreign Studies, Japan. He received his PhD from the University of Reading, UK. He has participated in a number of research projects, including national education surveys and the development of several English proficiency tests in Japan. He heads the CEFR-J Project, and his current interests include the application of the CEFR to language teaching in Japan and the development of tests based on the CEFR-J.

Brian North is a researcher and consultant to the Council of Europe. After developing the CEFR levels and descriptors, he co-authored the CEFR itself, the prototype European Language Portfolio, and the manual *Relating Language Examinations to the Common European Framework of Reference for Languages* (Council of Europe, 2009). He coordinated the CEFR *Companion Volume*. Other project involvement includes EAQUALS core inventories (English and French) and, more recently, the investigation of CEFR use in Canada and Switzerland, the alignment of the Canadian Language Benchmarks to the CEFR, and the ECML's CEFR QualiMatrix. Recent publications include *The CEFR in Practice* (Cambridge University Press, 2014), and (with Mila Angelova, Elżbieta Jarosz and Richard Rossner) *Language Course Planning* (Oxford University Press, 2018) and most recently (with

Enrica Piccardo) *The Action-oriented Approach* (Multilingual Matters, 2019).

Barry O'Sullivan is the British Council's Head of Assessment Research & Development. He has worked on numerous test development and validation projects globally and advises ministries and institutions on assessment policy and practice. He has undertaken research across many areas of language testing and assessment and has worked on the development and refinement of the socio-cognitive model of test development and validation since 2000. He is the author of more than 100 publications, which have appeared in a range of international journals, books and technical reports. He is Advisory Professor to Shanghai Jiao Tong University, and Visiting Professor at the University of Reading.

Introduction

David Little and Neus Figueras

Since its publication in 2001, the *Common European Framework of Reference for Languages* (CEFR; Council of Europe, 2001) has established itself as an indispensable reference point for all aspects of second and foreign language education. The publication of a *Companion Volume* (CEFR-CV), first in a provisional and then in its definitive version (Council of Europe, 2018, 2020), promises to reinforce its influence. Used worldwide by individuals, institutions and policymakers in different contexts with different aims and with varying degrees of rigour, the CEFR has become *de facto* an open source apparatus that is a great deal more than a collection of documents. Making systematic and effective use of the CEFR and the CEFR-CV is the responsibility of Council of Europe member states (Council of Europe, 2008; Goullier, 2007) and of language education agencies and language education professionals in Europe and beyond. Taking that responsibility seriously means exploring ways of developing research methodologies and projects of various kinds that can help to extend and further develop the CEFR and its implementation.

These considerations prompted the organization of a two-day conference entitled The CEFR: Towards a Road Map for Future Research and Development. The conference took place at St Martin-in-the-Fields in London on 7 and 8 February 2020; it was sponsored by EALTA (European Association for Language Testing and Assessment) and UKALTA (UK Association for Language Testing and Assessment) and hosted by the British Council. The organizing team comprised members of EALTA, UKALTA and the British Council: Jamie Dunlea, Neus Figueras, Vincent Folny, David Little, Barry O'Sullivan and Mina Patel. The conference was attended by 130 language education professionals from 23 countries.[1]

The first session of the conference introduced past, present and future perspectives on the CEFR. In his keynote address, David Little reminded participants of the origin, ethos and impact of the CEFR and explored the themes to be addressed in the second, third and fourth sessions: the action-oriented approach, plurilingualism and pluriculturalism, and the use of descriptors and scales in curriculum, teaching/learning and assessment. With an eye to the present and the future, Masashi Negishi described the impact of the CEFR in Japan, and Margaret E. Malone reported on the collaborative efforts of ACTFL (American Council on the Teaching of Foreign Languages) and the Council of Europe to explore the relation between the CEFR reference levels and scales and the ACTFL Proficiency Guidelines. Brian North opened up future vistas by providing a comprehensive introduction to the CEFR-CV.

The organizing team wanted the conference to take account of curricular and pedagogical issues as well as tests and other forms of assessment; to focus, in other words, on the three dimensions referred to in the second half of the CEFR's title – learning, teaching, assessment. This determined the choice of invited speakers, each of whom was asked to focus on one of these dimensions. Speakers were provided with guidance as follows.

Session 2: the action-oriented approach

Invited speakers: John H.A.L. de Jong, Mark Levy, Constant Leung

Does the CEFR-CV represent a change of paradigm as regards our understanding of the action-oriented approach? Does it make aspects of the CEFR's descriptive scheme that were already present in the 2001 version more explicit? Or does it add completely new dimensions, especially in relation to mediation? Either way, how can the new content presented in the CEFR-CV be reflected in curricula? Can it contribute to a stronger implementation of the action-oriented approach in the classroom? And what does it imply for test development?

Session 3: plurilingualism and pluriculturalism

Invited speakers: Bessie Dendrinos, Déirdre Kirwan, Peter Lenz

The first chapter of the CEFR declares the Council of Europe's commitment to a 'plurilingual approach' to language education, contrasting multilingualism – 'the knowledge of a number of languages' – with plurilingualism, 'a communicative competence to which all knowledge and experience of language contributes and in which languages interrelate and interact'. This contrast is intended to challenge the tradition of teaching and learning languages in isolation from one another.

According to the CEFR, plurilingual competence is just one component of pluricultural competence. Perhaps recognizing that this view left the CEFR open to the charge of cultural essentialism, the Council of Europe's project, 'Languages in Education, Languages for Education', abandoned 'pluricultural' in favour of 'intercultural'. The CEFR-CV nevertheless provides three scales for 'plurilingual and pluricultural competence'.

These considerations prompt the following questions: What kinds of curricula are implied by the plurilingual and pluricultural/intercultural approach? What kinds of classroom practice are apt to develop plurilingual repertoires, and how should they deal with 'culture'? And what are the implications of the plurilingual and pluricultural/intercultural approach for assessment?

Session 4: the use of descriptors and scales in curriculum, teaching/learning and assessment

Invited speakers: Elaine Boyd, Armin Berger, Elif Kantarcıoğlu

The profusion of new descriptors in the CEFR-CV (35 new scales, plus the supplementary descriptors in Appendix 9, to be added to the 54 scales in the CEFR) is evidence of the Council of Europe's aim to take the CEFR descriptors beyond the area of foreign language learning to encompass language education across the curriculum.

If CEFR descriptors are to be an 'inspiration for curriculum development and teacher education' (Council of Europe, 2018: 22), they also 'commonly act as the *de facto* framework' (Berger, 2018: 8). Thus, a lot of work lies ahead in order to identify the descriptors that are relevant in each context, explain why that is the case, and show how to incorporate them in curricula, classroom practice and assessment.

Such procedures will facilitate the localization of language programmes and assessment, but an additional effort will be required to communicate objectives and outcomes in ways that support rather than constrain comparability, avoiding a return to 'Is my B1 the same as your B1?'

The discussion at the end of each session confirmed a high level of interest in the idea of developing a CEFR road map. This book, in which the speakers at the conference expand on their oral presentations, is offered as a first step. It follows the same structure as the conference, but each part begins with a short introduction based on the relevant section of David Little's keynote presentation, and Part 5 adds a coda by Barry O'Sullivan. The book cannot claim to be a road map, not least because its chapters point in many different directions. Nonetheless, we believe that it brings together the diversity of perspectives, richness of insights and multiplicity of questions that must inform the development of such a road map.

Note

(1) A report on the conference is available on the EALTA website: https://www.ealta.eu.org/documents/EALTA_UKALTA_CEFR_report_final.pdf (accessed 1 January 2021).

References

Berger, A. (2018) What the new 'can do' descriptors can do for classroom assessment. In D. Little (ed.) *The CEFR Companion Volume with New Descriptors: Uses and Implications for Language Testing and Assessment* (pp. 8–9). Report on VIth EALTA CEFR SIG, Trinity College Dublin, 27 January. http://www.ealta.eu.org/events/Report%20on%20VIth%20EALTA%20CEFR%20SIG%20rev%2023.02.18.pdf (accessed 23 November 2020).

Council of Europe (2001) *Common European Framework of Reference for Languages: Learning, Teaching, Assessment.* Cambridge: Cambridge University Press.

Council of Europe (2008) Recommendation CM/Rec(2008)7 to member states on the use of the Council of Europe's 'Common European Framework of Reference for Languages' (CEFR) and the promotion of plurilingualism. Strasbourg: Council of Europe. https://search.coe.int/cm/Pages/result_details.aspx?ObjectId=09000016805d2fb1 (accessed 24 August 2020).

Council of Europe (2018) *Common European Framework of Reference for Languages: Learning, Teaching, Assessment. Companion Volume with New Descriptors.* Strasbourg: Council of Europe. https://rm.coe.int/cefr-companion-volume-with-new-descriptors-2018/1680787989 (accessed 1 January 2021).

Council of Europe (2020) *Common European Framework of Reference for Languages: Learning, Teaching, Assessment. Companion Volume.* Strasbourg: Council of Europe. Available at https://rm.coe.int/common-european-framework-of-reference-for-languages-learning-teaching/16809ea0d4 (accessed 21 August 2020).

Goullier, F. (2007) The *Common European Framework of Reference for Languages* (CEFR) and the development of language policies: Challenges and responsibilities. Policy Forum presentation. Strasbourg: Council of Europe. Available at https://rm.coe.int/impact-of-the-common-european-framework-of-reference-for-languages-and/16805c28c7 (accessed 20 August 2020).

Part 1: The *Common European Framework of Reference for Languages*: Past, Present and Future

Introduction to Part 1

David Little

The publication of the *Common European Framework of Reference for Languages* 20 years ago (CEFR; Council of Europe, 2001a) marked the culmination of three decades of work on foreign language teaching and learning by a succession of Council of Europe projects. To begin with, the work was carried out under the aegis of the Committee for Out-of-School Education and focused on the needs of adult learners. Traditionally, language learning had been conceived as a years-long progress from 'zero beginner' to (rarely attained) 'native-like' proficiency; the learner's progress was measured with reference to the target language system (Trim, 1984: 11). Against this tradition, the first Council of Europe modern languages project sought ways of developing programmes of limited duration that would enable learners to meet clearly defined communicative objectives. This entailed a shift of focus from language system to learner needs, from lexicogrammatical features to communicative purposes. The project's earliest products were proposals for a European unit/credit scheme of adult language learning (Trim, 1978) and *The Threshold Level* (van Ek, 1975), which specified the repertoire needed to cross the threshold into temporary membership of the target language community. The unit/credit scheme turned out to be shortlived, but *The Threshold Level*'s functional approach had a profound impact on the development of communicative approaches to language teaching and laid the foundations on which, in due course, the CEFR was built.

From the beginning, the Council of Europe's modern languages projects were informed by the organization's core values: human rights, democratic governance and the rule of law. The projects aimed to facilitate the free movement of people and ideas, to make the language learning process more democratic, and to provide a framework for international cooperation (Trim, 1984: 9). The CEFR was developed with the same goals in mind. In 1991 the Rüschlikon Symposium, 'Transparency and Coherence in Language Learning in Europe', hosted by the federal Swiss authorities, recommended that the Council of Europe should establish 'a comprehensive, coherent and transparent framework for the description of language proficiency' (Council of

Europe, 1992: 39). This task was undertaken by the project 'Language Learning for European Citizenship'. At an intergovernmental conference held in Strasbourg in 1997, the second draft of the CEFR (Council of Europe, 1996) was launched for dissemination, discussion and feedback, and over the next three years further work resulted in the version of the CEFR that was published in English and French in 2001 (Council of Europe, 2001a, 2001b).

Those who are unfamiliar with the CEFR often assume that it consists entirely of proficiency 'standards' expressed in scales of 'can do' descriptors. But to focus on the scales without engaging with their immediate and broader context is to miss a large part of their point. The CEFR's illustrative scales are embedded in detailed taxonomic descriptions of communicative language activities (CEFR, Chapter 4) and the language user/learner's competences (Chapter 5). These central chapters are preceded by a summary of the political and educational context in which the CEFR was developed (Chapter 1), an explanation of its action-oriented approach to the description of proficiency (Chapter 2) and an overview of the common reference levels on which the illustrative scales are based (Chapter 3). Chapter 6 discusses the processes of language learning and the methodological options available for language teaching, Chapter 7 considers the role of tasks in language learning and teaching, Chapter 8 explores the implications of linguistic diversification for curriculum design, and Chapter 9 focuses on the purposes and types of assessment.

In keeping with the CEFR's underlying ethos, the second half of its title puts learning before teaching and teaching before assessment. Nevertheless, over the past 20 years the CEFR's impact has been most obvious in the area of language testing. Its proficiency levels were quickly adopted by major testing agencies across Europe; in some countries, so-called reference level descriptions were developed as a way of putting language-specific flesh on the CEFR's language-neutral skeleton;[1] and the Council of Europe developed manuals for linking language tests to the CEFR (Council of Europe, 2009) and developing new language tests in conformity with the CEFR (Council of Europe, 2011a). In addition, there has been a large number of alignment projects, and additional descriptors have been developed by language-testing and other agencies in many countries in Europe and around the world.

Projects linking curricula to the CEFR's proficiency levels in a systematic and detailed way have been undertaken especially by organizations in the private and semi-state sectors; one thinks, for example, of the *Core Inventory for English* developed by EAQUALS and the British Council[2] and, on a more limited scale, Integrate Ireland Language and Training's *English Language Proficiency Benchmarks*, based on the first three proficiency levels (A1, A2, B1) of the CEFR (Integrate Ireland Language and Training, 2003a, 2003b) and used to support the educational inclusion of pupils and students from immigrant families. As regards foreign language learning in the school sector, it was widely assumed that A1 and A2 applied to lower secondary, B1 and B2 to upper secondary and C1 and C2 to tertiary education. This may help to explain why, soon after publication of the CEFR, ministries of education began to attach CEFR proficiency levels to the learning outcomes proposed in their curricula without following systematic linking procedures (see Part 4). The *First European Survey on Language Competences* (European Commission, 2012), based on the CEFR, showed that in many cases actual learning outcomes fell a long way short of the levels specified in curricula.

As for teaching and learning, the Rüschlikon Symposium recommended that 'once the Common Framework has been elaborated, there should be devised, at the European level, a common instrument allowing individuals who so desire to maintain a record of their language learning achievement and experience, formal or informal' (Council of Europe, 1992: 39). Instead of developing this common instrument, destined to become the European Language Portfolio (ELP), the Council of Europe issued Principles and Guidelines that described the ELP's structure and purposes (Council of Europe, 2011b). The ELP was to have three obligatory components: a language passport that would summarize the owner's experience of foreign language learning and use; a language biography that would provide a reflective accompaniment to learning; and a dossier in which the owner would keep evidence of learning achievement. The pedagogical function of the ELP was to promote learner autonomy, plurilingualism and intercultural awareness and competence. It was linked to the CEFR by checklists of 'I can' descriptors derived from the illustrative scales and used for the purposes of goal-setting and self-assessment.

From 1998 to 2000 versions of the ELP were developed and piloted in 15 member states of the Council of Europe, in private language schools under the auspices of EAQUALS, and in universities in various countries under the auspices of CercleS (Confédération Européenne des Centres de Langues de l'Education Supérieure) and the European Language Council (Little *et al.*, 2011: 8–10). Thereafter it was left to interested agencies and institutions to develop their own ELPs and submit them to the ELP Validation Committee in Strasbourg for validation and accreditation. By the end of 2010, when validation was replaced by registration, the committee had accredited 118 ELPs from 32 Council of Europe member states and 8 INGOs/international consortia (Little *et al.*, 2011: 10).[3] Between 2001 and 2009 some eight European seminars were organized to support ELP development and implementation.[4]

To begin with, there was a widespread expectation that the ELP would effect a transformation of language teaching and learning across Europe. Ministries of education funded projects to develop, pilot and disseminate ELPs, and the European Centre for Modern Languages in Graz funded a succession of projects designed to support ELP development and use.[5] But pilot projects came to an end, continuation funding was scarce, and several years before validation came to an end it was already difficult to find evidence of widespread ELP use. By now, the ELP is mostly history, though in some countries there are echoes of its influence in the self-assessment component of language coursebooks.

There are multiple and complex reasons for the ELP's failure to take root in Europe's education systems (Little, 2019a). Chief among them perhaps is the fact that the ELP was rarely part of an integrated and coherent reform of curricula, teaching/learning and assessment. As a consequence, in most contexts it was extraneous to established classroom practice and its checklists of 'I can' descriptors bore little discernible relation to curriculum goals. The idea of learners setting their own learning targets and assessing their own progress was alien to most education systems, the concept of interculturality was poorly understood, and the plurilingual approach to language education advocated by the CEFR (Council of Europe, 2001a: 4–5; see Part 3) was mostly overlooked. The ELP's early demise is a fair measure of the extent to which the CEFR has failed to make its mark on language education in schools, colleges and universities across Europe. It is also a measure of the need for a renewed effort following the publication of the CEFR's *Companion Volume* (CEFR-CV), first in a provisional and then in its definitive version (Council of Europe, 2018, 2020).

Since the provisional version was released in 2018, the CEFR-CV has been received with a great deal of interest, especially by associations of language education professionals. Inevitably there is a risk that existing users will discard and new users will ignore the CEFR in favour of the CEFR-CV. In doing so they will easily lose sight of the human rights basis of Council of Europe language education policy, and they will deprive themselves of the detailed taxonomic description of communicative language activities and the language user/learner's competences contained in Chapters 4 and 5 of the CEFR. If the CEFR-CV is to make a lasting impact on language curricula, teaching/learning and assessment, we must explore critically the relevance and utility of its illustrative scales – especially in relation to mediation and plurilingual/pluricultural competences – in conjunction with the CEFR's taxonomy of language use in different contexts. It has always been the Council of Europe's intention that the CEFR should be used selectively, taking account of local priorities and issues. The large number of new scales and descriptors included in the CEFR-CV means that the need for a disciplined approach to selection and localization is more urgent than ever.

Outside Europe the impact of the CEFR has nowhere been greater than in Japan, which developed its own version, CEFR-J, to guide the teaching and learning of English in Japanese schools and colleges. Chapter 1, by Masashi Negishi, provides a detailed summary of this work. As in Europe so in Japan: most interest seems to centre around levels and can-do descriptors; much less attention is paid to key concepts like the action-oriented approach, the social agency of language user/ learners, plurilingualism and pluriculturalism, and mediation. In Negishi's view more time is needed for these concepts to filter through to language learning, teaching, and assessment. At the same time, he argues that principled localization of the CEFR as exemplified in the work inspired by CEFR-J has the potential to strengthen the original framework by reflecting back local contexts and needs.

In the US the ACTFL Proficiency Guidelines perform much the same function as the CEFR does in Europe (for a detailed comparison of the two systems, see Little, 2019b). In Chapter 2, Margaret E. Malone reports on the progress of a transatlantic initiative to explore the feasibility of creating a 'crosswalk' between the ACTFL Proficiency Guidelines and the CEFR and considers possible next steps in light of the publication of the CEFR-CV and the growing importance of plurilingualism. Drawing on her experience with the ACTFL Proficiency Guidelines, Malone argues that the success of the CEFR-CV is likely to depend on a sustained effort of public education. It will be necessary, for example, to find ways of communicating the complexity of its content in relatively straightforward terms and persuading the general public that language learning is a challenging process that takes a long time.

Chapter 3, by Brian North, provides an essential point of reference for the remainder of the book. As one of the authors of the 2001 CEFR and coordinator of the project that developed the CEFR-CV, Brian North is ideally placed to outline the CEFR-CV's aims, summarize its content, explain its conceptualization of mediation, and detail the conceptual and technical achievements on which it rests.

Notes

(1) For details see the Council of Europe's CEFR website: https://www.coe.int/en/web/ common-european-framework-reference-languages/reference-level-descriptions-rlds-developed-so-far (accessed 20 August 2020).
(2) Available at https://www.eaquals.org/resources/the-core-inventory-for-general-english/ (accessed 24 August 2020).
(3) Full details of accredited and registered ELPs are provided on the Council of Europe's ELP website: https://www.coe.int/en/web/portfolio/accredited-and-registered-elp (accessed 21 August 2020).
(4) The reports on the ELP seminars are available on the Council of Europe's ELP website: https://www.coe.int/en/web/portfolio/reports (accessed 21 August 2020).
(5) Details of these projects will be found on the ECML website: https://www.ecml.at.

References

Council of Europe (1992) *Transparency and Coherence in Language Learning in Europe: Objectives, Evaluation, Certification.* Report on the Rüschlikon Symposium. Strasbourg: Council of Europe.

Council of Europe (1996) *Modern Languages: Learning, Teaching, Assessment. A Common European Framework of Reference.* Draft 2 of a Framework proposal. Strasbourg: Council of Europe.

Council of Europe (2001a) *Common European Framework of Reference for Languages: Learning, Teaching, Assessment.* Cambridge: Cambridge University Press. https://rm.coe.int/1680459f97 (accessed 20 August 2020).

Council of Europe (2001b) *Cadre européen commun de référence pour les langues: Apprendre, enseigner, évaluer.* Paris: Didier. https://rm.coe.int/16802fc3a8 (accessed 17 December 2020).

Council of Europe (2009) *Relating Language Examinations to the Common European Framework of Reference for Languages: Learning, Teaching, Assessment (CEFR): A Manual.* Strasbourg: Council of Europe. https://rm.coe.int/CoERMPublicCommonSearchServices/DisplayDCTMContent?documentId=0900001680667a2d (accessed 20 August 2020).

Council of Europe (2011a) *Manual for Language Test Development and Examining. For Use with the CEFR.* Produced by ALTE on behalf of the Language Policy Division of the Council of Europe. Strasbourg: Council of Europe. Available at https://rm.coe.int/CoERMPublicCommonSearchServices/DisplayDCTMContent?documentId=0900001680667a2b (accessed 20 August 2020).

Council of Europe (2011b) *European Language Portfolio (ELP) Principles and Guidelines, with added explanatory notes.* Strasbourg: Council of Europe. Available at https://rm.coe.int/CoERMPublicCommonSearchServices/DisplayDCTMContent?documentId=09000016804586ba (accessed 21 August 2020).

Council of Europe (2018) *Common European Framework of Reference for Languages: Learning, Teaching, Assessment. Companion Volume with New Descriptors.* Strasbourg: Council of Europe. https://rm.coe.int/cefr-companion-volume-with-new-descriptors-2018/1680787989 (accessed 17 December 2020).

Council of Europe (2020) *Common European Framework of Reference for Languages: Learning, Teaching, Assessment. Companion Volume.* Strasbourg: Council of Europe. Available at https://rm.coe.int/common-european-framework-of-reference-for-languages-learning-teaching/16809ea0d4 (accessed 21 August 2020).

European Commission (2012) *First European Survey on Language Competences.* Brussels: European Union. Available at https://op.europa.eu/en/publication-detail/-/publication/42ea89dc-373a-4d4f-aa27-9903852cd2e4/language-en/format-PDF/source-119658026 (accessed 21 August 2020).

Integrate Ireland Language and Training (2003a) *English Language Proficiency Benchmarks for non-English-speaking Pupils at Primary Level.* Dublin: Integrate Ireland Language and Training. Available at https://ncca.ie/media/2064/english_language_proficiency_benchmarks.pdf (accessed 24 August 2020).

Integrate Ireland Language and Training (2003b) *English Language Proficiency Benchmarks for non-English-speaking Students at Post-primary Level.* Dublin: Integrate Ireland Language and Training. Available at https://www.ecml.at/Portals/1/ELP_Portfolios/English%20language%20proficiency%20benchmarks%20post%20primary.pdf?ver=2019-02-11-151109-203 (accessed 24 August 2020).

Little, D. (2019a) The European Language Portfolio: Past success, present reality, future prospects. In S. Ballweg and B. Kühn (eds) *Portfolioarbeit im Kontext von Sprachenunterricht* (pp. 17–35). Göttingen: Universitätsverlag Göttingen.

Little, D. (2019b) Proficiency guidelines and frameworks. In J.W. Schwieter and A. Benati (eds) *The Cambridge Handbook of Language Learning* (pp. 550–574). Cambridge: Cambridge University Press.

Little, D., Goullier, F. and Hughes, G. (2011) *The European Language Portfolio: The Story So Far (1991–2011).* Strasbourg: Council of Europe. Available at https://rm.coe.int/CoERMPublicCommonSearchServices/DisplayDCTMContent?documentId=09000016804595a7 (accessed 21 August 2020).

Trim, J.L.M. (1978) *Some Possible Lines of Development of an Overall Structure for a European Unit/Credit Scheme for Foreign Language Learning by Adults.* Strasbourg: Council of Europe. Republished 1980 as *Developing a Unit/Credit Scheme of Adult Language Learning.* Oxford: Pergamon.

Trim, J.L.M. (1984) Chapter one: A unit scheme. In J.A. van Ek and J.L.M. Trim (eds) *Across the Threshold: Readings from the Modern Languages Projects of the Council of Europe* (pp. 11–17). Oxford: Pergamon.

van Ek, J.A. (1975) *The Threshold Level.* Strasbourg: Council of Europe.

1 The Impact of the CEFR in Japan

Masashi Negishi

This chapter presents an overview of the impact of the CEFR in Japan, which includes the development of the CEFR-J and its related resources, the start of the CEFR-J x 28 project, the alignment of various language tests and language surveys to the CEFR-J, the adoption of can-do descriptors in the Courses of Study (national curricula) for foreign languages, the use of the CEFR for Japanese language teaching, and the alignment of NHK (Nihon Hoso Kyokai) English radio and TV programmes with the CEFR. The CEFR offers transparency and coherence between curriculum, teaching and assessment of languages in Japan. However, interest seems to centre around levels and can-do descriptors, while other important concepts such as the action-oriented approach, learners as social agents, plurilingualism/pluriculturalism, and mediation tend to be overlooked. More time might be needed for these concepts to be reflected in language learning, teaching, and assessment in Japan. The use of the CEFR in Japan shows that principled localization may be able to contribute back to the original CEFR, and that hopefully this reciprocal relationship will strengthen the framework by reflecting local contexts and needs.

The Impact of the CEFR in Japan

Since its publication in 2001, the *Common European Framework of Reference for Languages* (CEFR; Council of Europe, 2001) has made a significant impact on various aspects of language learning, teaching and assessment in Europe. Initially the CEFR might not have exerted its impact as it does today. It took some years to be fully recognized across Europe; it had to be aligned to language teaching and assessment practices in concrete ways in each local context. For example, language teaching materials needed to be aligned to the CEFR as well as language tests. Tangible impacts of the CEFR came later in Japan. However, the impacts are increasing, and now the CEFR is extending its reach into layers of language teaching and assessment practices of not only English but also other languages. We will look at these impacts one by one in the sections that follow.

The development of the CEFR-J

One of the most significant impacts of the CEFR in Japan is the development of the CEFR-J, a modified version of the original CEFR to support the learning, teaching and assessment of English in Japan. As Table 1.1 shows, it is the outcome of many years of collaborative research by CEFR-J project members (Negishi *et al.*, 2013; Negishi & Tono, 2016; Tono, 2013).

Our project started in 2004; the period of our first Grant-in-Aid for Scientific Research <KAKENHI> (Kiban A) was 2004–2008. The purpose of our project during this period was to analyse how the achievement targets for English were set at each stage of school education and in business settings in Japan and to examine whether or not the target was attainable based on findings of second language acquisition research. At that time, textbooks, teaching objectives and language tests were developed independently of each other or locally aligned to each other in Japan. Different language tests had different scoring and/or grading systems and therefore their results could not be compared. Most papers presented at academic conferences in Japan claimed that the participants in their studies were 'intermediate'. However, the test results in the studies ranged widely, so 'intermediate' participants in one study were in fact at a 'basic' level in other studies. In order to resolve these issues, we carried out a number of surveys in Asia and Europe and began to notice the expanding influence of the CEFR in Europe. In the final report of our first-stage project,[1] we concluded that the use of the CEFR as a common language framework could not be overlooked.

Our research project started to evolve around the CEFR. Initially we attempted to use the CEFR as it was, but the surveys the present author undertook showed that 80% of Japanese learners of English were at A level (Negishi *et al.*, 2013). Also, it turned out that some of the descriptors were not familiar to Japanese learners of English, e.g. READING INSTRUCTIONS A2,

Table 1.1 A brief history of the CEFR-J project

2008	Launch of the CEFR-J alpha version
2012	Release of the first version of the CEFR-J
2012–2016	CEFR-J Reference Level Description Projects: Grammar Profile, Text Profile, Error Profile
2016–2020	Development of CEFR-J-based tests Alignment of local English tests with the CEFR-J
2018–2020 and beyond	Applying the CEFR-J to other languages; CEFR-J x 28 project at TUFS

*Can understand simple instructions on equipment encountered in everyday life – such as a **public telephone**.* Therefore, we decided to adapt the original CEFR to English education in Japan. First, we created a framework consisting of granular levels towards the lower end with a set of can-do descriptors. These can-do descriptors were made by adapting the original CEFR can-do descriptors and those available at the time of development in Japan. After compiling a list of can-do descriptors, we released it in 2008 as a CEFR-J alpha version.

Since then we have received four more Grants-in-Aid for Scientific Research <KAKENHI> (Kiban A; 2008–2012, 2012–2015, 2015–2020, 2020–2025).[2] After the release of the alpha version, we conducted a number of studies, the most important of which at this stage administered can-do self-assessment questionnaires to English learners from primary to tertiary education, put the can-do descriptors on a common scale, and validated the difficulty of each descriptor. Based on this research, we revised the alpha version, taking account of teachers' comments. We compiled the first version of the CEFR-J and published it in 2012. We then embarked on the CEFR-J Reference Level Description (RLD) Projects in 2012: Grammar Profile, Error Profile and Text Profile (Tono, 2013). One of the most important achievements at this stage might be the development of CVLA: CEFR-based Vocabulary Level Analyzer (ver. 1.1),[3] which is an online programme that provides the user with an estimated CEFR-J level of any input text based on four textual features (Uchida & Negishi, 2018).

The unique feature of the 2015–2020 project is the development of CEFR-J-based language tests with specifically-designed language resources, i.e. the CEFR-J wordlist, the CEFR-J Grammar Profile, and the CEFR-J Text Profile (Tono & Negishi, 2020). In 2016, we started to develop CEFR-J-based tests from the CEFR-J can-do descriptors and administered the tests to secondary school students. We checked if the difficulties of the items were ordered as we had planned.

Now these English resources created for the CEFR-J are used in preparing teaching resources for 27 other languages taught at Tokyo University of Foreign Studies (see Table 1.2). The project was named CEFR-J x 28.[4] The resources used in this project include the framework itself, a vocabulary list, CEFR-J-based tests and e-learning tools and apps – at the time of writing, the Flash Card Vocab Builder, the Can Do Sentence Builder and the Can Do Task-Based Spoken/Written Corpus Collection Tool. Tono states:

> the evaluation of our multilingual resource development based on the CEFR-J is yet to be seen, but the approach taken by the CEFR-J x 28 project is moving in a promising direction in that resource-rich languages such as English could give support to under-resourced languages [see Table 1.2] in terms of language teaching and learning contents and methods. (Tono, 2019: 16)

Table 1.2 The list of languages for the CEFR-J x 28 project

English	Japanese	German	French	Spanish
Cambodian	Russian	Chinese	Korean	Czech
Vietnamese	Thai	Urdu	Polish	Uzbek
Portuguese	Malay	Filipino	Turkish	Hindi
Mongolian	Laotian	Italian	Arabic	Persian
Indonesian	Burmese	Bengali		

Today, the CEFR-J is gaining attention both inside and outside Japan. There are four references to the CEFR-J in the CEFR *Companion Volume* (CEFR-CV). Some of the Pre-A1 descriptors developed by the CEFR-J project have been included in the CEFR-CV.

In the 2020–2025 project, the focus of our research has shifted from assessment to learning and teaching. The relevance of the key concepts proposed in the CEFR-CV, such as mediation and plurilingualism/pluriculturalism, are being discussed among the project members. At this moment, we agree that we need to clarify how those concepts change the procedure and communication in the language classroom, which I think in turn will make us explore new approaches to assessment.

The use of the CEFR for test alignment

In Japan, a number of commercial English tests are available for different purposes. Some of them are used for assessment at school and others for assessment in business settings. In recent years, the number of universities that use commercial English tests for admission purposes has been growing steadily.

The National Center Test, which is a standardized exam designed for students who are graduating or who have already graduated from upper secondary school and want to enter a university, has been replaced by a new Common Test for University Admissions from 2020 (for 2021 university entrants).[5] In this new test, the Ministry of Education, Culture, Sports, Science and Technology (MEXT) decided to assess speaking and writing for English in addition to reading and listening. After a series of discussions, the National Center for University Entrance Examinations announced that it was going to use commercial English tests for its new Common Test for University Admissions instead of developing and administering the English test on its own. Since there were a number of candidate tests on the market, they needed to be comparable with each other. Some attempts were made to compare the tests, and eventually it was decided to align them with the CEFR.

At that time, some tests had already been aligned with the CEFR, while others had not. The test developers of the latter tests carried out their alignment projects and eventually all the candidate tests came to be aligned with the CEFR (e.g. Dunlea & Matsudaira, 2009). Based on these alignment studies, MEXT produced a conversion table of the English tests.[6] People found this conversion table very useful because each university sets the CEFR level to indicate its admission standard and the candidates can use the conversion table to tell whether they can meet the requirements. It should be noted, however, that the table might have given many Japanese people a false impression that the scores for each test were interchangeable in spite of the fact that those tests had different test designs with different purposes. However, the plan to use commercial English tests as a part of the Common Test for University Admissions was suspended at the last moment in November 2019. It is worth mentioning that, notwithstanding this sudden suspension, the existence of the CEFR itself became more widely known in Japan.

The use of the CEFR for national surveys

As shown above, based on a couple of surveys that the present author carried out, it was predicted that 80% of Japanese learners of English would be at level A. However, it should be borne in mind that the samples in those surveys were not necessarily representative of the Japanese population. In this respect, it is very meaningful for MEXT to administer CEFR-aligned English proficiency tests to lower and upper secondary school students. The English Proficiency Survey for the Improvement of English Education was conducted annually between 2014 and 2017.[7] The tests used in the survey measured all four skills and the test results were aligned with the CEFR. In objectives and design this survey is quite similar to the *First European Survey on Language Competences* (European Commission, 2012).

The results were rather shocking to Japanese teachers, researchers, and policymakers. The first survey, in 2014, indicated that about 75% of third-year upper secondary school students were at A1 level in reading and listening, while about 85% of them were at A1 level in writing and speaking. In the 2017 survey, there was substantial improvement in writing and speaking, with about half the students above A1 in writing and about 35% above A1 in speaking, while there was only slight improvement in reading and listening. These survey results are presumed to have contributed to the setting of the attainment targets of secondary education by MEXT. The Third Basic Plan for the Promotion of Education[8] defines a measurement indicator as follows:

> Achieve the percentage [50%] of lower and upper secondary school students whose English ability is equivalent to or higher than A1 level of CEFR when they graduate from lower secondary schools, and equivalent to or higher than A2 level of CEFR when they graduate from upper secondary schools

Before the surveys were conducted, some people wanted to have more ambitious targets, like C1, but when the survey results came out, people realized that they needed to set more realistic and attainable targets by lowering the target levels.

The setting of can-do based teaching objectives in the Courses of Study

Another impact would be the adoption of can-do descriptors for the Courses of Study for primary and secondary schools. MEXT determines 'the Courses of Study as broad standards for all schools, from kindergarten through upper secondary schools, to organize their programs in order to ensure a fixed standard of education throughout the country'.[9] The new Course of Study for primary schools was released in 2017 and that for secondary schools in 2018. In the previous Courses of Study, although the general teaching objectives were presented in a kind of can-do form, nouns were used to express the contents of language activities. In the new Courses of Study, the teaching objectives are presented in the form of can-do descriptors. Strictly speaking, however, those in the new Courses of Study do not adopt the form of standard can-do descriptors: instead they use the form 'to enable (students) to do ...'. The subject of the descriptors is the teacher, although this is not specified explicitly (see Table 1.3).

The objectives consist of five categories: listening, reading, spoken interaction, spoken production and writing, following the CEFR's Common Reference Levels: Self-assessment Grid (Council of Europe, 2001: 26–27).

The new Courses of Study are expected to have a substantial impact on teaching and assessment in primary and secondary schools in Japan. However, it should be noted that transparent teaching objectives do not guarantee fundamental changes in teaching practice. This is where the authorized textbooks come in: they present English teachers with concrete examples of classroom tasks suggested by the Courses of Study. Without authorized textbooks, it would not be easy to adopt a can-do based action-oriented approach in the classroom because not many teachers are familiar with the approach.

Table 1.3 Examples of can-do descriptors from the new Course of Study for lower secondary schools

1. Listening

   A: Enable (students) to catch necessary information about everyday topics if spoken clearly.

   B: Enable (students) to get the gist of a talk on everyday topics if spoken clearly.

   C: Enable (students) to catch the main point of a brief explanation of a social topic if spoken clearly.

The use of the CEFR for Japanese language teaching

As the number of learners of Japanese increases at home and abroad, so Japanese proficiency tests have been mushrooming in recent years. The FY 2018 Comprehensive Survey on Japanese Language Education[10] shows that at least 16 tests of Japanese as a second or foreign language are used in Japan and elsewhere. However, the structures and proficiency ranges measured by these tests vary greatly. For example, some of the tests measure only receptive skills, while others measure the four skills, and some focus on speaking. The tests were developed independently of each other, and their relationships are not known to their users. Some of the tests claim that they are aligned with the CEFR, but generally the procedures used in the alignment are not open to the public. Therefore, the Agency for Cultural Affairs, which is responsible for Japanese language teaching inside and outside Japan, proposes to use the CEFR as a common framework of reference for Japanese language teaching. They launched their project in 2019, and at the time of writing it is still in progress. The framework the Agency is developing now is tentatively referred to as the Common Framework of Reference for Japanese. This framework 'is expected to contribute to the realization of a symbiotic society by improving the quality of Japanese language education at home and abroad'.[11] Basically, all the important features in the CEFR are included in this framework, although mediation and online communication have not yet been fully adopted.

The use of the CEFR for radio and TV English programmes

A national television station in Japan (Nihon Hoso Kyokai or NHK) has been broadcasting radio and TV language programmes since the first English radio programme in 1925, with an intermission during the wartime period. The languages covered by NHK comprise English, Chinese, Korean, Italian, German, French, Spanish, Russian, Arabic and Portuguese, as of 2020. Today there are as many as 11 English radio programmes. Although the levels of the programmes were indicated with numbers (e.g. 1, 2, 3) or labels (e.g. 'introductory', 'advanced'), the relationship between them was not very clear. Therefore, NHK attempted to align all radio and TV language programmes with the CEFR levels. Initially all language programmes were labelled using the CEFR levels (Tono & Negishi, 2012), but eventually NHK gave up the labelling except for English, probably because the other languages have a limited number of programmes – perhaps just one or two for each language – which means that an individual programme covers a wide range of levels. Right now, NHK provides listeners and viewers with a chart that shows a clear relationship between the English radio and TV programmes along with can-do descriptors for each level.[12]

The Impact of the CEFR *Companion Volume* in Japan

As of October 2020, six months have passed since the publication of the *Common European Framework of Reference for Languages: Learning, Teaching, Assessment. Companion Volume* (CEFR-CV; Council of Europe, 2020), which is the product of a large-scale project. The Council of Europe website states:

> It [the CEFR-CV] presents the key aspects of the CEFR for teaching and learning in a user-friendly form and contains the complete set of extended CEFR descriptors, replacing the 2001 set. These now include descriptors for mediation, online interaction, plurilingual/pluricultural competence, and sign language competences.[13]

The changes to the illustrative descriptors in the CEFR-CV are summarized in a table (Council of Europe, 2020: 24–25).

The CEFR-CV is beginning to attract the attention of researchers in Japan, but probably not of practitioners. Again, interest seems to centre around levels. Pre-A1 and the concept of plus levels (introduced to Japan via the CEFR-J before the launch of CEFR-CV) were not particularly new to Japanese teachers and researchers. The levels of the CEFR-J consist of Pre-A1, A1.1, A1.2, A1.3, A2.1, A2.2, B1.1, B1.2, B2.1, B2.2, C1 and C2. The CEFR-J project team has replaced the phrase 'native speakers' in some of their can-do descriptors with 'speakers of the language', following the change made in CEFR-CV.

A closer look at the document, however, reveals the importance of other changes. For example, online interaction will assume major significance in an era of ever-increasing electronic communication. Especially, the concept of online written interaction gives us a wider perspective on the definition of writing ability. Online written interaction is fundamentally different from conventional writing by hand and word-processing in a number of ways. Performances observed in online written interaction are affected greatly by various help functions for input, such as the 'spell check' function.

In the case of Japanese, online written interaction with a smartphone is a matter of speaking into the machine: candidate letters appear on the screen and all you have to do is choose the ones you need. Modern Japanese is written in a mixture of three main systems: kanji (Chinese characters) and two syllabaries, hiragana and katakana. Generally, learners of Japanese from non-kanji areas are likely to have great difficulty writing Japanese texts with kanji. In this sense, Japanese online writing will open doors for the wider definition of 'writing' proficiency because, with modern technology, if you can talk and read, you can write. This may well be the case with other languages as well.

Another important change would be the creation of descriptors for mediation and the strengthening of the concept of plurilingual and pluricultural competence. These ideas should be very meaningful in Japan as well. However, discussion regarding these issues has only just started, and so far is limited to researchers. More time will be needed for them to make an impact on Japanese language classrooms.

Issues Regarding the Use of the CEFR in Japan

The greatest advantage of the CEFR is in providing us with a broad and coherent framework for language learning, teaching, and assessment for languages learnt and taught in Japan. The CEFR enables us to relate our language teaching in different contexts to a common framework, and the framework sheds light on the trajectory of language learning. Along this pathway, learners and teachers come across various textbooks and tests. The CEFR functions as a language learning GPS. With this tool, we can get access to and utilize a large number of resources designed to support the use of the CEFR inside and outside Japan, e.g. the Council of Europe website,[14] the English Profile website,[15] the CEFR-J website,[16] etc. Had we developed our framework independently of the CEFR, we would have had to develop all the necessary supports from scratch, and studies conducted on the CEFR might have had little relevance for us.

However, along with these positive influences comes a number of potential problems. One might be that people's interest still centres around the levels. CEFR levels are in fact a double-edged sword. As the CEFR-CV states: 'the existence of fixed points of common reference offers transparency and coherence, a tool for future planning and a basis for further development' (Council of Europe, 2020: 175). At the same time, however, the CEFR-CV gives us a clear warning regarding levels:

> Levels are a necessary simplification. We need levels in order to organise learning, to track progress and to answer questions like 'How good is your French?' or 'What proficiency should we require from candidates?' However, any simple answer like B2 – or even B2 receptive, B1 productive – hides a complex profile. The reason the CEFR includes so many descriptor scales is to encourage users to develop differentiated profiles. Descriptor scales can be used firstly to identify which language activities are relevant for a particular group of learners and, secondly, to establish which level those learners need to achieve in those activities in order to accomplish their goals. (Council of Europe, 2020: 38)

In relation to this, the fact that the method of determining the level differs depending on the test provider makes the matter even more complicated. Some test providers use average test scores, others the minimum requirement for a level, and some use a combination of levels. So there is a possibility of the same test results leading to different overall levels depending on the methods used.

Another problem might be that people tend not to pay due attention to important concepts of the CEFR other than the levels. Such concepts include the action-oriented approach and learners as social agents. What is happening in Japan seems to be that textbooks and tests that are not necessarily based on the action-oriented approach, and hence in which learners and test-takers are not seen as social agents, claim that they are aligned with the CEFR. Generally, their claim is based on the judgement of the linguistic difficulty of the materials and/or test items used in their products.

Another potential problem is test providers claiming that their tests are aligned to the CEFR without having followed the proper procedure. The CEFR-CV states:

> the Council of Europe's Language Policy Division has published a manual for relating language examinations to the CEFR [Council of Europe, 2009], now accompanied by a toolkit of accompanying material and a volume of case studies published by Cambridge University Press, together with a manual for language test development and examining [Council of Europe, 2011]. The Council of Europe's ECML has also produced *Relating language examinations to the Common European Framework of Reference for Languages: Learning, teaching, assessment (CEFR) – Highlights from the Manual* [Noijons et al., 2011] and provides capacity building to member states through its RELANG initiative. (Council of Europe, 2020: 29)

So documents for aligning examinations with the CEFR are available to test developers. However, the technical requirements of these documents may be daunting for some institutions; for example, statisticians familiar with test alignment methods may not be readily available.

As the CEFR-CV points out: 'there is no body monitoring or even coordinating [the CEFR's] use' (Council of Europe, 2020: 29). People worried about a rather chaotic situation in Japan, however, want to have some kind of monitoring institution to validate claims of test alignment and test quality.

Conclusion

Since its publication in 2001, the CEFR has impacted in many different ways on language learning, teaching and assessment in Japan. However, the impacts appear to centre around levels and can-do descriptors; the impact of other aspects of the CEFR remains to be seen.

Compared with the CEFR, the impact of the CEFR CV in Japan has so far been limited. This is presumably because, at the time of writing, only six months have passed since the publication of the CEFR-CV, and two years since that of the provisional version in 2018. The introduction of Pre-A1 and the strengthening of the description of 'plus' levels might not have been particularly new to Japanese teachers and researchers because they were already familiar with them via the

CEFR-J. However, it should be noted that there are other changes made in the CEFR-CV, which may have an impact in the future, e.g. the concept of online interaction, the creation of descriptors for mediation, and the strengthening of the concepts of plurilingual and pluricultural competence. More time may be needed, however, for these concepts to be reflected in classroom practice.

As the CEFR-CV clearly states: 'It [the CEFR] aims to facilitate transparency and coherence between the curriculum, teaching and assessment within an institution and transparency and coherence between institutions, educational sectors, regions and countries' (Council of Europe, 2020: 27). This is the case in Japan as well. However, there are a number of problems regarding the use of the CEFR. One of them is that people's attention seems to centre around levels, and they often forget the core concepts of the CEFR, such as its action-oriented approach and learners as social agents. Test alignment with the CEFR might be another problem because of the technicality of the alignment methods suggested in the Council of Europe's documents. In order to promote a valid use of the CEFR in Japan, it remains to be seen whether we need some kind of monitoring institution or not.

The impact of the CEFR is spreading across Europe and beyond, and the framework is used in different contexts for different purposes. This accords with the findings of Runnels and Runnels (2017). At a glance, the impact seems unidirectional, i.e. from Strasbourg to all corners of the world. However, the impact may in fact be reciprocal. Principled localization may be able to contribute to the further development of the CEFR. Such a contribution will make the CEFR grow further and possibly strengthen it in the long run, enabling it to respond more adequately to local contexts and needs.

Notes

(1)   The report (in Japanese) is available at http://www.cefr-j.org/PDF/KoikeKaken 16202010_FinalReport.pdf (accessed 25 November 2020).

(2)   For reports (in Japanese) go to http://www.cefr-j.org/research.html#reports (accessed 25 November 2020).

(3)   Available at http://dd.kyushu-u.ac.jp/~uchida/cvla.html (accessed 25 November 2020).

(4)   For details (in Japanese) go to: https://tufs-sgu.com/cefr-jx28/ (accessed 25 November 2020).

(5)   For further information go to: https://www.nicjp.niad.ac.jp/en/japanese-system/ admission.html (accessed 25 November 2020).

(6)   The conversion table is available at https://www.mext.go.jp/a_menu/koutou/koudai/ detail/__icsFiles/afieldfile/2019/09/25/1420500_3_2.pdf (accessed 25 November 2020).

(7)   The results of the survey (in Japanese) are available at https://www.mext.go.jp/a_ menu/kokusai/gaikokugo/index.htm (accessed 25 November 2020).

(8)   For further information go to https://www.mext.go.jp/en/policy/education/lawand-plan/title01/detail01/1373799.html (accessed 25 November 2020).

(9)   For further information go to https://www.mext.go.jp/en/policy/education/elsec/ title02/detail02/1373859.htm (accessed 25 November 2020).

(10)   The results of the survey (in Japanese) are available at https://www.bunka.go.jp/ tokei_hakusho_shuppan/tokeichosa/nihongokyoiku_sogo/pdf/r1393077_01.pdf (accessed 25 November 2020).

(11)   Available (in Japanese) at https://www.bunka.go.jp/seisaku/bunkashingikai/kokugo/ hokoku/pdf/92664201_01.pdf (accessed 25 November 2020).

(12)   Available (in Japanese) at https://eigoryoku.nhk-book.co.jp/cefr (accessed 25 November 2020).

(13)   https://www.coe.int/en/web/common-european-framework-reference-languages (accessed 25 November 2020).

(14)   https://www.coe.int/en/web/common-european-framework-reference-languages (accessed 25 November 2020).

(15)   https://www.englishprofile.org/ (accessed 25 November 2020).

(16)   http://cefr-j.org/ (accessed 25 November 2020).

References

Council of Europe (2001) *Common European Framework of Reference for Languages: Learning, Teaching, Assessment*. Cambridge: Cambridge University Press.

Council of Europe (2009) *Relating Language Examinations to the Common European Framework of Reference for Languages: Learning, Teaching, Assessment (CEFR). A Manual*. Strasbourg: Council of Europe.

Council of Europe (2011) *Manual for Language Test Development and Examining*. Strasbourg: Council of Europe.

Council of Europe (2020) *Common European Framework of Reference for Languages: Learning, Teaching, Assessment. Companion Volume*. Strasbourg: Council of Europe. https://rm.coe.int/common-european-framework-of-reference-for-languages-learning-teaching/16809ea0d4 (accessed 7 October 2020).

Dunlea, J., and Matsudaira, T. (2009) Investigating the relationship between the EIKEN tests and the CEFR. In N. Figueras and J. Noijons (eds) *Linking to the CEFR Levels: Research Perspectives* (pp. 103–110). Arnhem: Cito, Council of Europe and EALTA. http://www.ealta. eu.org/documents/resources/Research_Colloquium_report.pdf (accessed 7 October 2020).

European Commission (2012) *First European Survey on Language Competences*. Brussels: European Commission. https://op.europa.eu/en/publication-detail/-/publication/ 42ea89dc-373a-4d4f-aa27-9903852cd2e4/language-en/format-PDF/source-119658026 (accessed 7 October 2020).

Negishi, M. and Tono, Y. (2016) An update on the CEFR-J project and its impact on English language education in Japan. In C. Docherty and F. Barker (eds) *Language Assessment for Multilingualism, Proceedings of the ALTE Paris Conference, April 2014* (pp. 113–133). Cambridge: Cambridge University Press.

Negishi, M, Takada, T. and Tono, Y. (2013) A progress report on the development of the CEFR-J. In E.D. Galaczi and C.J. Weir (eds) *Exploring Language Frameworks: Proceedings of the ALTE Kraków Conference, July 2001* (pp. 135–163). Cambridge: Cambridge University Press.

Noijons, J., Bérešová, J., Breton, G. and Szabó, G. (eds) (2011) *Relating Language Examinations to the Common European Framework of Reference for Languages: Learning, Teaching, Assessment (CEFR). Highlights from the Manual*. Graz: European Centre for Modern Languages and Strasbourg: Council of Europe. https:// www.ecml.at/Portals/1/documents/ECML-resources/2011_10_10_relex._E_web. pdf?ver=2018-03-21-100940-823 (accessed 7 October 2020).

Runnels, J. and Runnels, V. (2017) Impact of the Common European Framework of Reference – A bibliometric analysis of research from 1990–2017. *CEFR Journal – Research and Practice*, 18–32. https://cefrjapan.net/images/PDF/Newsletter/CEFR-1-1-art2_JRunnels_VRunnels.pdf (accessed 7 October 2020).

Tono, Y. (ed.) (2013) *The CEFR-J Handbook*. Tokyo: Taishukan Shoten.

Tono, Y. (2019) Coming full circle – From CEFR to CEFR-J and back. *CEFR Journal – Research and Practice*, 2–17. https://cefrjapan.net/images/PDF/Newsletter/CEFR-1-1-art1_YTono.pdf (accessed 7 October 2020).

Tono, Y. and Negishi, M. (2012) The CEFR-J: Adapting the CEFR for English language teaching in Japan. *Framework & Language Portfolio SIG Newsletter* (Japan Association for Language Teaching) 8, 5–12.

Tono, Y. and Negishi, M. (eds) (2020) *The CEFR-J Resource Book*. Tokyo: Taishukan Shoten.

Uchida, S. and Negishi, M. (2018) Assigning CEFR-J levels to English texts based on textual features. In Y. Tono and H. Isahara (eds) *Proceedings of the 4th Asia Pacific Corpus Linguistics Conference (APCLC 2018)* (pp. 463–467). https://apcla.net/conf.html (accessed 7 October 2020).

2 ACTFL and CEFR: Relationships, Influences and Looking Forward

Margaret E. Malone

In 2010, ACTFL (American Council for the Teaching of Foreign Languages) and colleagues from across Europe launched an international initiative to expand understanding of the two most commonly used proficiency and assessment systems: the ACTFL Proficiency Guidelines and the Common European Framework of Reference for Languages. *The initiative resulted in several in-person meetings of language proficiency assessment and curriculum experts from two continents, as well as a variety of research projects and publications. This chapter explores the history of the relationship, the resulting publications and connections, and suggests next steps for continuation with close attention to the role of plurilingualism in both contexts.*

Introduction

Standards-based teaching and assessment allows learners and instructors to understand the purposes and goals of a programme. National and international standards, especially when linked to reliable and valid assessments, allow for mutual communication and understanding across learners, teachers, schools, programmes and countries. There are several commonly used standards and assessments employed across the world, including the Interagency Language Roundtable (ILR) Scale, used in US government agencies; the Bureau for International Language Coordination's (BILC) Standardized Agreement (STANAG 6001), a proficiency scale implemented across NATO-serving countries that allows for comparison of proficiency across languages, agencies and countries; the ACTFL Proficiency Guidelines (ACTFL, 2012), a set of criteria that describe what language users can do with language specific to listening, speaking, reading and writing; and the *Common European Framework of Reference for Languages* (CEFR; Council of Europe, 2001), which provides a shared way to describe language teaching and learning, as well as assessment, primarily across Europe. The ILR scale, developed by the US Foreign Service Institute in the 1950s and adapted for a variety of US government agencies, is considered the original and has informed the development of subsequent standards-based language teaching, learning and assessment efforts (Cox *et al.*, 2018). Because both the ILR and STANAG are used primarily in governmental and military contexts, the tests and instructional methods related to them are generally unavailable to the public. Therefore, the CEFR and ACTFL Guidelines are most commonly used in teaching and learning environments, and the majority of non-governmental collaboration in the US, Europe and even beyond focuses on these systems. However, although governments and the military can mandate cooperation, crosswalk and comparisons across systems, universities, employers and schools generally do not. Thus, the incentive for cooperation must be self-motivated rather than imposed.

Shared standards are critical to establishing, maintaining and improving language teaching and learning. However, one issue that frequently arises is the comparison of systems across countries or world regions. When US students come to Europe for study-abroad programmes, they may find their course outcomes and proficiency being aligned to those of the CEFR and return home confused by their results or, worse yet, unable to generalize the language results they gained in Europe to a US context. European students face a similar issue when studying in the US. Of equal importance is the comparability of the two systems when seeking employment based on such results. Thus, being able to compare the two systems in a valid and reliable way is important for encouraging language teaching and learning, as well as for communicating the results of such efforts, internationally.

Background

In June 2010, ACTFL, in collaboration with TestDaf, the University of Leipzig, Cambridge English and other European language-testing scholars, convened a three-day meeting in Leipzig, Germany. The meeting included several plenary presentations by prominent language and language-testing scholars proficient in one or both systems or in language testing in general. The focus of the meeting was to find ways to establish a crosswalk between the two systems. Some of the issues that arose included the major differences between the two systems as well as how to talk through these differences in a way that allows for common understanding.

When examining ways to align the scales, Lowe (2012), Chapelle (2012), Luoma, (2004) and others have highlighted the many basic theoretical differences that underpin each of the two systems and the limitations of an alignment approach rather than a crosswalk. Whereas alignments between two systems generally highlight the similarities to produce a simple 1:1 comparison of scores, crosswalks serve not only to show how ratings and scores are linked but also how the systems and thus the ratings and scores are different (Luoma, 2004). As mentioned earlier, one outcome of the meetings was an acceptance of some of the fundamental differences between the two systems and the challenge of finding efficient and accurate ways to show how scores on one system can be compared with scores on the other. Therefore, it was decided to pursue a crosswalk, which would demonstrate respect for the underlying constructs of each system, rather than a straightforward alignment, which, while more straightforward, would fail to acknowledge important aspects of each system.

Perhaps the most important outcome – in addition to bringing together developers of the ACTFL Guidelines, the CEFR and the related tests, as well as psychometricians and language testers – was an increased understanding of the differences between the perception of how the two scales are used. Most American participants consider the ACTFL Guidelines a proficiency scale that helps inform language teaching, learning and testing and encourages a proficiency focus. The contrast is clear with the perception of the CEFR as a framework or system to guide and develop language teaching and learning. In other words, even the names used to describe them – guidelines versus framework – suggest that, although the two are used for some overlapping purposes, they were developed with different aims in mind. Namely, the ACTFL Guidelines, adapted from the ILR scale, have assessment as their focus, or 'an instrument for the evaluation of functional language ability',[1] while the CEFR, although modelled in part on the ACTFL Guidelines and ILR,

> was designed to provide a transparent, coherent and comprehensive basis for the elaboration of language syllabuses and curriculum guidelines, the design of teaching and learning materials, and the assessment of foreign language proficiency.[2]

Thus, the ACTFL–CEFR collaboration began with a focus on the inherent cultural difference and priorities of the foci of the two systems. During the first days of the meeting, participants familiar with one system participated in an orientation to the other, which resulted in many questions, queries and discussions. At one point the group even asked if a crosswalk was possible. However, discussion continued, and the participants formed professional working groups to pursue several research areas to crosswalk the two systems.

In considering the first and subsequent meetings from a standpoint of problem solving and dispute resolution, it is possible to map the discussion onto Moore's (1986) triangle of satisfaction *vis-à-vis* conflict resolution. If the conflict in this case was about creating a crosswalk between two systems with some overlapping and some conflicting uses and purposes, then the group needed to focus on Moore's three areas of interest to solve the problem, or, in this case, to reach a solution in providing a crosswalk. Moore (1986) identifies process, substance and relationship as the interests that need to be satisfied to reach a solution. In this case, the process was convening meetings to discuss the issue and to include regular check-ins with research programmes. The relationship or emotional interest was to develop cordial, professional interactions among developers and primary users of the two systems as well as with psychometricians and language testers. Finally, the substance was to understand the two systems, within the contexts in which they are used, and to pursue ways to crosswalk the two systems. By meeting the criteria of the three aspects of the triangle of satisfaction, the group not only produced results but also developed ongoing connections for future work on both sides of the Atlantic.

To continue the work begun in 2010, a follow-up meeting was held during August 2011 in Provo, Utah. This second meeting included 43 participants, featured two plenaries and eight presentations and added US-based language-testing and psychometrics experts who had not travelled to Leipzig the previous year. The topics of the presentations allowed the group to dig more deeply into the logistical and theoretical challenges of crosswalking the two systems. To address some of these challenges through an authentic activity, the organizing group developed a benchmarking activity for the participants to experience together. In four groups (each focusing on speaking, reading, writing or listening), participants rated samples, reading texts or listening passages according to either ACTFL or CEFR descriptors. This activity not only allowed increased understanding of the two systems as they are used in assessment, but also resulted in a study that explored the correspondence among ratings. Of equal importance, participants experienced with each system were able not only to learn about but also to practise using a system in collaboration with other experts. Moore (1986) would likely suggest that, by putting the focus on both substance (rating using the two scales) and process (determining how to rate using the two scales), the group moved forward both intellectually and procedurally. Thus, the research efforts begun in 2010 were cemented, while new ones were initiated.

A third meeting marked the beginning of a formal agreement between European and US-based language assessment systems. Held in Graz, Austria, in June 2012, at the European Centre for Modern Languages (ECML) of the Council of Europe, the group expanded beyond the previous efforts at establishing relationships and understanding the systems. The first outcome of the meeting was the establishment of a formal, signed relationship between ACTFL and the ECML. The second outcome was a discussion of the research conducted to date and a plan to publish a volume of research focused on issues of correspondence between the CEFR and ACTFL systems. Finally, the group was able to review the report of the first European Survey on Language Competences, a comprehensive, multi-country study of students' proficiency in their first and second foreign languages at the end of compulsory schooling.

A final meeting was held in Alexandria, Virginia (near ACTFL headquarters) in June 2013. At that point, great strides had been made, and some group members were pursuing together and individually different research projects to further the work. Thus, no further meetings were held until February 2020, when ACTFL, participating in an EALTA/UKALTA meeting on the CEFR and the CEFR *Companion Volume* (CEFR-CV), hosted by the British Council, suggested reviving and repositioning the group to focus on language assessment literacy to provide support for stakeholders, especially students, to understand the two systems, their purposes and how to navigate the two successfully.

Outcomes

The outcomes, both tangible and intangible, from the multi-country initiative, have been substantial. Publications include a volume edited by Erwin Tschirner, with 13 chapters each focusing on a different issue in establishing a CEFR/ACTFL crosswalk and exploring how to tackle each challenge (Tschirner, 2012). In addition, a few peer-refereed journal articles have been published (including Tschirner, 2013; Tschirner *et al.*, 2012) and have contributed to heightened awareness of the two systems beyond their traditional borders of the US and Europe. Several technical reports have been published to detail specific crosswalks between tests (Bärenfänger & Tschirner, 2012; Tschirner & Bärenfänger, 2013a, 2013b, 2015; Tschirner *et al.*, 2015). In addition, ACTFL, in cooperation with two German researchers, has published a correspondence between ACTFL assessments and CEFR ratings.[3] The publication of this correspondence means that test takers can receive a CEFR score on some of ACTFL's listening and reading assessments. This accommodation means that students can literally translate their ratings from one system to another, thus making results on these tests more relevant for the European language learner who has studied in the US or taken an ACTFL test.

A second outcome was ACTFL's agreement with ECML. From 2012 until the pandemic, ACTFL sent at least one representative to the annual meeting of ECML's Professional Network Forum. The meeting, attended by ECML partners from across Europe as well as Canada, was expanded to include ACTFL as a non-voting US member. Thus, an ACTFL representative was able to participate in these meetings to stay abreast of language testing and teaching issues in Europe. In addition to maintaining and further expanding relationships, ACTFL contributed to the ECML's position statements on the value of international education. In turn, the ECML is regularly represented at the ACTFL Convention via presentations and an annual meeting to discuss CEFR/ACTFL projects. By meeting on both sides of the Atlantic, awareness of new and ongoing efforts and collaborations beyond the original group can occur.

The third outcome has been continued formal and informal relationships, efforts, research and invitations from both sides of the Atlantic. For example, being invited to the February 2020 conference as one of the few US-based researchers shows that ACTFL has made inroads not only in providing information and data on US-based systems but has also shown a willingness to listen, learn and collaborate with our colleagues who use the CEFR.

Lessons Learned

The process is not over and there is still a great deal of work and mutual effort needed to advance the progress we have made. One success of the project was an improved understanding of the similarities between the two systems and an appreciation for the rigour, thoughtfulness, research and consensus-building inherent in developing, maintaining and constantly improving the two systems. In addition to the research and relationships described above, the release of a correlation between the CEFR and TOEFL scores[4] has allowed for more robust research and comparison for test developers, graduate students and other researchers when trying to compare and provide correspondences between two systems that were previously unaligned. It is also important to note that most of the crosswalking efforts between the two systems have been conducted by a small group in one or two languages rather than across languages and organizations.

One important lesson learned was the amount of time and effort it takes to build a community around such systems and to develop and execute studies that contribute to a valid crosswalk. By engaging in a multiple-years process, there was time to truly engage both with content and colleagues. As a result, the similarities and differences between the systems emerged; in addition to foci on substantive differences, participants were able to discuss shared challenges, such as frequent misunderstanding among stakeholders about the meaning of and uses for both systems.

The CEFR *Companion Volume*

The newly released CEFR *Companion Volume* (CEFR-CV; Council of Europe, 2020) has expanded the previous focus to include mediation or the negotiation of meaning, either within one language or across languages As stated in the CEFR: 'Mediation language activities – (re)-processing an existing text – occupy an important place in the normal linguistic functioning of our societies' (Council of Europe, 2001: 14). The ACTFL Guidelines, which refer to circumlocution and negotiation of meaning, and professional development related to the ACTFL Guidelines, as well as rater readiness for the speaking and writing tests, address in detail whether and how mediation occurs at different levels of proficiency. Consistent with previously addressed differences in the two systems, the ACTFL Guidelines and the CEFR address mediation differently. The CEFR-CV separates mediation from receptive and productive skills. By contrast, the ACTFL Guidelines incorporate many aspects of mediation within specific proficiency levels within a domain.

By focusing on mediation and thus negotiation of meaning, those working with the ACTFL Guidelines and the CEFR can explore additional areas of overlap. After all, words alone do not assure communication: it is the interaction between language and behaviour that leads to understanding (or misunderstanding) and is critical to successful transmission of ideas. As mediation is further defined and explored in context, there may be ways that ACTFL-influenced systems can both benefit from and support the emphasis on mediation. For example, by addressing mediation both monolingually and plurilingually, the CEFR-CV tackles how negotiation of meaning occurs in real life, when speakers either share or do not share more than one common language.

Ongoing Challenges

Despite early and ongoing successes, challenges remain. First, a clear, unambiguous crosswalk between the two systems remains elusive and likely unrealistic. The two systems remain fundamentally and philosophically different; the ACTFL Guidelines' primary focus is language proficiency assessment and the CEFR's is language learning and teaching. These differences are striking and important to take into account when describing the systems. In terms of testing, ACTFL is one US-based organization that provides certified, reliable ratings across languages. By contrast, CEFR ratings may or may not be consistent across languages because there is no single organization that serves as the arbiter of the CEFR as ACTFL does for its Proficiency Guidelines. This divide has resulted in numerous presentations with titles such as, 'Is your B1 my B1?' and the assertion that some CEFR tests in some languages are more rigorous than others. These differences can be traced to the diversity of examination organizations that employ the CEFR. Because there is no one arbiter for CEFR, as there is for the ACTFL Guidelines, organizations can interpret the CEFR differently, thus resulting in lack of alignment.

In addition to fundamental differences between the systems, when crosswalks have been explored, the challenge of establishing a 1:1 correspondence between the two systems remains. Initially, attempts were made to develop a crosswalk based on the criteria of the two systems across domains. In other words, by comparing the terminology of the two systems within the domains (speaking, reading, writing and listening), it was thought possible to set up a comparison where an Intermediate Mid on the ACTFL scale, for example, was comparable to an A1 across languages and domains in the CEFR. Research shows, however, that such an approach was ineffective. Instead, each test needs to be compared, via a standard setting study, to establish the correspondence. For example, Bärenfänger and Tschirner (2012) found a correspondence between receptive skills (listening and reading), meaning that a crosswalk could be made between scores on ACTFL and CEFR-based listening and reading tests. They also found a correspondence between productive skills (speaking and writing). However, the crosswalk was different depending on the domain. For example, a rating of ACTFL Intermediate Mid on listening and reading tests corresponds to a CEFR A2, while a rating of ACTFL Intermediate Low on ACTFL speaking and writing tests corresponds to a CEFR A2. In other words, the correspondence is nuanced and complicated; one cannot claim that there is a straightforward alignment between A2 and a specific ACTFL proficiency level across all domains. The lack of generalization across languages and domains means that any crosswalk will require a domain-specific correspondence. In addition, the correspondences established via recent research is one-way, meaning that an ACTFL test can produce a CEFR rating but not the reverse.

Additional limitations are evident in the CEFR-CV itself, including approaching plurilingual assessment development and validation, examining the role of the CEFR in assessing young learners, and making the document accessible and comprehensible. The emphasis on plurilingualism is exciting. However, providing validity evidence for plurilingual tests is a daunting venture. Documenting such validation efforts, including opening them to critique and improvement by experts in the field, will be critical to the success of future plurilingual assessment.

A second issue is that of assessing young learners. ACTFL has developed tests for primary and secondary school language learners, and it has been a rewarding, and often difficult, venture. It would be enlightening for CEFR leaders to work with ACTFL to explore both the successes and challenges in developing these assessments and accompanying outreach to students, parents, teachers and administrators. With the explosion of dual-language immersion programmes in the United States, more students than ever are learning languages at younger ages, and we may be able to support our European colleagues with our own lessons learned.

Perhaps the most profound difficulty, however, is not in making correspondences between the two systems and their tests but, instead, in the general understanding of the two systems and of language and how it is assessed. Related to this issue is the length, density and complexity of the CEFR-CV. Although the volume itself is interesting and compelling, its length may be daunting to many readers. Thus, finding engaging ways to transmit the information in the CEFR-CV may be critical to its success. Moreover, determining *what* in the volume is of interest to many stakeholders as well as *how* to convey it, may be the secret to its success outside language professionals.

As Deygers and Malone (2019), Kremmel and Harding (2020), Malone (2013), Pill and Harding (2013) and others have pointed out, many stakeholders – from teachers to administrators to students and policymakers – understand neither the system nor what can be expected after learning a language in school or via in-country immersion. In other words, the general public, language learners and language teachers, lack basic understanding of how long it takes to learn a language, what can be expected after different sequences and how such outcomes differ based on contact hours, language teaching method, other languages studied, intensity and language typology. The failure of both the general public and consumers of language education to understand the time investment and processes critical to language proficiency is one of the greatest barriers to understanding language assessment in general and the CEFR and ACTFL Guidelines specifically.

To further confound the issue, many websites have emerged that compare the ACTFL and CEFR systems. Although some, such as the ACTFL website, show crosswalks based on empirical results, others do not represent research-based outcomes. There is a large discrepancy between the research-based comparisons and the others. Continued misrepresentation and simplification of the correspondence will further the divide between providing a clear, accurate and complex crosswalk between the systems and providing an uncomplicated but inaccurate one. Thus, the issue goes beyond a mutual understanding of and correspondence between the two systems, and drifts into the need to both ascertain and then improve users' understanding of language, language assessment and the systems most commonly used in both countries. It is critical to note, however, that most language assessment literacy efforts focus on the assessment part rather than the comprehensive assessment systems that provide information to stakeholders.

Kremmel and Harding's (2020) international study of stakeholders' understanding of language assessment also shows a gap in information about users of language assessment. The survey shows that most responses came from teachers while few came from parents and students. While teachers are, of course, important, other language users, such as parents and students, need to develop an understanding of language, language proficiency and language outcomes, and assessment is integral both to set reasonable goals and to pursue realistic outcomes for language proficiency. An examination of both Kremmel and Harding's (2020) findings and any insight they shed on the general population's perceptions could help identify ways to improve understanding of language assessment. An international effort to understand parents', test-takers', administrators' and teachers' perceptions of language development, language assessment and the ACTFL Proficiency Guidelines and the CEFR would allow leaders working with both systems to identify gaps in understanding and begin to address them.

Thus, I propose a transatlantic effort to develop, administer, analyse and implement the results of a needs assessment focused on parent, student, administrator and non-language-instructor knowledge of the ACTFL Guidelines and the CEFR to show the current holes in the system. Kremmel and Harding (2020) have created a strong model for such an approach to language assessment literacy. By working from both sides of the Atlantic, perhaps with an international questionnaire of both common and region-specific (CEFR versus ACTFL) questions, it would be possible to conduct a thorough needs assessment and find out how to address the knowledge gap to increase understanding of the systems. The proposed questionnaire and its results could be shared widely with relevant groups to support an international effort to improve knowledge of how languages are learned and to increase awareness of how to attain proficiency in languages.

Notes

(1) The ACTFL Guidelines are available at https://www.actfl.org (accessed 21 September 2020).
(2) https://www.coe.int/en/web/common-european-framework-reference-languages/introduction-and-context (accessed 21 September 2020).
(3) https://www.actfl.org/resources/assigning-cefr-ratings-actfl-assessments (accessed 25 November 2020).
(4) https://www.ets.org/Media/Research/pdf/RM-15-06.pdf (accessed 21 September 2020).

References

ACTFL (2012) ACTFL Proficiency Guidelines 2012. Alexandria, VA: ACTFL.
Bärenfänger, O. and Tschirner, E. (2012) *Assessing Evidence of Validity of Assigning CEFR Ratings to the ACTFL Oral Proficiency Interview (OPI) and the Oral Proficiency Interview by computer (OPIc) (Technical Report 2012-US-PUB-1)*. Leipzig: Institute for Test Research and Test Development.
Chapelle, C. (2012) Seeking solid theoretical ground for the ACTFL–CEFR crosswalk. In E. Tschirner (ed.) *Aligning Frameworks of Reference in Language Testing: The ACTFL Proficiency Guidelines and the Common European Framework of Reference for Languages* (pp. 35–48). Tübingen: Stauffenburg.

Council of Europe (2001) *Common European Framework of Reference for Languages: Learning, Teaching, Assessment*. Cambridge: Cambridge University Press.

Council of Europe (2020) *Common European Framework of Reference for Languages: Learning, Teaching, Assessment. Companion Volume*. Strasbourg: Council of Europe.

Cox, T.L., Malone, M.E. and Winke, P. (2018) Future directions in assessment: Influences of standards and implications for language learning. *Foreign Language Annals* 51 (1), 104–115.

Deygers, B. and Malone, M.E. (2019) Language assessment literacy in university admission policies, or the dialogue that isn't. *Language Testing* 36 (3), 347–368.

Kremmel, B. and Harding, L. (2020) Towards a comprehensive, empirical model of language assessment literacy across stakeholder groups: Developing the Language Assessment Literacy Survey. *Language Assessment Quarterly* 17 (1), 100–120.

Lowe Jr, P. (2012) Understanding 'hidden features' of the ACTFL speaking guidelines as an intermediate step to comparing the ACTFL Guidelines and the CEFR for speaking assessment. In E. Tschirner (2012) *Aligning Frameworks of Reference in Language Testing: The ACTFL Proficiency Guidelines and the Common European Framework of Reference for Languages* (pp. 93–106). Tübingen: Stauffenburg.

Luoma, S. (2004) *Assessing Speaking*. Cambridge: Cambridge University Press.

Malone, M.E. (2013) The essentials of assessment literacy: Contrasts between testers and users. *Language Testing* 30 (3), 329–344.

Moore, C.W. (1986) *The Mediation Process: Practical Strategies for Resolving Conflict*. San Francisco: Jossey-Bass.

Pill, J. and Harding, L. (2013) Defining the language assessment literacy gap: Evidence from a parliamentary inquiry. *Language Testing* 30 (3), 381–402.

Tschirner, E. (ed.) (2012) *Aligning Frameworks of Reference in Language Testing: The ACTFL Proficiency Guidelines and the Common European Framework of Reference for Languages*. Tübingen: Stauffenburg.

Tschirner, E. (2013) El Marco Común Europeo de Referencia en diálogo con el ACTFL: Indicadores de competencia. *Verbum et Lingua* 1, 25–34. http://verbumetlingua.cucsh.udg.mx/sites/default/files/vel_1_etschirner.pdf (accessed 19 November 2020).

Tschirner, E. and Bärenfänger, O. (2013a) *Assessing Evidence of Validity of the ACTFL CEFR Reading Proficiency Test (RPT) (Technical Report 2013-US-PUB-5)*. Leipzig: Institute for Test Research and Test Development.

Tschirner, E. and Bärenfänger, O. (2013b) *Assessing Evidence of Validity of the ACTFL CEFR Listening Proficiency Test (LPT) (Technical Report 2013-US-PUB-6)*. Leipzig: Institute for Test Research and Test Development.

Tschirner, E. and Bärenfänger, O. (2015) *The ACTFL CEFR Listening and Reading Proficiency Tests (LPT and RPT) Reliability and Validity Report 2015: Spanish, French, and German (Technical Report 2015-EU-PUB-1)*. Leipzig: Institute for Test Research and Test Development.

Tschirner, E., Bärenfänger, O. and Wanner, I. (2012) *Assessing Evidence of Validity of Assigning CEFR Ratings to the ACTFL Oral Proficiency Interview (OPI) and the Oral Proficiency Interview by Computer (OPIc) (Technical Report 2012-US-PUB-1)*. Leipzig: Institute for Test Research and Test Development.

Tschirner, E., Bärenfänger, O. and Wisniewski, K. (2015) *Assessing Evidence of Validity of the ACTFL CEFR Listening and Reading Proficiency Tests (LPT and RPT) Using a Standard-setting Approach (Technical Report 2015-EU-PUB-2)*. Leipzig: Institute for Test Research and Test Development.

3 The CEFR *Companion Volume* Project: What Has Been Achieved

Brian North

This chapter outlines the aims of the Companion Volume *project – updating the CEFR model and descriptors and addressing some misunderstandings about the CEFR – as well as outlining innovative aspects of the CEFR that are further developed in the CEFR-CV. It then considers the outcomes from the project – an accessible explanation of the CEFR vision, updated and extended CEFR descriptors, including those for mediation, online interaction, plurilingual/pluricultural competence, phonology and signing competences, the compilation of descriptors for young learners, and related reports (for mediation, phonology, the young learner compilation and the validation). It is pointed out that the new descriptors offer tools to inspire classroom tasks that generate and monitor languaging on the part of learners. The conceptual achievements of the project – regarding mediation, the action-oriented approach, agency, plurilingualism and inclusivity – and the technical achievements – extending the descriptors to radically different areas while maintaining the integrity of the calibration – are then outlined. Finally, the chapter notes that the project has already sparked a revival of interest in the CEFR, inspired a number of other projects, provided a clearer definition of the action-oriented approach, clarified the links between mediation and plurilingualism, and suggested a direction of travel towards an action-based pedagogy of plurilingualism.*

Introduction

It is perhaps a little early to be discussing the achievements of the project that developed the CEFR *Companion Volume* (CEFR-CV; Council of Europe, 2020) when we are actually still studying the impact of the CEFR itself (Council of Europe, 2001). In many respects, an evaluation of the CEFR-CV in about another 20 years' time might be more appropriate, since achieving change in language education is notoriously difficult and slow (Borg, 2018; Freeman, 2016; Thornbury, 2016). However, we can envisage how the CEFR-CV may fuel innovation in language education.

As was the case with the CEFR at the time of its publication, the CEFR-CV is a forward-looking document intended to give an impulse to both teaching practices and research over the next decade(s). It is not actually the case that research precedes changes in practices, or that new models are the direct result of research. Lado's (1961) model of the four skills and three elements (grammar, vocabulary, pronunciation), which the CEFR model replaces, gradually had a revolutionary effect on practices, but was not based on research, which in that period had a very narrow base in structural linguistics. The CEFR model was in fact inspired by research and insights from applied linguistics and applied psychology (see North, 1997, 2000; Richer, 2017), and elements of it show similarities to other models developed at the same time (e.g. Bachman, 1990; Bachman & Palmer, 1996; Celce-Murcía *et al.*, 1995; Cook, 1991, 1992), but it was not based directly on research, although a lot of research went into the production of the descriptors (North, 1995, 2000; North & Schneider, 1998; Schneider & North, 2000).

As Piccardo and North (2019) explain, the action-oriented approach and the concept of the user/learner as a social agent, mentioned but not developed in the CEFR, are also inspired by research, but have developed since 2001 in a bottom-up way through experimentation by practitioners in different contexts as they thought through the implications of the CEFR model. Indeed, it would not be an exaggeration to say that, in the language profession, progress tends to happen through a symbiotic relationship between practices and research, often kick-started by an inspiring document or forum. The CEFR-CV aims to be that kind of document, as EALTA aspires to be that kind of forum.

Aims of the CEFR *Companion Volume*

The *Companion Volume* project had several aims:

(1) to update the CEFR model and clarify its role, taking account of academic developments since 2001, particularly as regards mediation;
(2) to update the 2001 descriptor scales, mainly on the basis of descriptors validated and calibrated since 2001,[1] in order to fill noticeable gaps in them, particularly at the A levels and C levels; and
(3) to develop descriptors for important aspects that, for one reason or another, had been left to one side in 2001.

The first and third aims led to the conceptualization of mediation and related areas (mediation activities, mediation strategies), plurilingual and pluricultural competence, online interaction, and reactions to creative text, including literature – which is included in the final version under mediating a text (North & Piccardo, 2016, 2019; Piccardo *et al.*, 2019).

There was also an underlying desire to redress some of the myths that have developed around the CEFR: for example, that it takes a monolingual approach, with a native speaker model, or that it is exclusively an instrument for assessment and standardization (Piccardo, 2020). This explains the focus on plurilingualism, the steps taken to remove what might be called the ghost of the native speaker – particularly from where it was most prominent, in the scale for phonological control, and the emphasis on teaching and learning (as in the title – *Common European Framework of Reference for Languages: Learning, Teaching, Assessment*). It is made clear that the descriptors are intended to be sources for curriculum aims and task design, to facilitate showing plurilingual profiles across languages, ensuring transparency and coherence between an integrated language curriculum and its enactment in action-oriented teaching and assessment (Graves, 2008). The CEFR-CV's short and accessible text on the key aspects of the CEFR aims to bring these CEFR messages closer to classroom practitioners. This text also contributes to dispelling yet another myth about the CEFR 2001: that because it was non-prescriptive, it was pedagogically neutral.

In fact, the CEFR contained pioneering pedagogical concepts that were ahead of their time: for example, the social agent, a new way of seeing communicative activities and strategies, mediation, the action-oriented approach, plurilingualism (see Piccardo & North, 2019, for detailed discussion). The CEFR-CV seeks to flesh out and operationalize these concepts and, in so doing, facilitate a conceptual shift from (Cartesian) division (e.g. the four skills, strict separation of languages) to an integrationist (Harris, 1981; Orman, 2013), ecological (van Lier, 2004, 2007), complex (Larsen-Freeman, 2017) vision. The hope is that this vision, taking account of both conceptual development and bottom-up classroom experimentation over the past 20 years, will broaden the scope of language education.

The Outcomes of the Project

Perhaps it is useful to briefly outline the various outcomes from the 2013–2020 project. Firstly there is the CEFR-CV itself, with an accessible text (CEFR-CV, Chapter 2) on key aspects of the CEFR for teaching and learning. This explains the aims of the CEFR and how to implement the action-oriented approach. The CEFR model (descriptive scheme) is outlined, with a particular emphasis on the concepts of plurilingual and pluricultural competence and mediation. As Piccardo (2012) pointed out, the CEFR model with the user seen as a social agent implies a far broader and more central role for mediation than has been widely appreciated. The text on key aspects of the CEFR also deals with misunderstandings about the common reference levels, gives examples of needs and proficiency profiles based on the levels, and concludes by explaining the nature and role of the descriptors, suggesting ways in which they can be used, before listing some useful resources for CEFR implementation.

The complete, updated and extended set of CEFR descriptors follows in Chapters 3–6. In the spirit of inclusive education, all the descriptors have been edited to be gender-neutral and modality-inclusive, with the ghost of the native speaker removed. In fact, C2 has never been associated with so-called native-speaker competence. However, since this misconception just would not go away, 16 descriptors at B2 and C2 have been revised slightly and, as mentioned, the scale for phonological control has been replaced. Most additions to the 2001 scales are for reception, production and interaction, to each of which one new scale is also added (Reading as a Leisure Activity; Giving Information; Using Telecommunications), as well as the new section on online interaction. Here the description for listening and reading, a weak point of the 2001 scales, has been substantially improved. The 'plus levels' have also been more systematically fleshed out, with the distinction between 'criterion levels' and 'plus levels' re-emphasized in the text. For all the descriptor scales, the generally acknowledged dearth of descriptors at the top and bottom levels has been addressed, with the 2001 'Tourist band' developed into Pre-A1, of particular relevance to young learners.

The newly developed scales bring descriptors for aspects of mediating a text (11 scales), mediating concepts (4 scales), mediating communication (3 scales), mediating strategies (5 scales), online interaction (2 scales) and plurilingual/pluricultural competence (3 scales). Finally, there are descriptors for signing competences (7 scales each for receptive and productive respectively), which were developed in a separate project (Keller, 2019).

There is also, as mentioned, a new – analytic – scale for phonological control, based on a review of research in a subproject (Piccardo, 2016). This new scale has subscales for sound articulation and for prosody (stress and intonation). It moves away from native-speaker norms, adopting intelligibility as the guiding feature and acknowledging the possible retention of an accent at all levels. It offers realistic objectives at each level and will hopefully encourage teachers to re-engage with explicit work on phonology.

All scales, new and old, come with a short rationale to aid interpretation. All the descriptors are available on the homepage of the CEFR website[2] in an Excel file with filters that enable the user to choose the language(s), level(s), main category/ies and actual scales that they want to download. In addition, there are appendices giving: the three general scales used to introduce the levels in 2001; the writing assessment scale developed in 2009; examples across the four domains – public, personal, occupational and educational – for all the new descriptors; a brief report on the project; supplementary descriptors dropped in fine-tuning; and a list of online resources related to the CEFR.

There are several other products from the project. Firstly, there is a separate compilation of CEFR-based descriptors for the age groups 7–10 and 11–15, available on the CEFR website (Szabo & Goodier, 2018). In this subproject, each of the CEFR-CV descriptors was assessed for relevance to the two age groups concerned and any descriptors adapted for younger learners from the 19 sources that relate to the CEFR descriptors were listed next to it. In practice, for the moment the collection is restricted to adaptations of the older descriptors, since adaptations of the new descriptors have not yet been undertaken.

Then, there are three other reports from the project. Firstly, there is the Mediation Report (North & Piccardo, 2016). This explains the conceptualization of mediation and summarizes the process of developing and validating the descriptors for mediation and related areas. The report outlines the presentation of mediation in the CEFR and, based on the work of Piccardo (2012), explains the way in which this implies cultural, social and pedagogic mediation in addition to the more obvious (cross-)linguistic mediation. It then develops a richer model of mediation before outlining the categories adopted for the descriptors and the rationales for the different scales. Finally, it briefly summarizes the development and validation of the descriptors, outlining the validation phases, before discussing the relevance of the mediation descriptors for different contexts.

Secondly there is the report on the Phonology Project (Piccardo, 2016). This report analyses the existing CEFR construct for phonology and its operationalization in the 2001 scale, pointing out a discrepancy between the two, and proposes a rationale for revising the scale. There follows a review of research and other pronunciation scales and, with input from pronunciation experts, the identification of key concepts for a new scale. The drafting of the scales, consultation with experts and the validation stages are then described.

Finally, there is a Validation Report (North, 2020) that discusses criticisms of the CEFR descriptors, outlines the different stages of the overall project and describes the validation process in detail. This report is an update and amalgamation of the series of reports on the various validation phases that were made available online during the formal process of consultation on the descriptors. In addition, in a long appendix, the report provides the difficulty estimates and standard errors for all the descriptors, new and old, for which this information is available, matched to the formulations actually calibrated.

The (Re)Conceptualization of Mediation in the *Companion Volume*

The conceptualization of mediation in the CEFR-CV is considerably broader than in the CEFR 2001. In fact, mediation has largely been interpreted as the sole transfer of information across languages (for critique, see North, forthcoming; North & Piccardo, forthcoming). The approach in the CEFR-CV, building on Piccardo (2012) and Coste and Cavalli (2015), is more in line with the view of mediation in research in language education (see Piccardo, forthcoming; Piccardo & North, 2019), focused on the (co-)construction of meaning and advocating learner agency and creativity in action-oriented tasks. With its focus on interaction and the concept of the social agent, the CEFR 2001 made the social, situated nature of language use a key feature of its descriptive model. With the elaboration of mediation in the CEFR-CV, the focus changes from negotiation of meaning in the sense of getting onto the same wavelength (social language use in interaction) to the (co-)construction of new meaning and knowledge. This puts an emphasis on collaborative language use in mediation, in *languaging* (Cowley & Gahrn-Andersen, 2018), the process of thinking things through by articulating thoughts in language. Languaging is touched on in the Mediation Report (North & Piccardo, 2016) and discussed in detail in Piccardo (forthcoming). As she points out, the notion of language as an action rather than an entity is not new:

> In Halliday's systemic functional linguistics the focus is on 'meaning potential' – van Lier's (2004: 74) 'semiotic potential of the affordances' … – and languaging refers to both the 'action in the making' and the way each individual experiences that act, that language use. (Piccardo, forthcoming)

This relates to mediation as follows:

> The social agent mediates while languaging, because languaging is the manifestation of mediation. If we think of the three main categories in which mediation is presented in the CEFR-CV, in MEDIATING CONCEPTS, social agents are quite obviously languaging as they think things through together, in MEDIATING COMMUNICATION they are languaging in the process of self–other regulation, and in MEDIATING A TEXT they are languaging to find formulations that enable understanding of the text itself for themselves and for or with others. (Piccardo, forthcoming)

The new descriptor scales offer teachers tools to inspire classroom tasks that generate this languaging and then to monitor the way learners do this. The language activity may be taking place across two languages in a form of structured codeswitching, it may be fully open, allowing learners to draw on their full repertoire in *plurilanguaging* (Lüdi, 2014, 2016; Piccardo, 2017, 2018, forthcoming), or it may take place all in the one language/variety. The CEFR-CV makes clear that the talk here is not just with regard to standard named languages. In the introduction to the section on mediating a text, it states:

> For all the descriptors in the scales in this section, Language A and Language B may be different languages, varieties or modalities of the same language, different registers of the same variety, or any combination of the above. However, they may also be identical: the CEFR 2001 is clear that mediation may also be in one language. Alternatively, mediation may involve several languages, varieties or modalities; there may be a Language C and even conceivably a Language D in the communicative situation concerned. The descriptors for mediation are equally applicable in each case. Users may thus wish to specify precisely which languages/varieties/modalities are involved when adapting the descriptors to their context. For ease of use, reference is made in the descriptors to just Language A and Language B. (Council of Europe, 2020: 92)

From the beginning, mediation was understood as 'acting upon all three of the other categories Reception, Interaction and Production' (North, 1994: 10) with 'tasks where participants engage in interaction, production, reception or mediation, or a combination of two or more of these' (Council of Europe, 2001: 157). In a multi-phase action-oriented task there is a natural development through:

- sourcing and understanding information and ideas (reception);
- processing them for oneself or others and possibly reporting on the content to the collaborative group (mediating a text);
- discussing that content and people's reactions (interaction);
- developing a concept/solving a problem together on the basis of this input (mediating concepts and possibly mediating communication); and
- creating the proposal, report or artefact (poster, video, presentation, etc.) (production)

Feedback during the validation process and the piloting, as well as from the case studies (North *et al.*, forthcoming), suggests that the project is already starting to have an impact in the way mediation is conceived. North (2021) summarizes a series of practical examples from these pilots and studies that demonstrates the breadth and variety of interpretations involved.

Conceptual Achievements of the Project

To return to the title of this chapter, while it is a little early to state 'achievements' one could list some of the contributions that the project makes to the ongoing development of language education. The most obvious is the way in which the core messages of the CEFR – such as the integrated view of communicative activity, mediation, plurilingualism, learner agency – are spelled out in a clear, accessible text. The CEFR model is also brought up to date by being related to recent developments in language education (ecological approach, sociocultural theory, complexity theory, etc.; see Piccardo & North, 2019).

Mediation

As discussed above, the CEFR-CV offers a comprehensive operationalization of the concept of mediation in descriptors. After its appearance in CEFR 2001, mediation had tended to be interpreted in a rather reductive, transactional manner in those, mainly German-speaking, countries that had adopted it in their curricula (but see, for example, Nied Curcio, 2017, for a view outlining the potential of that approach). Kolb (2016) pinpoints the problem as being a lack of contextualization in the tasks typically appearing in materials: 'it is sometimes the case that the contextualization with a particular addressee is considerably underspecified [so that the context given] can be seen as above all an excuse for a summary' (2016: 52; my translation). The CEFR-CV shows a way of overcoming this problem by proposing the classroom itself and online research as real life contexts in which affordances can stimulate the embodied 'perception in action' (van Lier, 2007: 97) that is key to successful learning. A learning module, linked through a scenario, can comprise an integrated series of lessons involving reception, interaction, mediation and final production.

Action-oriented approach

The CEFR-CV puts the emphasis back on learning and teaching, explaining that the descriptors are intended as stimuli for needs analysis, the design of teaching tasks, the monitoring of the action by the learners, and self-assessment. The clear explanation of this action-based (van Lier, 2007) approach shows the way that the CEFR model works, with competences and strategies being mobilized through the communicative language activities required by tasks, and being reinforced and extended in that process. Language is seen as a process not just as an inert product, a verb (languaging) as well as a noun (language). With regard to assessment, the descriptors provide the means to operationalize a classroom-based alternative to standardized testing, integrated in teaching, with transparent and coherent feedforward (clear expectations) and feedback, so building agency and self-efficacy (Bandura, 2001).

Agency

The CEFR-CV promotes both teacher and learner agency. Descriptors offer teachers a practical tool to systemize and justify their professional decisions and an inspiration for devising classroom tasks. The language user/learner is seen as a '"social agent" acting in the social world and exerting agency in the learning process' (Council of Europe, 2020: 22). The centrality of learner agency in the action-oriented approach can be seen as the defining feature of the difference to task-based teaching. As the CEFR-CV goes on to explain: 'This implies a real paradigm shift in both course planning and teaching by promoting learner engagement and autonomy' (2020: 22). This was already part of the CEFR 2001 message, but the CEFR-CV highlights it.

Plurilingualism

The CEFR-CV clarifies the position of the concept of plurilingualism in the language policy of the Council of Europe, citing the CEFR 2001:

> ... the aim of language education is profoundly modified. It is no longer seen as simply to achieve 'mastery' of one or two, or even three languages, each taken in isolation, with the 'ideal native speaker' as the ultimate model. Instead, the aim is to develop a linguistic repertoire, in which all linguistic abilities have a place. (CEFR 2001, Section 1.3; Council of Europe, 2020: 123)

More fundamentally, the CEFR-CV promotes the operationalization of a plurilingual approach with tangible tools for teachers. A modest number of CEFR descriptors at each level, presented like those for other language learning aims, encourages the inclusion of plurilingual and pluricultural competence in curriculum and teaching aims, thus putting plurilingualism on the map in a practical way.

Inclusivity

The move to gender and modality neutrality and the provision of descriptors specifically for sign languages are the most obvious contributions to inclusivity. But in addition to the glossing of Language A and Language B mentioned previously, the expression 'standard language' has been replaced with 'standard language or a familiar variety' in all the descriptors. The foreword explicitly states that the CEFR has never been intended to be used as a gate-keeping instrument, and the provision of descriptors for Pre-A1 values low levels of achievement.

Technical Achievements of the Project

Extending descriptors used internationally to radically different areas, while maintaining the integrity of the calibration, was not a simple undertaking. An overview of how this was achieved is given by North and Piccardo (2016), with full details in North (2020). Technical achievements of the project include:

- incorporating expertise from 7 CEFR-related projects and confirming in that process the relationship of the descriptors in those projects to the CEFR levels;
- mobilizing a wide international network of 190 institutions for validation activities;
- confirming the levels of the new descriptors through analyses with different anchoring and standard-setting approaches, thus solving the issue of how to anchor the calibration values of the descriptors of new areas to the scale underlying the CEFR levels created 20 years earlier; and finally,
- assuring the coherence of the calibration of the descriptors to levels: within scales; across categories; across groups of respondents; across occasions (1995/2015); across specialists and generalists (for plurilingual/pluricultural); and across languages.

Conclusion

The project has already had a certain impact through the revival of interest in the CEFR that it sparked, which has led to many events organized around the CEFR-CV and indeed to this volume. Almost 2000 language professionals from around the world were involved at one time or another, more than 1000 of whom took part in all the validation activities. The focus on plurilingualism and removing the ghost of the native speaker in the descriptors (especially for phonology) suggests a rethink of language policy at the institutional, curricular and classroom levels. The provision of descriptors specific to signing competences will help to develop CEFR-based curricula for sign languages.

The project has already inspired a number of related and follow-up projects, including two in the 2020–2023 programme of the European Centre for Modern Languages and the series of 19 case studies mentioned (North *et al.*, forthcoming). With its focus of mediation, plurilingualism and pluriculturalism, the CEFR-CV moves beyond a narrow view of modern language education and brings the CEFR closer to the wider Council of Europe mission. Apart from obvious relevance to CLIL (Content and Language Integrated Learning) and languages across the curriculum, there are synergies with the Council of Europe's *Reference Framework of Competences for Democratic Culture*,[3] with the European Commission's 'comprehensive approach' to language education,[4] as well as with various initiatives concerning 21st-century skills.

Above all, the project has provided a clearer definition of the action-oriented approach, clarified the links between mediation and plurilingualism, and suggested a direction of travel, a roadmap, towards an action-based pedagogy of plurilingualism.

Notes

(1)   The ALTE Can Do Statements; the Finnish AMKKIA project; the Cambridge English Assessment 'common scales'; the CEFR-J; Lingualevel; English Profile (C levels); and Pearson's Global Scale of English.
(2)   https://www.coe.int/en/web/common-european-framework-reference-languages (accessed 2 November 2020).
(3)   https://www.coe.int/en/web/education/competences-for-democratic-culture (accessed 14 October 2020).
(4)   http://data.consilium.europa.eu/doc/document/ST-9229-2018-ADD-2/EN/pdf (accessed 14 October 2020).

References

Bachman, L.F. (1990) *Fundamental Considerations in Language Testing.* Oxford: Oxford University Press.

Bachman, L.F. and Palmer, A.S. (1996) *Language Testing in Practice.* Oxford: Oxford University Press.

Bandura, A. (2001) Social cognitive theory: An agentic perspective. *Annual Review of Psychology* 52, 1–26.

Borg, S. (2018) Teachers' beliefs and classroom practices. In P. Garrett and J. Cots (eds) *The Routledge Handbook of Language Awareness* (pp. 75–91). London: Routledge.

Celce-Murcia, M., Dörnyei, Z. and Thurrell, S. (1995) Communicative competence: A pedagogically motivated model with content specifications. *Issues in Applied Linguistics* 6 (2), 5–35.

Cook, V.J. (1991) The poverty-of-the-stimulus argument and multi-competence. *Second Language Research* 7 (2), 103–117.

Cook, V.J. (1992) Evidence for multicompetence. *Language Learning* 42 (4), 557–591.

Coste, D. and Cavalli, M. (2015) *Education, Mobility, Otherness: The Mediation Functions of Schools.* Strasbourg: Council of Europe. https://www.coe.int/en/web/common-european-framework-reference-languages/documents (accessed 14 October 2020).

Council of Europe (2001) *Common European Framework of Reference for Languages: Learning, Teaching, Assessment.* Cambridge: Cambridge University Press. http://www.coe.int/en/web/common-european-framework-reference-languages (accessed 10 October 2020).

Council of Europe (2020) *Common European Framework of Reference for Languages: Learning, Teaching, Assessment. Companion Volume.* Strasbourg: Council of Europe. https://book.coe.int/en/education-and-modern-languages/8150-common-european-framework-of-reference-for-languages-learning-teaching-assessment-companion-volume.html (accessed 14 October 2020).

Cowley, S.J. and Gahrn-Andersen, R. (2018) Simplexity, languages and human languaging. *Language Sciences* 71, 4–7. https://doi.org/10.1016/j.langsci.2018.04.008 (accessed 14 October 2020).

Freeman, D. (2016) *Educating Second Language Teachers.* Oxford: Oxford University Press.

Graves, K. (2008) The language curriculum: A social contextual perspective. *Language Teaching* 41 (2), 147–181.

Harris, R. (1981) *The Language Myth.* London: Duckworth.

Keller, J. (2019) Deskriptoren für Textkompetenz in Gebärdensprachen [Descriptors for textual competence in sign languages]. In M. Barras, K. Karges, T. Studer and E. Wiedenkeller (eds) *IDT 2017. Band 2* (pp. 111–117). Berlin: Erich Schmidt Verlag.

Kolb, E. (2016) *Sprachmittlung: Studien zur Modellierung einer Komplexen Kompetenz* [Linguistic mediation: Studies to model a complex competence]. Münster: Waxmann.

Lado, R. (1961) *Language Testing*. London: Longman.

Larsen-Freeman, D. (2017) Complexity theory: The lessons continue. In L. Ortega and Z.H. Han (eds) *Complexity Theory and Language Development: In celebration of Diane Larsen-Freeman* (pp. 11–50). Amsterdam & Philadelphia: John Benjamins.

Lüdi, G. (2014) Dynamics and management of linguistic diversity in companies and institutes of higher education: Results from the DYLAN project. In P. Grommes and H. Wu (eds) *Plurilingual Education: Policies – Practices – Language Development* (pp. 113–138). Amsterdam: John Benjamins.

Lüdi, G. (2016) Language regime in the Swiss armed forces between institutional multilingualism, the dominance of German, English and situated plurilanguaging. In G. Lüdi, K. Höchle Meier and P. Yanaprasart (eds) *Managing Plurilingual and Intercultural Practices in the Workplace* (pp. 100–118). Amsterdam and Philadelphia: John Benjamins.

Nied Curcio, M. (2017) Sprachmittelnde Aktivitäten im akademischen DaF-Unterricht in Italien – aus der Sicht der Studierenden [Cross-linguistic mediation activities from the viewpoint of the learner]. In M.C. Moroni and F. Ricci Garotti (eds) *Brücken Schlagen Zwischen Sprachwissenschaft und Daf-Didaktik* [Building bridges between language research and the teaching of German as a foreign language] (pp. 77–94). Bern: Peter Lang.

North, B. (1994) Perspectives on language proficiency and aspects of competence: A reference paper defining categories and levels: Possible categories of description and possible levels for a Common European Framework of Reference. A Reference Paper prepared for the second meeting of the Council of Europe Working Party for the development of a Common European Framework for Language Learning and Teaching, 24–25 May 1994. *CC-LANG* vol. 94, no. 20. Strasbourg: Council of Europe.

North, B. (1995) The development of a common framework scale of descriptors of language proficiency based on a theory of measurement. *System* 23 (4), 445–465.

North, B. (1997) Perspectives on language proficiency and aspects of competence. *Language Teaching* 30 (2), 93–100.

North, B. (2000) *The Development of a Common Framework Scale of Language Proficiency*. New York: Peter Lang.

North, B. (2020) The CEFR illustrative descriptors: Validation reference paper for researchers. Unpublished manuscript. Strasbourg: Council of Europe. https://www.researchgate.net/publication/350156412_North_CEFR_Validation_Reference_Paper_-_with_appendices (accessed 18 October 2021).

North, B. (2021) Plurilingual mediation in the classroom: Examples from practice. In E. Piccardo, G. Lawrence and A. Germain-Rutherford (eds) *Routledge Handbook of Plurilingual Language Education* (pp. 319–336). London: Routledge.

North, B. (forthcoming) Developing an action-oriented perspective on mediation: The new CEFR descriptors. In B. Dendrinos (ed.) *Mediation as Linguistic and Cultural Negotiation of Meanings and Plurilingualism*. London: Routledge.

North, B. and Schneider, G. (1998) Scaling descriptors for language proficiency scales. *Language Testing* 15 (2), 217–262.

North, B. and Piccardo, E. (2016) *Developing Illustrative Descriptors of Aspects of Mediation for the Common European Framework of Reference (CEFR)*. Strasbourg: Council of Europe. https://rm.coe.int/common-european-framework-of-reference-for-languages-learning-teaching/168073ff31 (accessed 14 October 2020).

North, B. and Piccardo, E. (2019) Developing new CEFR descriptor scales and expanding the existing ones: Constructs, approaches and methodologies. In J. Quetz and H. Rossa (eds) *The Common European Framework of Reference, Illustrative Descriptors, Extended Version 2017*. Special issue of *Zeitschrift für Fremdsprachenforschung* (ZFF) 30 (2), 142–160.

North, B. and Piccardo, E. (forthcoming) The conceptualisation of mediation in the new CEFR. In P. Katelhön and P. Marečková (eds) *Sprachmittlung im schulischen und universitären Kontext* [Linguistic mediation in the school and university context]. Berlin: Frank & Timme.

North, B., Piccardo, E., Goodier, T., Fasoglio, D., Margonis, R. and Rüschoff, B. (forthcoming) *Enriching 21st Century Language Education: The CEFR Companion Volume, Examples from Practice.* Strasbourg: Council of Europe.

Orman, J. (2013) New lingualisms, same old codes. *Language Sciences* 37, 90–98.

Piccardo, E. (2012) Médiation et apprentissage des langues: Pourquoi est-il temps de réfléchir à cette notion ? [Mediation and learning languages: Why is it time to reflect on this notion?] *ELA: Études de Linguistique Appliquée* [Studies in Applied Linguistics] 167, 285–297.

Piccardo, E. (2016) *Phonological Scale Revision Process. Report.* Strasbourg: Council of Europe. https://rm.coe.int/phonological-scale-revision-process-report-cefr/168073fff9 (accessed 14 October 2020).

Piccardo, E. (2017) Plurilingualism as a catalyzer for creativity in superdiverse societies: A systemic analysis. *Frontiers in Psychology*, 8. https://doi.org/10.3389/fpsyg.2017.02169 (accessed 14 October 2020).

Piccardo, E. (2018) Plurilingualism: Vision, conceptualization, and practices. In P. Trifonas and T. Aravossitas (eds) *Handbook of Research and Practice in Heritage Language Education* (pp. 1–19). New York: Springer.

Piccardo, E. (2020) The Common European Framework of Reference (CEFR) in language education: Past, present, and future. TIRF Language Education in Review (LEiR) Series. Monterey, CA & Baltimore, MD: TIRF and Laureate International Universities. https://www.tirfonline.org/2020/03/leir-cefr-past-present-future/ (accessed 14 October 2020).

Piccardo, E. (forthcoming) Mediation for plurilingual competence: Synergies and implications. In B. Dendrinos (ed.) *Mediation as Linguistic and Cultural Negotiation of Meanings and Plurilingualism.* London: Routledge.

Piccardo, E. and North, B. (2019) *The Action-oriented Approach: A Dynamic Vision of Language Education.* Bristol: Multilingual Matters.

Piccardo, E., North, B. and Goodier, T. (2019) Broadening the scope of language education: Mediation, plurilingualism, and collaborative learning: The CEFR Companion Volume. *Je-LKS* 15 (1), 18–36

Richer, J.-J. (2017) Quand le monde du travail peut venir en renfort de la didactique des langues … [When the world of work can come to reinforce language pedagogy]. *Revue TDFLE 70 : La pensée CECR* [TDFLE Review 70: The CEFR Concept] 1–34. http://revue-tdfle.fr/les-numeros/numero-70/28-quand-le-monde-du-travail-peut-venir-en-renfort-de-la-didactique-des-langues (accessed 14 October 2020).

Schneider, G. and North, B. (2000) *Fremdsprachen können: was heisst das? Skalen zur Beschreibung, Beurteilung und Selbsteinschätzung der fremdsprachlichen Kommunikationsfähigkeit* [Knowing a foreign language: What does that mean? Scales for the description, assessment and self-assessment of foreign language communicative proficiency]. Zürich: Verlag Rüegger.

Szabo, T. and Goodier, T. (2018) *Collated representative samples of descriptors of language competence developed for young learners. Resource for educators.* Strasbourg: Council of Europe. https://www.coe.int/en/web/common-european-framework-reference-languages/bank-of-supplementary-descriptors (accessed 14 October 2020).

Thornbury, S. (2016) Communicative language teaching in theory and practice. In G. Hall (ed.) *The Routledge Handbook of English Language Teaching* (pp. 224–237). London: Routledge.

van Lier, L. (2004) *The Ecology and Semiotics of Language Learning.* Dordrecht: Kluwer Academic.

van Lier L. (2007) Action-based teaching, autonomy and identity. *Innovation in Language Learning and Teaching* 1 (1), 1–19.

Part 2: The Action-oriented Approach: A Change of Paradigm?

Introduction to Part 2

David Little

'Action-oriented' is the term the CEFR uses to define its approach to the description of language proficiency. The approach 'views users and learners primarily as "social agents", i.e. members of society who have tasks (not exclusively language-related) to accomplish' (CEFR; Council of Europe, 2001: 9) and it is 'centred on the relationship between ... the agents' use of strategies linked to their competences ... and the task or tasks to be accomplished' (Council of Europe, 2001: 15). The CEFR's descriptive scheme, in other words, has a dual focus: the language activities that user/learners need to perform, and the communicative language competences required for successful performance.

Although the CEFR is careful not to advocate an action-oriented approach to language teaching and learning, it is by no means pedagogically neutral. As the CEFR-CV points out, the descriptive scheme 'implies that the teaching and learning process is driven by action' (CEFR-CV; Council of Europe, 2020: 29). In this connexion it is worth quoting what John Trim (2012), one of the CEFR's authors, wrote about its relation to the classroom: '... having had some experience of the deadening effect of the overlearning of dialogues and endless structure drills, [we] wished to see attention shift from excessive formalism to the processes of communicative face-to-face interaction' (2012: 25).

At the beginning of Chapter 2, the CEFR (2001) summarizes its action-oriented approach like this:

> Language use, embracing language learning, comprises the actions performed by persons who as individuals and as social agents develop a range of *competences*, both *general* and in particular *communicative language competences*. They draw on the competences at their disposal in various contexts under various *conditions* and under various *constraints* to engage in *language activities* involving *language processes* to produce and/or receive *texts* in relation to *themes* in specific *domains*, activating those *strategies* which seem most appropriate for carrying out the *tasks* to be accomplished. The monitoring of these actions by the participants leads to the reinforcement or modification of their competences. (Council of Europe, 2001: 9, italics in original; the words and phrases in italics, to which 'contexts' in the second sentence should be added, refer to the main components of the CEFR's descriptive scheme)

These three sentences provide a basis for exploring what the CEFR's action-oriented approach implies for language learning and teaching. The first five words – 'Language use, embracing language learning' – are explained in Chapter 4: '... it is assumed that the language learner is in the process of becoming a language user, so that the same set of categories will apply' (Council of Europe, 2001: 43). This formulation provides justification for both weak and strong versions of the communicative approach, respectively language learning *for* and language learning *through* communication. The first sentence goes on to focus on language user/learners 'as individuals and as social agents' (Council of Europe, 2001: 9), which reminds us of the interdependent individual–cognitive and social–interactive dimensions of language use and, by implication, language learning. The second sentence provides an action-oriented description of language use that is also by implication an action-oriented description of language learning. The third sentence is concerned with the role that monitoring (metacognitive agency) plays in the exercise and development of proficiency. The CEFR defines monitoring as the strategic component that 'deals with the updating of mental activities and competences in the course of communication' (Council of Europe, 2001: 92). Monitoring as the updating of mental activities is an essential component of Levelt's (1989) model of speech production, while monitoring as the updating of competences is the basis of Schmidt's (1990, 1994) 'noticing hypothesis', which argues that L2 learners need to pay conscious attention to the form of linguistic input in order to address gaps in their knowledge. In both these senses, and also when it is concerned with 'the communicative process as it proceeds, and with ways of managing the process' (Council of Europe, 2001: 92), monitoring is a conscious phenomenon. It plays a crucial role in the user–learner's exercise of agency in language use, of self-regulation in language learning, and of strategic control over the learning process (Little, 1996).

In light of these considerations, it seems reasonable to conclude that the CEFR's action-oriented approach to the description of proficiency implies the need for pedagogies that are characterized by three features. First, they assign a central role to language use that is spontaneous and interactive, arising from the immediate concerns of the classroom, and that is authentic, corresponding to the needs, interests and motivations of the learners. Second, they treat learners as individuals and social agents, recognizing that individual learning is in part driven by interaction with others and framed by the collaboration that is essential to an effective learning community. The combination of interaction and mediation that characterizes classroom talk should be genuinely dialogic in that it allows learners to take discourse initiatives. And third, the action-oriented approach implies pedagogies that set out to foster the development of learners' monitoring skills by engaging them in recursive reflection on the goals, processes and outcomes of their learning.

Interpreted in this way, the CEFR's action-oriented approach licenses teaching that fosters learner autonomy (see, for example, Little *et al.*, 2017).

The contributors to this part of the book were asked to consider whether the CEFR-CV represents a paradigm shift, adding completely new dimensions to the CEFR, especially in relation to mediation, or whether it simply makes aspects of the descriptive scheme that were already present in 2001 more explicit. Contributors were also asked to consider how the new content presented in the CEFR-CV can be reflected in curricula, how it can contribute to a more effective implementation of the action-oriented approach in the classroom, and what it implies for test development.

In Chapter 4 of this volume, John de Jong argues that although the CEFR-CV expands on concepts that were developed in a rudimentary way in the CEFR, the essence of the action-oriented approach was already fully elaborated in the earlier document. He points out, however, that the action-oriented approach has not been taken up either in teaching or in testing, where older paradigms still prevail notwithstanding the impact of the CEFR's reference levels and scales. He welcomes the prominence that the CEFR-CV gives to plurilingualism, an increasingly common feature of our societies, but suggests that the assessment of plurilingualism would require the development of more advanced technologies. As regards mediation, he expresses concern that its operationalization in language testing may threaten the fairness of the assessment.

In Chapter 5, Mark Levy and Neus Figueras focus on the situation in Spain, where they find no evidence that the CEFR-CV is effecting a paradigm shift. An online survey they conducted in 2020 confirms that knowledge of the CEFR's proficiency scales does not necessarily go hand in hand with an understanding of the action-oriented approach and its pedagogical implications. Their survey enabled them to identify three problems: the inaccessibility of the CEFR and the CEFR-CV to teachers; minimal reference to these instruments in official curricula and accompanying documentation; and the need for language teacher education to engage with the action-oriented approach. They conclude, however, that the existence of bilingual and plurilingual education in the Spanish mainstream offers an opportunity to embed the action-oriented approach in teaching and learning.

In Chapter 6, Constant Leung adopts a mediational and plurilingual perspective on the action-oriented approach, welcoming the greater prominence that the CEFR-CV gives to mediation as a component of language proficiency. He pays particular attention to emotional intelligence and plurilingualism as aspects of mediation in social interaction. Pointing to the incommensurability between plurilingualism-in-use and the monolingual framing of language proficiency, he concludes that emotional intelligence and plurilingualism are in need of further conceptual analysis and development before they can be operationalized systematically; in other words, they require detailed empirical exploration.

References

Council of Europe (2001) *Common European Framework of Reference for Languages: Learning, Teaching, Assessment.* Cambridge: Cambridge University Press. https://rm.coe.int/1680459f97 (accessed 25 August 2020).

Council of Europe (2020) *Common European Framework of Reference for Languages: Learning, Teaching, Assessment. Companion Volume.* Strasbourg: Council of Europe. https://rm.coe.int/common-european-framework-of-reference-for-languages-learning-teaching/16809ea0d4 (accessed 25 August 2020).

Levelt, W.J.M. (1989) *Speaking: From Intention to Articulation.* Cambridge, MA: MIT.

Little, D. (1996) Strategic competence considered in relation to strategic control of the language learning process. In H. Holec, D. Little and R. Richterich, *Strategies in Language Learning and Use. Studies towards a Common European Framework of Reference for Language Learning and Teaching* (pp. 9–37). Strasbourg: Council of Europe.

Little, D., Dam, L. and Legenhausen, L. (2017) *Language Learner Autonomy: Theory, Practice and Research.* Bristol: Multilingual Matters.

Schmidt, R.W. (1990) The role of consciousness in second language learning. *Applied Linguistics* 11 (2), 129–158.

Schmidt, R.W. (1994) Deconstructing consciousness in search of useful definitions for applied linguistics. In J.H. Hulstijn and R. Schmidt (eds) *Consciousness in Second Language Learning: Conceptual, Methodological and Practical Issues in Language Learning and Teaching.* Thematic issue of *AILA Review* 11, 11–26.

Trim, J.L.M. (2012) The Common European Framework of Reference for Languages and its background: A case study of cultural politics and educational influences. In M. Byram and L. Parmenter (eds) *The Common European Framework of Reference: The Globalisation of Language Education Policy* (pp. 14–34). Bristol: Multilingual Matters.

4 The Action-oriented Approach and Language Testing: A Critical View

John H.A.L. de Jong

This chapter discusses some of the innovative aspects of the Common European Framework of Reference for Languages *(CEFR; Council of Europe, 2001) in general and, more specifically, those of the* Companion Volume *(CEFR-CV; Council of Europe, 2020). It considers how far the conceptual approach of the latter has contributed to an extension of that of the former. The chapter argues that the CEFR-CV has provided the necessary elaboration of concepts introduced and called for in the CEFR but which had remained rudimentary. It concludes that, in spite of the wide proliferation of the CEFR and its adoption in national curricula and syllabi across Europe and beyond, its basic principles have failed to catch on in the everyday practice of language teaching and testing. The descriptive scheme of CEFR levels has been adopted widely but its deeper concept of an action-oriented approach seems to defy acceptance. Plurilingualism is welcomed as a concept meeting the current context of our multicultural societies, but its assessment would require the development of more advanced technologies. The concept of mediation as defined in the CEFR seems to encounter some, albeit limited, operationalization in language testing but its evaluation in a testing context using the broader definition of mediation developed by the CEFR-CV may threaten the fairness of the assessment.*

Introduction

Many applied linguists have understood that the CEFR-CV (Council of Europe, 2020) offers 'a change of paradigm', although the Council of Europe's preface to the CEFR-CV states that it does not 'impact on the construct described in the CEFR' but, rather, enriches its original apparatus (see also Piccardo & North, 2019). This misunderstanding may have resulted from the language used in introductory papers presented at the launching conference 'Building Inclusive Societies through Enriching Plurilingual and Pluricultural Education' (Council of Europe, 2018), where Enrica Piccardo (2018) presented a paper entitled 'Mediation – A paradigm shift in language education'.

To speak to the concept of paradigm change, or paradigm shift, we will discuss the shifts that have occurred in language testing over the last hundred years with respect to the main innovative aspects of the CEFR, which are the CEFR descriptive scheme, the action-oriented approach, mediation and plurilingualism. The CEFR descriptive scheme introduces a new categorization of language use into reception, production, interaction, and mediation. The action-oriented approach recognizes that the use of a language is aimed at performing real-world tasks in a social context. Plurilingualism is the ability of a person who has competence in more than one language to switch between languages depending on the situation for ease of communication; for example, they can speak in one language while understanding another.

The organizers of the joint EALTA/UKALTA conference asked us to address a number of questions: Does the CEFR-CV indeed represent a change of paradigm – for example, as regards our understanding of the action-oriented approach? Does it make more explicit aspects of the CEFR's descriptive scheme that were already present in the 2001 version? Or does it add completely new dimensions, especially in relation to mediation? Either way, how can the new content presented in the CEFR-CV be reflected in curricula? Can it contribute to a stronger implementation of the action-oriented approach in the classroom? And what does it imply for test development?

To address these questions, we must turn to the original CEFR, which states:

> From this perspective, the aim of language education is profoundly modified. It is no longer seen as simply to achieve 'mastery' of one or two, or even three languages, each taken in isolation, with the 'ideal native speaker' as the ultimate model. Instead, the aim is to develop a linguistic repertory, in which all linguistic abilities have a place. (Council of Europe, 2001: 5)

A few lines later it acknowledges: 'The full implications of such a paradigm shift have yet to be worked out and translated into action.' Thus, the paradigm change or paradigm shift was effectively initiated by the development and subsequent publication of the CEFR.

From Four Skills to Four Modes of Communication

According to the view expressed in the CEFR, the traditional division of language usage modes into speaking, listening, reading and writing is replaced by a set of language activities involving reception, production, interaction and mediation, where all four can occur in oral and/or written form, reception representing the traditional skills of reading and listening and production the skills of speaking and writing. More often than not, language communication occurs in interaction between two or more individuals exchanging information, views, observations or perceptions. Interaction therefore can also make use of both oral and written channels. Finally, mediation enables communication between language users who are unable to communicate with each other directly and need the intermediary intervention of a third party who is able to communicate directly with both the other language users and can relay to each of them what the other wishes to communicate or is required to understand. The CEFR rightly points out that 'Mediating language activities – (re)processing an existing text – occupy an important place in the normal linguistic functioning of our societies' (Council of Europe, 2001: 14). This type of activity can take place within the context of a single language, e.g. where a mother explains to her child what was said by some other individual who was using language opaque to the youngster, or across languages where a court interpreter explains the defence of an immigrant to a jury.

The CEFR-CV has developed a broader view of mediation, including language activities such as chairing a meeting, which involves summarizing the views of different participants and unwrapping their similarities and differences, thereby adding cognitive and interpersonal mediation activities and strategies. In addition, the CEFR-CV recognizes that mediation goes beyond language (textual mediation) and includes social and cultural mediation. Reflecting on this broader interpretation of mediation one may come to suggest that for any interaction activity or strategy to be successful it requires mediation skills from the actor. Yet the implication of this consideration leads to a dilemma on assessment criteria as communicative success in real life also depends on, for example, physical properties of the actor such as height and gender: attractiveness of features of the actor does impact on degree of success in communication (Mulford *et al.*, 1988). Can, therefore, an assessment taking interpersonal and social skills into account be acceptable, or should it be considered as a form of undue discrimination resulting in lack of equitability?

The enduring relevance of translation and interpretation in our present society is exemplified by the close to 60,000 people working in that area in the USA (Statista, 2020). This number is dwarfed by the 180,000 people working in the same area in Europe (Eurostat, 2019), where the European Union's parliament alone uses around 550 translators and 650 interpreters in its daily work – small surprise if we know that the addition of a single country (Croatia) in 2013 required the addition of 46 new language combinations to deal with one additional language (European Parliament, 2020). Human skills and hard work remain prevalent in this context because in spite of the advances of technology, automated translation still leaves much to wish for (Hofstadter, 2018).

Translation has also recently regained recognition in foreign language education (Tsagari & Floros, 2013) since it was ostracized together with the grammar-translation approach to language learning, teaching and assessment. It is probably good to recall that the development that came to define language assessment as the evaluation of the four skills arose in reaction to the grammar-translation approach, which had existed for centuries and originated from the classical method of the teaching of Ancient Greek and Latin. Transposing this approach to modern languages was recognized as ineffectual and language teaching briefly adopted the technocratic behaviouristic approach of drills and memorization to teach the 'four skills', soon to be disqualified by the findings of the Pennsylvania Foreign Language Project (Smith, 1970) and experiments carried out by Savignon (1972).

Meanwhile, scholars like Dell Hymes (1966, 1972) had advocated that the objective of learning a foreign language should be directed at enabling learners to use the language in social contexts for achieving communication goals and formulated the concept 'communicative competence'. The segregated (four) skills approach was established by Rivers (1968) and replacement of the grammar-translation approach to teaching was laid down in the Netherlands' Education Act on Secondary Education of 1963 (effective from 1968), popularly known as the 'Mammoth Law', where under the influence of van Ek (author of *The Threshold Level*, 1975) the traditional separate testing of vocabulary, grammar and translation in final secondary schools examinations was explicitly outlawed and replaced by the segregated testing of reading, listening, speaking and writing.

Language Testing: The Four Skills Live On

In language testing and assessment, the oldest international English language test, currently known as Cambridge English Proficiency (CPE; first administered in 1913), originally focused on translation and grammar, although an oral component was also involved (Weir, 2003). In the 1960s both the original TOEFL (Test of English as a Foreign Language) and the EPTB (English Proficiency Test Battery, predecessor of first ELTS and later IELTS) adopted a discrete-features, structural approach, testing linguistic elements such as grammar and vocabulary. By the 1980s, under the influence of a more communicative approach to language teaching, the international language testing field moved to a skills-based approach, addressing reading, listening, writing and speaking, but each separately under the narrow-minded conception that psychometrics required 'pure' measures and that the unidimensionality requirement necessitated a segregated skills methodology. Davies (2007: 86) concludes that 'the changes in academic English language proficiency testing in the U.K. over the second half of the 20th century ... were driven by the paradigmatic changes in the climate of opinion about language'.

TOEFL in its latest version (TOEFL iBT) takes this development a step further. Moving from the segregated-skills testing it implemented, by adding the Test of Spoken English (TSE) and Test of Written English (TWE) to the TOEFL in the 1980s, it finally reached its 'TOEFL 2000' ideal with the launching of TOEFL iBT in 2005. This replaces the focus on distinct language skills with a more integrated approach that addresses communication and comprehension. However, the structure of score reporting has remained in the traditional format, with an overall score and scores for each of the four traditional skills of reading, listening, writing and speaking.

The most recent addition to international English language tests is the Pearson Test of English Academic (PTE Academic), which also reports an overall score and sub-scores on the four skills of reading, listening, writing, and speaking. In addition, it reports scores on some enabling skills (grammar, oral fluency, pronunciation, spelling, vocabulary and written discourse). However, these are not based on separate test questions or modules as they were during the structural approach but are derived from automatically generated analytic scoring of items addressing the oral and written competencies.

In summary, not one of the major international English language tests has followed up on the proposal of the CEFR to replace the four-skills approach (based on graphic and acoustic phenomena) by the four-modes approach (based on language actions) introduced almost 20 years ago; neither has the recently published CEFR-CV yet been able to reinforce the message. Apparently, international English language test providers have shied away from introducing this aspect of the paradigm change introduced by the CEFR, undoubtedly because score users are not ready to appreciate the change. The concepts of reception, production, interaction and mediation may be too abstract for immigration and university admission officers to readily adopt. Their thinking about language abilities may by now have moved on from the structuralist understanding of language ability as being composed of grammar and vocabulary knowledge to the four-skills approach introduced by the communicative movement. But they may see no advantage in restructuring the four skills into the four modes, or they may simply be unaware of this change. Another issue may be that some may see little advantage in replacing 'listening' with 'reception – oral comprehension' or find it too complicated to replace 'reading' with 'reception – reading comprehension'. As de Jong and Verhoeven stated:

> If the outcome of educational measurement is to be expressed in terms of a position on a continuum, and the measurement is to be meaningful outside of the situation of measurement, it is necessary to define the

underlying variable in such a way that potential users of the outcome of the measurement are able to interpret its meaning. (de Jong & Verhoeven, 1992: 10)

It would seem that the categorization proposed 20 years ago by the CEFR of language ability into reception, production, interaction, and mediation, while intended to cause a paradigm shift, has not yet been fully adopted by the language teaching and testing fields. However, the concept of speaking as interactional was modelled by Dell Hymes (1966) and has been adopted widely.

Language Coursebooks Still Lingering Mainly in the Structuralist Approach

Although the CEFR has been widely adopted by governments and educational authorities and introduced into official syllabi all over Europe and beyond (e.g. East Asian countries), the basic principles have not penetrated broadly into the classroom (Figueras, 2012). Educational goals may have been set in terms of the descriptive scheme of levels, and teachers may be aware of the levels A1 to C2, but concepts such as plurilingual and pluricultural competence, even when they have been integrated into the national foreign language curriculum, remain largely unknown by the teachers (Çelik, 2013). This may be because, while language testing seems unable to really move on from the four-skills approach, the textbook market offers a possibly even more dire picture. Although most popular textbooks now claim to move students through the CEFR levels from A1 to C2, they hardly ever refer to production, reception, interaction and mediation. A review of English language coursebooks,[1] written to help teachers decide on choosing the best coursebook, offers among the top of its 'Incredible Resources' the following examples:

> [Coursebook 1] incorporates a wide range of activities covering all of the important language skills: speaking, listening, reading and writing. It includes plenty of visuals and exercises and focuses both on vocabulary and grammar rules.

> [Coursebook 2] There are 53 lessons in total, covering subjects such as verb tenses, possessive adjectives, prepositions, negative forms and more. New chapters on the future perfect tense, additional exercises for a thorough review of verb tenses ...

Introducing a selection of coursebooks for the teaching of grammar the website states: 'These course books cover grammar for speaking, writing and reading. ... On top of the grammar knowledge, you'll even get CDs to practice pronunciation, intonation and stress.' Typically, listening

Table 4.1 Number of book titles available on Book Depository (approach labels added, J. de Jong, 8 November 2020)

Pre-communicative era approach	
Language Grammar	16,957
Language Vocabulary	6,577
Language Pronunciation	1,847
Language Translation	3,539
Language Interpretation	1,065
Four-skills approach	
Language Speaking	8,068
Language Reading	11,632
Language Listening	760
Language Writing	8,188
CEFR approach	
Language Production	592
Language Reception	78
Language Interaction	1,396
Language Mediation	77

is not even mentioned; as authors past and present have pointed out, listening is often neglected (Elin, 1972; Çakır, 2018).

A quick search of categories of available language teaching books on Book Depository[2] reveals that the publishing market is still predominantly lingering in past approaches to language teaching (Table 4.1).

As is clearly apparent from Table 4.1, the vast majority of books available at Book Depository smack of the pre-communicative era approach to language teaching; within the four-skills approach least attention is again paid to listening; and the CEFR approach seems to have inspired coursebook authors the least.

Plurilingualism

Two further concepts are considered to be elements of the paradigm shift introduced by the CEFR: plurilingualism and mediation. The CEFR states:

> The introduction of a European Language Portfolio with international currency is now under consideration. The Portfolio would make it possible for learners to document their progress towards plurilingual competence by recording learning experiences of all kinds over a wide range of languages, much of which would otherwise be unattested and unrecognized. (Council of Europe, 2001: 20)

More than 10 years later David Little (2012: 275) concludes: 'Although more than 100 ELPs from 70% of the Council of Europe's member states were validated and accredited between 2000 and 2010, the ELP remains largely untried in most national education systems.' Likewise, Piccardo *et al.* (2019: 18) admit that the field of language education has been, in general, slow to pick up on plurilingualism. Meanwhile, international recognition still remains utopian, which undermines the practical social relevance. The promise of an ELP that would open doors across national borders and bring recognition of learners' language abilities remains unfulfilled.

True, a large number of European Language Portfolios and Language Passports is available. These seem to function mainly as pedagogical tools in the context of self-assessment and classroom assessment. One can imagine that an inventory of the range of languages of which citizens have partial mastery, and to which level of competence they can use those languages, could be of interest to a society. It is, however, hard to envisage how such an inventory could be based on efficient and objective assessment procedures. Questionnaires could be designed asking subjects to go through a number of can-do statements and provide the names of the languages in which they are able to perform those language tasks. Gathering evidence on the truthfulness of such claims could possibly become feasible when the sophistication of artificial intelligence systems allowing for oral and written input and output has acquired a degree of perfection sufficient to exclude the occurrence of translation errors. But currently there does not seem to be a real demand from score users for plurilingual language tests. Score users may have an interest in test takers' command of more than one language, but they seem to prefer to see separate outcomes for each.

Tests for translators and interpreters do, of course, set demands on proficiency in more than one language, but are mostly addressing 'language pairs', i.e. two languages, and would therefore be more appropriately categorized as addressing mediation.

Mediation

On the concept of mediation, the picture has been more promising. As language testing has followed insights consolidated and further elaborated by the CEFR in interpreting language proficiency as communicative competence, many tests have taken the CEFR as a development guideline, and any test seeking recognition has understood the need to align its scores to levels defined in the CEFR. It can also be asserted that modern language testing incorporates mediation in a number of its tasks.

Some unpublished examples from the item type specifications and guidelines for item writers from the Pearson Test of English Academic illustrate how tasks include integrative mediation, but also require test takers to produce either oral or written language that reproduces the information they have seen or heard in graphic, written and/or audio input, thus effectively performing mediation tasks some of which go beyond textual mediation (interpreting graphs):

> Item type # 08: Specifically, this task allows test takers to demonstrate their ability to summarize the key points of the academic information they have read. Test takers are required to synthesize information in the reading text and write a one-sentence summary.

> Item type # 15: The goal of items written to this item specification is to set integrative tasks that require test takers to analyse and synthesize information in listening texts and write a summary of the key points. Test takers listen to the audio recording, and then write a summary of what the speaker has said.

> Item type # 19: The goal of items written to this item specification is to set speaking tasks that assess test takers' sociolinguistic knowledge and achievement strategies in extended explanation and description of graphic input. After looking at the image(s) on full screen, test takers describe in detail the development or sequence of events presented graphically.

> Item type #20: The goal of items written to this item specification is to set integrative tasks that require test takers to make a short presentation based on information from audio/video recording and graphic input. Test-takers hear an audio recording/watch a video and retell what they have just heard/watched in their own words. Test takers are required to imagine a situation in which they have attended a lecture and retell the content to a friend who was unable to attend.

Conclusions

The CEFR-CV by itself does not represent a paradigm shift but, by offering the necessary and much called-for elaboration of descriptors for notions such as mediation and plurilingualism that were clearly signalled in the CEFR (2001), it enhances the paradigm-shifting potential of the CEFR. In addition, the launch of the CEFR-CV has rejuvenated interest in the CEFR. The CEFR-CV also offers a broader interpretation of mediation, which can definitely be beneficial for teaching but may threaten fair and equitable assessment. Likewise, the concept of plurilingualism offers advantages for enhancing the relevance of language teaching in our present multilingual and multicultural societies but is unlikely to be implemented in language testing until more sophisticated technologies become available.

Has then the CEFR caused a paradigm shift? Unfortunately, we must conclude that some of the ground-breaking concepts introduced by the

CEFR have not yet been able to reach their full potential. Language teachers and test score users continue to follow the four-skills model and have not (yet) adopted the four-modes model advocated by the CEFR. Although the concept of mediation seems to have been operationalized to some degree, the adoption of the concept of plurilingualism seems to remain mainly utopian with little practical advantage for language learners, many of whom in this era of massive migration could indeed benefit from their home and heritage language skills if only they were recognized.

Notes

(1) https://www.fluentu.com/blog/english/english-course-book/
(2) https://www.bookdepository.com

References

Çakır, İ. (2018) Is listening instruction neglected intentionally or incidentally in foreign language teaching contexts? *Journal of Language and Linguistic Studies* 14 (2), 154–172.

Çelik, S. (2013) Plurilingualism, pluriculturalism, and the CEFR: Are Turkey's foreign language objectives reflected in classroom instruction? *Procedia – Social and Behavioral Sciences* 70, 1872–1879. https://www.sciencedirect.com/science/article/pii/S1877042813002668 (accessed 17 November 2020).

Council of Europe (2001) *Common European Framework of Reference for Languages: Learning, Teaching, Assessment.* Cambridge: Cambridge University Press.

Council of Europe (2018) Building Inclusive Societies through Enriching Plurilingual and Pluricultural Education, a conference organized by the Council of Europe, 16–17 May 2018. https://www.coe.int/en/web/common-european-framework-reference-languages/home/-/asset_publisher/bsir5Sz9Ku0J/content/building-inclusive-societies-through-enriching-plurilingual-and-pluricultural-education?inheritRedirect=false (accessed 1 October 2020).

Council of Europe (2020) *Common European Framework of Reference for Languages: Learning, Teaching, Assessment. Companion Volume.* Strasbourg: Council of Europe. https://www.coe.int/en/web/education/-/common-european-framework-of-reference-for-languages-learning-teaching-assessment-companion-volume (accessed 30 September 2020).

Davies, A. (2007) Assessing academic English language proficiency: 40+ years of U.K. language tests. In J. Fox, M. Wesche, D. Bayliss, L. Cheng, C.E. Turner and C. Doe (eds) *Language Testing Reconsidered* (pp. 73–86). Ottawa: University of Ottawa Press.

de Jong, J.H.A.L. and Verhoeven, L. (1992) Modeling and assessing language proficiency. In L. Verhoeven and J.H.A.L. de Jong (eds) *The Construct of Language Proficiency* (pp. 3–19). Amsterdam: John Benjamins.

Elin, R. (1972) Listening: Neglected and forgotten in the classroom. *Elementary English* 49 (2), 230–232.

European Parliament (2020) Interpretation. https://www.europarl.europa.eu/interpretation/en/introduction.htm (accessed 30 September 2020).

Eurostat (2019) How many translators and interpreters are in the EU? https://ec.europa.eu/eurostat/web/products-eurostat-news/-/EDN-20190930-1?inheritRedirect=true#:~:text=Your%20key%20to%20European%20statistics&text=In%202018%2C%20there%20were%20around,0.1%25%20of%20total%20EU%20employment (accessed 30 September 2020).

Figueras, N. (2012) The impact of the CEFR. *ELT Journal* 66 (4), 477–485.

Hofstadter, D. (2018) The shallowness of Google Translate. *The Atlantic*, 30 January 2018. https://www.theatlantic.com/technology/archive/2018/01/the-shallowness-of-google-translate/551570/ (accessed 30 September 2020).

Hymes, D.H. (1966) Two types of linguistic relativity. In W. Bright (ed.) *Sociolinguistics* (pp. 114–158). The Hague: Mouton.

Hymes, D.H. (1972) On communicative competence. In J.B. Pride and J. Holmes (eds) *Sociolinguistics. Selected Readings* (pp. 269–293). Harmondsworth: Penguin.

Little, D. (2012) The European Language Portfolio in whole-school use. *Innovation in Language Learning and Teaching* 6 (3), 275–285.

Mulford, M., Orbell, J., Shatto, C. and Stockard, J. (1988) Physical attractiveness, opportunity, and success in everyday exchange. *American Journal of Sociology* 103 (6), 1565–1592.

Piccardo, E. (2018) Mediation: A paradigm shift in language education. Paper presented at the Council of Europe conference, Building Inclusive Societies through Enriching Plurilingual and Pluricultural Education, a conference organized by the Council of Europe, 16–17 May 2018. https://rm.coe.int/mediation-a-paradigm-shift-in-language-education-piccardo/16808ae720 (accessed 1 October 2020).

Piccardo, E. and North, B. (2019) *The Action-oriented Approach: A Dynamic Vision of Language Education*. Bristol: Multilingual Matters.

Piccardo, E., North, B. and Goodier, T. (2019) Broadening the scope of language education: Mediation, plurilingualism and collaborative learning: the CEFR Companion Volume. *Journal of e-Learning and Knowledge Society* 15 (1), 17–36. https://www.je-lks.org/ojs/index.php/Je-LKS_EN/article/view/1612/1032 (accessed 15 October 2020).

Rivers, W. (1968) *Teaching Foreign-language Skills*. Chicago, IL: University of Chicago Press.

Savignon, S.J. (1972) *Communicative Competence: An Experiment in Foreign-language Teaching*. Berkeley, CA: Center for Curriculum Development, University of California.

Smith, P.D. (1970) *A Comparison of the Cognitive and Audiolingual Approaches to Foreign Language Instruction: The Pennsylvania Foreign Language Project*. Philadelphia, PA: Center for Curriculum Development.

Statista (2020) Number of employees in interpreting and translating services in the United States from 2022 to 2019 (in 1,000s). https://www.statista.com/statistics/320340/number-of-employees-in-interpreting-and-translating-services-us/#:~:text=Number%20of%20interpreters%20and%20translators%20in%20the%20U.S.%202012%2D2019&text=There%20were%20approximately%2058%2C870%20interpreters,U.S.%20as%20of%20May%202019 (accessed 30 September 2020).

Tsagari, D. and Floros, G. (eds) (2013) *Translation in Language Teaching and Assessment*. Newcastle upon Tyne: Cambridge Scholars.

van Ek, J.A. (1975) *The Threshold Level*. Strasbourg: Council of Europe.

Weir, C. (2003) A survey of the history of the Certificate of Proficiency in English (CPE) in the twentieth century. In C. Weir and M. Milanovic (eds) *Continuity and Innovation: Revising the Cambridge Proficiency in English Examination 1913–2002*. Cambridge: Cambridge University Press.

5 The Action-oriented Approach in the CEFR and the CEFR *Companion Volume*: A Change of Paradigm(s)? A Case Study from Spain

Mark Levy and Neus Figueras

The action-oriented approach to teaching and learning is at the heart of the Common European Framework of Reference for Languages (CEFR) *and the* CEFR Companion Volume (CEFR-CV): *a focus on linking language and action and enabling learners of a foreign language to use the language to communicate effectively. This has been identified by some as a paradigm shift, but in this chapter we will argue that, in Spain at least, there is little evidence of this. While there seems to be considerable knowledge of the CEFR proficiency levels and scales among educators, and especially assessment specialists, there appears to be little or no recognition of the action-oriented approach, especially at school level. We suggest that this is largely due to three factors: inaccessibility of the CEFR and the CEFR-CV to classroom teachers; minimal reference to the CEFR, the CEFR-CV and the action-oriented approach in official curricula and documentation; and the need for a greater focus on what the action-oriented approach means in practice at all stages of teacher education. Nonetheless, we finish by suggesting that mainstreamed plurilingual and bilingual education in Spain potentially offers a real opportunity to embed the action-oriented approach in teaching and learning, as long as teachers can be engaged and the realities of state sector teaching contexts addressed.*

Introduction: The (Real) Impact of the Action-oriented Approach

The CEFR advocates an action-orientated approach to teaching and learning in order to prepare learners to communicate effectively in a second/foreign language outside the classroom. This focus on 'action' and viewing user/learners as 'social agents' has been highlighted as one of the key features of the CEFR in training sessions and seminars, and the boxed paragraph at the beginning of Chapter 2 of the CEFR (Council of Europe, 2001: 9) has been widely quoted for more than 20 years. The CEFR *Companion Volume* (CEFR-CV) reinforces what the action-oriented approach implies in terms of approach and content for learning, teaching and assessment and aims at expanding and making more explicit the main aspects that 'were already implicit in the CEFR 2001, though not developed' (North, 2020: 10). The theory behind the updating of the CEFR descriptive scheme in the CEFR-CV is explained by North and Piccardo (2016, 2019), while Piccardo and North (2019) provide an extensive account of the background, sources and practical implications of the action-oriented approach, which they describe as a 'paradigm shift' (2019: 283) in pedagogy.

The publication of the CEFR-CV has resulted in a renewed interest in the principles that underlie the CEFR's descriptive scheme, from which the level labels and descriptors (often referred to as the vertical dimension of the CEFR) have tended to divert attention (Byram & Parmenter, 2012; Martyniuk & Noijons, 2007; North, 2014, 2020). The action-oriented approach, what it means, what it implies, how it can be implemented, and why it is key in language education, is currently being revisited and theorized, 50 years after John Trim and David Wilkins 'sketched out the *action-oriented approach* that became the basis of *The Threshold Level*' (North, 2014: 16).

John Trim (1980) summarized the essence of the action-oriented approach in his preface to the 1980 edition of *The Threshold Level*, a document which remains, like the CEFR, one of the best-known documents issued by the Council of Europe, *adopted* in many countries and translated into many languages:

> The *Threshold Level* remains a most powerful tool for those teachers and course planners who are converting language teaching from structure-dominated scholastic sterility into a vital medium for the freer movement of people and ideas, and for those language learners who travel faster and more purposively for knowing where they are going. (Trim, 1980: viii)

Our use of italics for *adopted* is meant to problematize what adoption means in education, and in particular what adoption has meant for the CEFR in general and the action-oriented approach in particular. A survey by Martyniuk and Noijons (2007) collected information on the impact of the CEFR in Council of Europe member countries. Released on the occasion of an intergovernmental forum held in Strasbourg, the results of the survey indicated concrete actions that would help achieve a fuller and more rigorous use of the CEFR (Goullier, 2007). One of the first actions taken by the Council of Europe after the forum was to issue a Recommendation of the Committee of Ministers to member states on the use of the CEFR and the promotion of plurilingualism (Recommendation CM/Rec (2008) 7).[1]

However, despite the efforts of researchers and the Council of Europe itself to document and disseminate the ethos and content of the CEFR beyond level labels and descriptors (Council of Europe, 2008), not much seems to have changed in 15 years. Whereas little has been published on how the action-oriented approach has materialized in classrooms, researchers (Little, 2011; North, 2014), studies and surveys (Diaz-Bedmar & Byram, 2019; European Parliament, 2013; Figueras, 2013), and professional fora (EALTA–UKALTA London Event, February 2020) conclude that the CEFR needs a renewed impetus to increase its effect.

It is important to consider why it is necessary to 'go back to' and 'go deeper into' a document that was published 20 years ago and has been widely influential but is seemingly still not fully understood. On the one hand, accessing Council of Europe materials and documents is not easy: they are difficult to find, often more than 100 pages in length, and usually written in what has been referred to as Council of Europe jargon. Even the documents specifically written for practitioners (e.g. Bailly et al., 2001) are long and not user-friendly, so it is not surprising that they have not succeeded in reaching classrooms. On the other hand, and although change in education takes time, the real 'paradigm shift' that adoption of the action-oriented approach implies was not highlighted in the CEFR as it is in the CEFR-CV:

> The CEFR presents the language user/learner as a 'social agent', acting in the social world and exerting agency in the learning process. This implies a real *paradigm shift* in both course planning and teaching promoting learner engagement and autonomy. (Council of Europe, 2020: 28; emphasis added)

Moreover, what the action-oriented approach represented was often underplayed in teacher training seminars, either because it was not fully understood or in order to gain acceptance in contexts where the CEFR was seen as a threat to well-established practice. Even professionals closely linked to the Council of Europe somehow diminished what adopting the approach might represent:

> The stress on an action-oriented approach found throughout the Council of Europe document does not in itself mean any drastic change of perspective for language teaching in France. (Goullier, 2006: 51)

Indeed, at the risk of oversimplifying, we could say that the CEFR's action-oriented approach reflects a familiar truth, that one essential difference between good and bad language teaching is the extent of and the sophistication of the connections between language and action, between controlled and free use, between exercise and task. (North, 2014: 100)

Our chapter focuses on Spain, on how the content of the CEFR, and in particular the action-oriented approach, is understood and implemented, and on whether a paradigm shift has taken place. We report on how the CEFR is referred to in legislation and official curricula and we present the results of a small-scale survey that aimed at finding out how practitioners working at different education levels in Spain perceive the principles underlying the CEFR and the CEFR-CV.

The CEFR in Spain and the Initial Impact of the CEFR-CV

The Spanish government has always claimed to follow the recommendations of the Council of Europe, as have the regional governments that are responsible for the development and implementation of royal decrees issued by Spain's highly decentralized state. These decrees fix curriculum content and assessment criteria from primary to *bachillerato* (sixth form in the UK) and vocational training, and also for the Escuelas Oficiales de Idiomas [Official Language Schools] (EOI), a system of public language schools for adults. No such legislation exists for university language centres, which write their own syllabi to suit their needs following the guidelines of the Conferencia de Rectores de las Universidades Españolas [Conference of Spanish University Rectors] (CRUE, 2011) and award their certificates according to the regulations of the Asociación de Centros de Lenguas en la Enseñanza Superior [Association of Language Centres in Higher Education], organizations which also claim to follow Council of Europe guidelines (ACLES, 2014).

We were prompted to undertake our survey because personal observations and anecdotal evidence from teachers working in a variety of contexts seemed to indicate that there are huge differences across the different educational levels and that, despite claims asserting the CEFR's impact, all too often there has been no real shift in how languages are taught, learnt and assessed since its publication in 2001.

As a starting point, a 'vox pop' was conducted in January 2020 amongst a small group of teachers, trainers, examiners and materials writers, some in the ELT sector and others in state sector education. The responses showed that there was clearly some understanding of the CEFR, especially amongst examiners and materials writers, but that very few had enough knowledge to, for example, chart a learning path from B1 to B2. Apart from those working in the EOIs, barely anyone

Table 5.1 Explicit references to the CEFR and related terms in Spanish curricular documentation for languages

Document	CoE	CEFR	CEFR-CV	AoA	Other
Primary (Ministerio de Educación, Cultura y Deporte, 2014)	1	2	–	–	European Union (4 times)
Secondary & *bachillerato* (Ministerio de Educación, Cultura y Deporte, 2015)	1	2	–	3	–
EOI curriculum (Ministerio de Educación, Cultura y Deporte, 2017)	4	6	–	–	Mediation (15 times)
EOI certificates (Ministerio de Educación, Cultura y Deporte, 2019)	2	2	–	–	Mediation (5 times)
CRUE (Conferencia de Rectores de las Universidades Españolas, 2011)	–	3	–	–	–
ACLES (Asociación de Centros de Lenguas en la Enseñanza Superior, 2014)	1	10	–	–	–

had heard of mediation or seen the CEFR-CV or the mediation scales; and no one had heard of, or could identify any features of, the action-oriented approach.

Following this initial sampling of the state of affairs in Spain, we accessed the available official curricula and documentation to find references to the CEFR and the action-oriented approach at the different levels of education. As reported in the study carried out by the European parliament (European Parliament, 2013) on the implementation of the CEFR in European education systems, explicit references are surprisingly scarce. Table 5.1 summarizes the number of explicit references to the Council of Europe (CoE), the CEFR, the *Companion Volume* (CEFR-CV), the action-oriented approach (AoA) and other CEFR-related terms (Other) in the official documents consulted, which are listed in the first column and can be accessed using the references at the end of this chapter. The rows are organized according to education levels and not the year of publication.

It is revealing that explicit references to the CEFR and related terms are so limited, although the principles and recommendations in the CEFR can actually be traced in the documentation. In the case of the curriculum for secondary and *bachillerato*, for example, the action-oriented approach is described most faithfully, relaying the content of the boxed paragraph at the beginning of Chapter 2 in the CEFR (Council of Europe, 2001: 9). In most cases, reference to the CEFR is made in general terms, with reference to domains of use and to the competences pertaining to each level (including mediation in the case of the curriculum decree for the EOIs, which predates the publication of the CEFR-CV in its provisional version in 2017). In other cases, however, the CEFR is mentioned as evidence of internationalization (as, for example, in the EOIs or in the ACLES documentation), or to justify a decision that is not supported by the CEFR. In the EOI certificates decree, for example, it is surprising to find that the Council of Europe and the CEFR are used to support the decision that the overall language proficiency certificates must include a separate paper on mediation, carrying the same weight as the other four papers (oral and written comprehension and oral and written expression and interaction). Regarding the cut score of the exam, we are told that 'following the indications of the Council of Europe on the adequate use of the European Language Portfolio and the CEFR, in order to pass the general competence exam it will be necessary to obtain a minimum score of 65% of the total possible score' (Ministerio de Educación, Cultura y Deporte, 2019: 2263).

The decision to evaluate mediation independently of the other papers in the certificate exams has impacted not only on the EOIs themselves but also on secondary schools with bilingual programmes in those regions of Spain where the EOIs are responsible for assessing learner performance (B1 level). Perhaps because of the decision to include mediation in the evaluation of student performance, and thus to include it in the curriculum, the 'vox pop' suggested that there had been no significant impact in secondary school classrooms beyond the inclusion of a number of exam preparation activities. There was also no evidence that teachers understood the action-oriented approach or implemented it in their classrooms.

Following the search for CEFR-related references in Spanish language legislation, we were interested to see whether the spirit of the CEFR and recommendations regarding its use had reached classrooms by 2020, twenty years after the CEFR's first publication. As the initial 'vox pop' was limited to Madrid and the Castilla-la Mancha region, a survey was drafted to gather information about the state of affairs across Spain. The following section focuses on the results of the survey.

The Survey: Results and Discussion

The survey (in Spanish) was released on 31 August 2020 and circulated to ACLES and GIELE (Grupo de Interés en Evaluación de Lenguas en España [Interest Group on Language Assessment in Spain])[2] lists and through a British Council newsletter, in the hope of attracting as many responses as possible. The number of responses was smaller than expected (127), with a small majority of these (55.9%) coming from teachers of English. Only 11 respondents had been teaching for five years or less, while 72 had more than 15 years' teaching experience. All but three questions were answered by all 127 respondents, the exceptions being question 8 (126 respondents) and questions 7 and 16 (125 respondents). (Differences in knowledge of and attitudes to the CEFR amongst teachers of different languages or those with different levels of experience might be an interesting study for the future.)

Most of the responses came from the language centres at universities (57) and from the Escuelas Oficiales de Idiomas (42), while there was a particularly low response from primary (9) and secondary (13) teachers. The difficult and stressful return to work in the COVID-19 context in September 2020 may have been responsible for the small number of responses from mainstream schoolteachers; it may also reflect their perception of the CEFR as a distant instrument not especially relevant to their situation. In any case, the results of our survey for secondary teachers were similar to those reported by Diaz-Bedmar and Byram (2019).

The survey asked 17 questions related to the CEFR and the CEFR-CV. For reasons of length we have chosen to focus on those responses that we feel most clearly add to the discussion. It is important to emphasize that an important limitation of our survey is that we were reliant on the respondents' own perception of their knowledge of the CEFR and the CEFR-CV rather than some external measure, and it is therefore perfectly possible that some have over-estimated their understanding while others have done the opposite.

That said, we can still usefully compare answers to the questions asked. Something that is immediately striking (Figure 5.1) is the difference between the 84.3% of respondents (107) who said that they were able to identify the main characteristics of each level of the CEFR (Question 5) and the 40.2% who said that they had consulted the *Companion Volume* (Question 17). Given the almost universal use of the CEFR levels in language testing and the widespread reference to the CEFR in teaching materials, it is not surprising that only two teachers (1.6%) admitted to

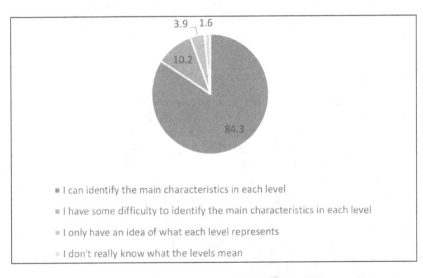

3.9 1.6

10.2

84,3

- I can identify the main characteristics in each level
- I have some difficulty to identify the main characteristics in each level
- I only have an idea of what each level represents
- I don't really know what the levels mean

Figure 5.1 Responses to the questions: How familiar are you with the CEFR levels? How would you rate your knowledge in identifying each level?

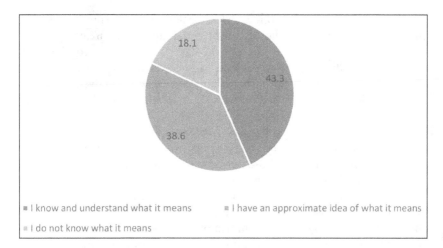

Figure 5.2 Responses to the question: How familiar are you with the action-oriented approach as described in the CEFR?

not really knowing what the levels stand for. In the earlier 'vox pop' (see above), when asked a follow-up question, few of those who knew the levels were confident in articulating them.

Lack of knowledge of the CEFR-CV is of special concern, given that a main aim of this volume is to reinforce understanding of the action-oriented approach and to encourage transfer of this knowledge into the classroom to create a paradigm shift in teaching and learning. It is significant that 28.3% (36 teachers) said they knew nothing at all of the CEFR-CV, while another 31.5% (40) had only heard of it (19) or of its content areas (21) from others.

Responding to specific questions about the action-oriented approach, 55 teachers (43.3%) said that they knew of and understood it (Question 6, Figure 5.2), which is a similar number to those who said they had consulted the *Companion Volume*. However, the vast majority of those who took the survey were teachers either in university language centres or the Escuelas Oficiales de Idiomas (99 of 127), who are likely to have been very much influenced by the fact that they issue official certificates that claim to be aligned with the CEFR. Furthermore, and as we have stated, these results reflect self-perception and not externally measured knowledge, so we think it unlikely that they allow us to talk about paradigm changes in teaching and learning, even amongst those who might well be expected to have a greater knowledge of both the CEFR and the CEFR-CV than primary and secondary teachers. On the contrary, we think it is a matter of concern that even in this small sample group, 18.1% said that they did not know what the action-oriented approach meant, while 38.6% claimed only to have some idea of what is meant by the term.

In response to Question 7, which asked respondents to identify the best description of the action-oriented approach, 62.4% (78) of those who answered chose the option describing it as a combination of the communicative approach and task-based learning, while 18.4% (23) felt it was a new approach to language teaching. Given that only 55 respondents (43.3%) had previously said that they knew of and understood the action-oriented approach, there were clearly a number of teachers who were making a guess, however educated that guess might be. Some 19.2% (24), a large number for this survey, said that they did not know, and two people chose not to answer the question.

The responses to a follow-up to Question 7 – 'Could you define in your own words the action-oriented approach?' – in many cases echoed the responses given in Question 7, but some responses hinted that although many teachers may not be able to define the action-oriented approach as described in the CEFR, some do actually have an understanding of what it means and entails – autonomy, successful communication, context relevance, authenticity, learner-centredness:

'It's about being independent and satisfactorily resolving situations in communication in a foreign language.'

'It is the fact of learning a language as a member of society.'

'A foreign language teaching methodology where the learner plays an active part in their own learning and is a user of the language. An approach oriented to being able to use the language in concrete situations.'

One respondent even suggested that talking about the action-oriented approach is unnecessary because it is so obvious:

'It seems to me that we are discovering "hot water", it is teaching so that learners can use the language in real situations.'

These responses raise the issue of teachers' familiarity with terminology in language teaching research and may imply that they have changed their approach as a natural response to the needs of their students. However, as stated before in this chapter, we need to remember that the survey responses reflect perceptions and beliefs that would need to be confirmed by in-depth interviews and classroom observation.

Perhaps the most illuminating response about the action-oriented approach was to the question of whether sufficient attention has been paid to it in language teaching (Question 8, Figure 5.3) A large majority either did not think so (48.4% – 61) or did not know (31.7% – 40), and only 19.8% (25) answered affirmatively. There would appear to be a clear need for a greater focus on the action-oriented approach, whether in teacher training and development, in coursebooks or in making the CEFR-CV more accessible to teachers. We give our own opinion in the following section.

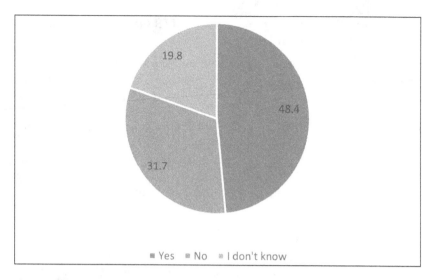

Figure 5.3 Responses to the question: Do you think that the action-oriented approach has received sufficient attention in the field of language learning?

The survey also included a number of questions on mediation. While we cannot make direct links between teaching context and areas of knowledge, we think it is plausible that, given the legal imperative to focus on mediation in the EOIs (see above), the 51 teachers (40.2%) who answered that they had consulted the *Companion Volume* and know what it contains is likely to include a significant number of the 42 EOI teachers who took the survey, and who represented 33% of the respondents. This speculation may be supported by the fact that an even higher number (64 teachers, 51.2%) said that they knew the mediation scales in the CEFR-CV (Question 16), and the difference is perhaps the result of teachers learning about the scales on training courses (Question 18: How did you learn about the CEFR-CV?). More interestingly still, in answer to Question 18, only 41 teachers (32.3%) said that they had read the CEFR-CV compared to 51 (40.2%) in Question 17.

Finally, and perhaps encouraging for the future, 83.5% (106 respondents) of the people who answered our survey wanted more information about the CEFR and the CEFR-CV, though this perhaps also further reflects that they do not feel they have had enough so far.

In summary, while we are aware of the numerous limitations of our survey and the danger of drawing too many conclusions from it, it is interesting – if not surprising – that even amongst teachers in university language centres and Escuelas Oficiales de Idiomas, self-perceived knowledge of the CEFR-CV, and of the action-oriented approach and mediation, is considerably lower than self-perceived knowledge of the CEFR levels. And of course, the question remains whether teachers knowing about any of this has any observable effect on what actually happens in their classrooms.

The Action-oriented Approach and the CEFR *Companion Volume*: A Window of Opportunity

Although our evidence base is limited, both the initial 'vox pop' and this wider questionnaire survey suggest that classroom teachers' knowledge of the CEFR and the CEFR-CV does not go much beyond some understanding of the CEFR proficiency levels and certainly does not include familiarity with the CEFR-CV or recognition of the action-oriented approach, even if good teaching practice may well include examples of what the action-oriented approach means and entails.

It seems that despite the best intentions of all involved, the CEFR and CEFR-CV remain either largely inaccessible or unknown to classroom teachers and, therefore, irrelevant to their day-to-day teaching. There is clearly a huge information gap between policymakers and assessment specialists who understand and use the CEFR and the CEFR-CV on the one hand and teachers and the classroom on the other. Until this gap is bridged and the CEFR and the CEFR-CV are made accessible and relevant to classroom teachers, any talk of a paradigm shift is premature.

We would suggest that a crucial factor in remedying this is a different approach to teacher training, rather than another teacher-focused publication or another series of seminars describing 'new' approaches and why and how current teaching practice(s) should change. Disseminating existing good practice(s) and listening to teachers' views on what they think their classrooms need and on how satisfied they are with what they are doing (or what was done to them, in the case of trainee teachers) should be the point of departure. There will be time after that to discuss how near to or far from the recommendations of the CEFR and the CEFR-CV existing practices are.

The implementation of the action-oriented approach suggests a different sort of teacher, a different sort of learner and a different sort of classroom, but the starting point has to be the teacher. Teachers make the biggest difference. As Hattie (2003) argues, of the main sources of variance in students' achievement the one we can most influence to really make a difference is the teacher. In his work on visible learning, Hattie (2012) shows that Collective Teacher Efficacy – teachers' collective belief in their ability to positively affect students – is strongly correlated with student achievement. If the action-oriented approach is to be implemented successfully teachers need to believe in it.

Teacher education, and perhaps especially pre-service and early career teacher training, plays an important role in helping to establish teacher identity: how we see ourselves as teachers. The action-oriented approach may require new and less experienced teachers to take on roles that are different to the ones they are used to and comfortable with, whether they have learned these roles as teachers or as learners. At the same time, more experienced teachers will also need to be supported if they are expected to change what may be a core part of their teacher identity.

Training and development, whether expert-led or peer-supported, are therefore fundamental, and the appropriate methodologies and approaches for implementing the action-oriented approach will need to be developed throughout a teaching career. If the CEFR and the CEFR-CV are to influence teaching practice more widely and more effectively than at present, then there is a lot of work to be done in ensuring that the key messages are part of training and development programmes

But to end on a more positive note, we feel that in Spain at least, the reality of mainstreamed plurilingual and bilingual education and the internationalization of tertiary education (see the ACLES 2020 survey in the list of references) offer real possibilities for more widespread take-up of the action-oriented approach, though only if teachers can be engaged. The latest official Spanish Ministry of Education figures[3] show that during 2018–2019, some 1,609,141 students in primary, secondary and vocational education received some of their education in a non-official language, overwhelmingly in English (96.2%), with more than a third of primary and secondary schools across the country offering families this option. Learning school subjects through a second or third language is a real-life task, with outcomes that are not only linguistic but require intercultural and plurilingual awareness, that have a social and cognitive– strategic dimension, involve competences and communicative activities, and develop student autonomy. So perhaps the opportunity is here, but if we are to be successful we need to address real teacher needs and concerns and the realities of state sector teaching contexts.

Notes

(1) https://www.ecml.at/Portals/1/documents/CoE-documents/Rec-CM-2008-7-EN. pdf?ver=2016-11-29-112711-910 (accessed 22 November 2021).
(2) http://giele.webs.upv.es/ (accessed 16 November 2020).
(3) https://www.educacionyfp.gob.es/dam/jcr:b921d3a6-a17a-483e-bd5b-9d80fba13756/ nota-18-19.pdf (accessed 16 October 2020).

References

ACLES (2014) CertAcles: ACLES Model for the Accreditation of Language Competence. https://www.acles.es/uploads/archivos/examenes/model-accreditation-language-competence.pdf (accessed 30 September 2020).

ACLES (2020) The internationalisation of Spanish universities: Impact in foreign language teaching and accreditation. https://acles.es/uploads/archivos/varios/ACLES_Int_Univ_English.pdf (accessed 2 November 2020).

Bailly, S., Devitt, S., Gremmo, M-J., Heyworth, F., Hopkins, A., Jones, B., Makosch, M., Riley, P., Stoks, G. and Trim, J. (eds) (2001) *Common European Framework of Reference for Languages: Learning, Teaching, Assessment. A Guide for Users.* Strasbourg: Council of Europe. https://rm.coe.int/1680697848 (accessed 30 September 2020).

Byram, M. and Parmenter, L. (eds) (2012) *The Common European Framework of Reference: The Globalisation of Language Policy*. Bristol: Multilingual Matters.

Council of Europe (2001) *Common European Framework of Reference for Languages: Learning, Teaching, Assessment*. Cambridge: Cambridge University Press. https://rm.coe.int/1680459f97 (accessed 30 September 2020).

Council of Europe (2008) Recommendation CM/Rec (2008) 7 to member states on the use of the Council of Europe's 'Common European Framework of Reference for Languages' (CEFR) and the promotion of plurilingualism. https://www.coe.int/en/web/common-european-framework-reference-languages/extracts-recommendation-2008-7 (accessed 30 September 2020).

Council of Europe (2020) *Common European Framework of Reference for Languages: Learning, Teaching, Assessment. Companion Volume*. Strasbourg: Council of Europe. https://rm.coe.int/common-european-framework-of-reference-for-languages-learning-teaching/16809ea0d4 (accessed 30 September 2020).

CRUE (2011) Propuestas Sobre La Acreditación De Idiomas Informe elaborado por la 'Comisión para el análisis y estudio de la acreditación y formación en idiomas' y aprobado en la Asamblea General de la CRUE (Santander, 8 de septiembre de 2011) [Report of the 'Commission for the analysis and study of the teaching and accreditation of languages' approved at the General Assembly of the CRUE in Santander, 8 September 2011]. https://www.acles.es/uploads/archivos/examenes/modelo-acreditacion-avalado-crue.pdf (accessed 30 September 2020).

Diaz-Bedmar, B. and Byram, M. (2019) The current influence of the CEFR in secondary education: Teachers' perceptions. *Language, Culture and Curriculum* 32 (1), 1–15. DOI: 10.1080/07908318.2018.1493492.

European Parliament (2013) *The Implementation of the Common European Framework for Languages in European Education Systems*. Brussels: European Parliament, Directorate-General for Internal Policies. https://www.europarl.europa.eu/RegData/etudes/etudes/join/2013/495871/IPOL-CULT_ET(2013)495871_EN.pdf (accessed 30 September 2020).

Figueras, N. (ed.) (2013) *The Impact of the CEFR in Catalonia*. APAC Monographs 9. Barcelona: APAC (Associació de Professors d'Anglès de Catalunya) [Association of Teachers of English in Catalonia].

Goullier, F. (2006) *Council of Europe Tools for Language Teaching: Common European Framework and Portfolios*. Paris: Didier. https://rm.coe.int/CoERMPublicCommonSearchServices/DisplayDCTMContent?documentId=090000168069ce6e (accessed 30 September 2020).

Goullier, F (2007) *The Common European Framework of Reference for Languages (CEFR) and the Development of Language Policies: Challenges and Responsibilities*. Language Policy Document, Report on an Intergovernmental Forum, Council of Europe, Strasbourg, 6–8 February 2007. https://www.coe.int/en/web/common-european-framework-reference-languages/documents (accessed 30 September 2020).

Hattie, J. (2003) Teachers make a difference: What is the research evidence? Paper presented at the ACER Research Conference, Building Teacher Quality: What does the research tell us?, Melbourne, Australia. Australian Council for Educational Research (ACER), 1997–2008, ACER Research Conference Archive. https://research.acer.edu.au/cgi/viewcontent.cgi?article=1003&context=research_conference_2003 (accessed 11 October 2020).

Hattie, J. (2012) *Visible Learning for Teachers. Maximizing Impact on Learning*. Abingdon: Routledge.

Little, D. (2011) The Common European Framework of Reference for Languages: A research agenda. *Language Teaching* 44 (3), 381–393. doi:10.1017/S0261444811000097.

Martyniuk, W. and Noijons, J. (2007) Executive summary of results of a survey on The Use of the CEFR at National Level in the Council of Europe Member States. Strasbourg: Council of Europe. https://rm.coe.int/CoERMPublicCommonSearchServices/DisplayDCTMContent?documentId=090000168069b7ad (accessed 30 September 2020).

Ministerio de Educación, Cultura y Deporte (2014) *Real Decreto 126/2014, de 28 de febrero por el que se establece el currículo básico de la Educación Primaria* [Royal Decree 126/2014, February 28, by which primary education basic curriculum contents are set]. https://www.boe.es/buscar/pdf/2014/BOE-A-2014-2222-consolidado.pdf (accessed 30 September 2020).

Ministerio de Educación, Cultura y Deporte (2015) *Real Decreto 1105/2014, de 26 de diciembre, por el que se establece el currículo básico de la Educación Secundaria Obligatoria y del Bachillerato* [Royal Decree 1105/2014, December 26, by which compulsory and post-compulsory secondary education basic curriculum contents are set]. https://www.boe.es/buscar/pdf/2015/BOE-A-2015-37-consolidado.pdf (accessed 30 September 2020).

Ministerio de Educación, Cultura y Deporte (2017) *Real Decreto 1041/2017, de 22 de diciembre, por el que se fijan las exigencias mínimas del nivel básico a efectos de certificación, se establece el currículo básico de los niveles Intermedio B1, Intermedio B2, Avanzado C1, y Avanzado C2, de las Enseñanzas de idiomas de régimen especial reguladas por la Ley Orgánica 2/2006, de 3 de mayo, de Educación, y se establecen las equivalencias entre las Enseñanzas de idiomas de régimen especial reguladas en diversos planes de estudios y las de este real decreto* [Royal Decree 1041/2017, December 22, by which the minimum standards for the basic level certification are set, the basic curriculum contents for Intermediate B1 and B2 and Advanced C1 and C2 levels of special language education regulated by the Organic Law of Education 2/2006, May 3 are established, and the equivalences between special regime language education studies formerly regulated and those regulated in the present Royal Decree]. https://www.boe.es/buscar/act.php?id=BOE-A-2017-15367 (accessed 30 September 2020).

Ministerio de Educación, Cultura y Deporte (2019) *Real Decreto 1/2019, de 11 de enero, por el que se establecen los principios básicos comunes de evaluación aplicables a las pruebas de certificación oficial de los niveles Intermedio B1, Intermedio B2, Avanzado C1, y Avanzado C2 de las enseñanzas de idiomas de régimen especial* [Royal Decree 1/2019, January 11, which establishes the basic common assessment principles to be implemented in official certificates of levels Intermediate B1 and B2 and Advanced C1 and C2 of the special regime language education]. https://www.boe.es/diario_boe/txt.php?id=BOE-A-2019-317 (accessed 30 September 2020).

North, B. (2014) *The CEFR in Practice*. Cambridge: Cambridge University Press.

North, B. (2020) Trolls, unicorns and the CEFR: Precision and professionalism in criticism of the CEFR. *CEFR Journal – Research and Practice* 2, 8–24. https://cefrjapan.net/images/PDF/Newsletter/CEFRJournal-2-1_BNorth.pdf (accessed 30 September 2020).

North, B. and Piccardo, E. (2016) Developing illustrative descriptors of aspects of mediation for the Common European Framework of Reference (CEFR). A Council of Europe project. *Language Teaching* 49 (3), 455–459.

North, B. and Piccardo, E. (2019) Developing new CEFR descriptor scales and expanding the existing ones: Constructs, approaches and methodologies. *Zeitschrift für Fremdsprachenforschung* 30 (2), 142–160.

Piccardo, E. and North, B. (2019) *The Action-oriented Approach: A Dynamic Vision of Language Education*. Bristol: Multilingual Matters.

Trim, J.L.M. (1980) Preface. In J.A. van Ek and L.G. Alexander (1980) *Threshold Level English in a European Unit/Credit System for Modern Language Learning by Adults*. Oxford: Pergamon.

6 Action-oriented Plurilingual Mediation: A Search for Fluid Foundations

Constant Leung

The CEFR Companion Volume has given greater prominence to mediation as a component part of language proficiency. This is a welcome development in that the amplification and elaborations on mediation can provide an enriched account of language-in-use. In this chapter, I will explore the articulation of mediation within the action-oriented approach to language modelling adopted by the CEFR. I will pay particular attention to the fluid and dynamic nature of emotional intelligence and plurilingualism as aspects of mediation in social interaction. The discussion will cover a number of thorny issues, including the relationship between emotional intelligence and language proficiency, and the incommensurability between plurilingualism-in-use and monolingual framing of language proficiency. It will be argued that both emotional intelligence and plurilingualism are in need of further conceptual analysis and development before they can be operationalized systematically.

Introduction

Many language education professionals welcome the action-oriented approach adopted by the *Common European Framework of Reference for Languages* (CEFR; Council of Europe, 2001) because conceptually it grounds curriculum, pedagogy and assessment in language use. While the action-oriented approach, as it is characterized in the CEFR, does not obviate the need to take account of the many cognitive and social dimensions of language learning and teaching, it offers a conceptual frame for the articulation of can-do statements in the proficiency scales that afford immediacy and transparency in terms of identifiable objectives and observable activities. It is no accident that in the 20 years since its publication, the CEFR has been widely regarded as a standard reference and as a friendly and ready-to-use resource for myriad curricular applications for different purposes at different levels of education and in different world locations, many of which are far from its European home.

The more recently published *Companion Volume* of the CEFR (CEFR-CV; Council of Europe, 2020) provides an expansion on some aspects of the original framework. Of note is the considerable amplification of the notion of mediation. Although mediation figures in the 2001 CEFR, it was largely discussed in relation to interpreting and translating. The prominence given to mediation in the CEFR-CV represents a significant recognition of the complex and dynamic nature of language in communication. Mediation, as seen in the CEFR-CV, is no longer primarily concerned with the use of another language for interpretation and translation: it is now an important part of language users' action-oriented competence to enact communication in social interaction. The expanded mediation has also raised the importance of plurilingualism as part of action-oriented competence. Given this reconfiguration, it seems important to revisit the formulation of the action-oriented approach and the underlying competences associated with it, and to examine how far it is companionably articulated to the expanded notion of mediation and plurilingualism.

In the first part of this discussion, I will look at the ways in which the action-oriented approach has been characterized in the 2001 and 2020 volumes with a view to laying out the epistemic basis of the concept of action. Next, I will describe the 'actions' involved in mediation and plurilingualism as they have been elaborated in the CEFR-CV, paying particular attention to the underlying assumptions regarding models of language and multilingualism. Building on the discussions in the first two parts, I will move on to the overall conceptual articulation between the action-oriented approach, competences involved in language use, and the notion of mediation, highlighting areas of compatibility and tension between them. In the final part of the chapter, I will consider some issues that would benefit from further exploration.

Action-oriented Approach

In the CEFR the action-oriented approach explicitly links language use to the actions of individuals seen as social agents:

> Language use, embracing language learning, comprises the actions performed by persons who as individuals and as social agents develop a range of *competences*, both *general* and in particular *communicative language competences*. They draw on the competences at their disposal in various contexts under various *conditions* and under various *constraints* to engage in *language activities* ... (Council of Europe, 2001: 9; italics in original)

This action-oriented approach is re-affirmed in the CEFR-CV, where it is stated that 'competence exists only in action' (Council of Europe, 2020: 138). And user/learner action, represented by can-do statements, is the point of departure for curriculum planners and teachers as they are advised to work 'backwards from *what the users/learners need to be able to do in the language*' (2020: 28; italics in original). The use of language is underpinned, *inter alia*, by a set of competences.

Competent use of language in social activities is understood as not just a mechanical process of using language resources (e.g. vocabulary and grammar) to express one's meaning and to receive messages from others: there are other considerations to be taken into account. Language users call on a wider range of knowledge, skills and other personal capacities, referred to as competences, as they engage in social activities in context. Competences are defined as 'the sum of knowledge, skills and characteristics that allow a person to perform actions' (Council of Europe, 2001: 9). There are two categories of competences:

- *General competences* are not specific to language but are called upon for actions of all kinds, including language activities.
- *Communicative language competences* are those which empower a person to act using specifically linguistic means.

(Council of Europe, 2001: 9; italics in original)

Aspects of these competences are applied in particular contexts: '*Context* refers to the constellation of events and situational factors (physical and others), both internal and external to a person, in which acts of communication are embedded' (2001: 9; italics in original).

The salient components of these concepts, stated in highly abstract terms, can be summarized as follows.

General competences comprise everyday and professional/specialist knowledge, skills (automated know-how, e.g. riding a bicycle once learned), existential competence (e.g. personality dispositions and attitudes), and ability to learn (e.g. knowing how to learn about other people, new knowledge areas, etc.).

Communicative language competences comprise three components (Council of Europe, 2001, section 5.2): linguistic competences, which comprise knowledge of different aspects of lexicogrammar; sociolinguistic competences, which are concerned with knowledge and skills related to the social conventions of language use, such as forms of address and turn-taking; and pragmatic competences, which are related to the ways in which language resources are actually used in real-life communication, e.g. different ways of organizing the flow of information for different discourse purposes.

Plurilingual Competence

Plurilingualism is defined in contradistinction to the more conventionally understood meaning of multilingualism. Multilingualism can refer to individuals knowing more than one language and/or the presence of more than one language in a community. In the plurilingual approach advocated by the CEFR a plurilingual person does not keep their languages in 'separate mental compartments but rather builds up a communicative competence to which all knowledge and experience of language contributes and in which languages interrelate and interact' (Council of Europe, 2001: 4). In actual language use, a plurilingual 'can call flexibly upon different parts of this competence to achieve effective communication with a particular interlocutor' (Council of Europe, 2001: 4). This view of plurilinguals gives user/learners licence 'to use all their linguistic resources when necessary, encouraging them to see similarities and regularities as well as differences between languages and cultures' (Council of Europe, 2020: 30). The phrase 'all their linguistic resources' does not imply an equal amount or level of knowledge in the different languages involved, and 'language' can mean 'dialect' or 'variety'. This action-oriented approach to plurilingualism thus gives rise to the following characterization of plurilingual competence that involves the ability to call flexibly upon an inter-related, uneven, plurilinguistic repertoire to:

- switch from one language or dialect (or variety) to another;
- express oneself in one language (or dialect, or variety) and understand a person speaking another;
- call upon the knowledge of a number of languages (or dialects, or varieties) to make sense of a text;
- recognize words from a common international store in a new guise;
- mediate between individuals with no common language (or dialect, or variety), even with only a slight knowledge oneself;
- bring the whole of one's linguistic equipment into play, experimenting with alternative forms of expression;
- exploit paralinguistics (mime, gesture, facial expression, etc.).

(Council of Europe, 2020: 30)

This characterization suggests an approach to languages-in-use that is mediation-friendly, particularly in social settings where the participants have different linguistic repertoires, including different named languages (such as German, Japanese, Russian).

Mediation

In the CEFR, mediation is presented as a technical facilitation of communication involving two languages. It is described as 'written and/or oral activities ... [that] make communication possible between persons who are unable, for whatever reason, to communicate with each other directly' (Council of Europe, 2001: 14). It is elaborated in relation to translation as follows:

Writer (Lx) → text (in Lx) → USER → text (in Ly) → Reader (Ly) (Council of Europe, 2001: 99)

and in relation to interpretation:

Interlocutor (Lx) ↔ discourse (Lx) ↔ USER ↔ discourse (Ly) ↔ Interlocutor (Ly) (Council of Europe, 2001: 14)

This somewhat technical approach to mediation is expanded considerably in the CEFR-CV to include a personal quality component:

A person who engages in mediation activity needs to have a well-developed emotional intelligence, or an openness to develop it, in order to have sufficient empathy for the viewpoints and emotional states of other participants in the communicative situation. (Council of Europe, 2020: 91)

Empathetic sensitivity to interlocutors' linguacultural backgrounds seems to be part of the emotional intelligence needed for mediation because it is:

a social and cultural process of creating conditions for communication and cooperation, facing and hopefully defusing any delicate situations and tensions that may arise. Particularly with regard to cross-lingual mediation, users should remember that this inevitably also involves social and cultural competence as well as plurilingual competence. (Council of Europe, 2020: 91)

There are three types of activities in which mediation can occur:

- Mediating a text 'involves passing on to another person the content of a text to which they do not have access' and responding to creative texts.
- Mediating concepts 'refers to the process of facilitating access to knowledge and concepts for others, particularly if they may be unable to access this directly on their own'.
- Mediating communication 'aims to facilitate understanding and shape successful communication between users/learners who may have individual, sociocultural, sociolinguistic or intellectual differences in standpoint'.

(Council of Europe, 2020: 91)

Each of these three types of activities is accompanied by a set of scaled descriptors. It should be noted that mediation can involve different languages and/or different varieties of the same language. Given the interest in plurilingualism in this discussion, the next section of this chapter will focus on those aspects of mediation activities that involve the use of more than one language.

Mediation and Plurilingualism in Action

It may be important to spell out the line of reasoning that inheres in the conceptual frame of the CEFR as a whole: the action-oriented approach provides the basis for seeing language use as the locale for the analysis and description of language proficiency, making it epistemologically justifiable and empirically possible to formulate can-do statements to populate the proficiency scales within the framework. Underlying language use is a set of knowledge and skills based on general and language competences. Curricular planning and pedagogic decision-making should take account of the can-do statements, the level descriptors within the various scales, when construing user/learners' performances. 'Working backwards', they should use the can-do statements to devise teaching–learning activities that help develop the underlying general and language competences. This complex edifice of reasoning is premised on the conceptual soundness of the key component parts, and the commensurability between them.

Given the recency of the elaboration and foregrounding of mediation, it seems important to examine how far the component parts within its interiority are sound and well connected. The point of departure for this reflexive exercise, as noted earlier, is the can-do statements in the relevant scales. For reasons of scope and space, it is not the intention of this chapter to offer an exhaustive account of the analysis of all aspects of the CEFR-CV's mediation section. I will focus on emotional intelligence and plurilingualism in the ensuing discussion, with a view to foregrounding the issues that would benefit from further examination.

Emotional intelligence

The CEFR-CV's elaboration of mediation comes with a prerequisite: emotional intelligence. The user/learner needs to 'have sufficient empathy for the viewpoints and emotional states of other participants in the communicative situation' (Council of Europe, 2020: 91). This seems to be related to the 'characteristics that allow a person to perform actions', as part of the action-oriented approach that 'takes into account the cognitive, emotional and volitional resources and the full range of abilities specific to and applied by the individual as a social agent' (Council of Europe, 2001: 9). Mediation strategies are seen as 'ways of coping with the demands of using finite resources to process information and establish equivalent meaning' (2001: 87). In mediation activities the language user/learner is in effect an enabling messaging conduit – difficult or hard-to-follow meanings that have emerged in interaction are made (more) accessible through renditions that are more readily and happily understood by others involved. In the CEFR-CV, this view seems to continue to inform the scales.

On this view it makes sense to include emotional intelligence as part of general competence. The question now is: How has this individual user/learner quality been operationalized in the can-do statements? Put differently: can we see emotional intelligence being invoked in the level descriptors under mediation?

The terms 'emotion' and 'emotional' occur eight times in the mediation section of the CEFR-CV. Two of these occurrences are in the passage that introduces the term (Council of Europe, 2020: 91; Council of Europe, 2001: 14). The other six mentions appear in the section headed 'Expressing a Personal Response to Creative Texts (Including Literature)'. This activity is concerned with ways in which the user/learner expresses their response to literature. The following descriptor captures the way 'emotion' is framed in the descriptors in this scale:

> B1   Can relate the emotions experienced by a character in a work to emotions he/she has experienced. (Council of Europe, 2020: 107)

This is about reader response and it is clearly not the sense in which emotional intelligence is understood as an integral part of mediation as social interaction. Of course, it is possible to have an element of emotional intelligence built into the can-do statements without explicitly referring to the term itself. For instance, in the Overall Mediation scale there are four can-do descriptors that can be interpreted as emotional-intelligence related at B1, B2, C1 and C2 levels (but not at A1 and A2):

> C2   Can mediate effectively and naturally, taking on different roles according to the needs of the people and situation involved, identifying nuances and undercurrents and guiding a sensitive or delicate discussion …
>
> C1   Can act effectively as a mediator, helping to maintain positive interaction by interpreting different perspectives, managing ambiguity … intervening diplomatically in order to redirect talk …
>
> B2   Can establish a supportive environment for sharing ideas and facilitate discussion of delicate issues showing appreciation of different perspectives … and adjusting sensitively the way he/she expresses things …
>
> B1   Can collaborate with people from other backgrounds, showing interest and empathy by asking and answering simple questions … (Council of Europe, 2020: 91–92)

There are other descriptors in the mediation section of the CEFR-CV that can similarly be interpreted as being related, even if at a stretch, to emotional intelligence. For example, in the scale for Collaborating in a Group – Facilitating Collaborative Interaction with Peers, under Mediating Concepts, we can also see in these descriptors elements of 'a social and cultural process of creating conditions for communication and cooperation, facing and hopefully defusing any delicate situations and tensions that may arise' (Council of Europe, 2020: 91).

> C1   Can show sensitivity to different perspectives within a group, acknowledging contributions and formulating any reservations, disagreements or criticisms in such a way as to avoid or minimize any offence. Can develop the interaction and tactfully help steer it towards a conclusion.
>
> B2   Can, based on people's reactions, adjust the way he/she formulates questions and/or intervenes in a group interaction. (Council of Europe, 2020: 110)

However, there is no other invocation of emotional intelligence, even indirectly, in the other level descriptors in this scale. The reference to emotional intelligence in these scales seems to be truncated. It is also interesting to note, in passing, that the discussion on the progression up this scale seems to suggest that the rationale is more goal-oriented than emotional-intelligence related:

> At A2, the user/learner can collaborate actively in simple, shared tasks, provided someone helps him/her to express his/her suggestions. At B1, the focus is on posing questions and inviting others to speak. By B2, the learner/user can refocus the discussion, helping to define goals and comparing ways of achieving them. At C1, he/she can help steer a discussion tactfully towards a conclusion. (Council of Europe, 2020: 109)

So, I may have over-interpreted the links of the descriptors to emotional intelligence in the above discussion. It should also be pointed out that it is very difficult to detect any connection to emotional intelligence in many of the proficiency rating scales in the mediation section, e.g. Relaying Specific Information in Speech (Council of Europe, 2020: 94) and Processing Text in Speech (2020: 99). Taking the CEFR and CEFR-CV discussions on emotional intelligence as a whole, it would be fair to say that due recognition is given to the importance of emotional intelligence within the action-oriented approach. The question is whether its current manifestation needs further development.

Plurilingualism

The CEFR's argument that plurilingual user/learners do not keep their languages and cultures in separate mental compartments, and that they can develop a communicative competence calling on all their knowledge and experience of languages, is carried over into the

CEFR-CV. The can-do statements in the proficiency scales provide a close-up view of how this characterization has been operationalized. The following extracts of the scale Acting as Intermediary in Informal Situations (with Friends and Colleagues), under Mediating Communication, explicitly mentions the use of two languages compartmentally at all levels:

C2　Can communicate in a clear, fluent, well-structured way (in Language B) the sense of what is said (in Language A) on a wide range of general and specialized topics ...

C1　Can communicate fluently (in Language B) the sense of what is said (in Language A) on a wide range of subjects of personal, academic and professional interest ...

B2　Can communicate (in Language B) the sense of what is said in a welcome address, anecdote or presentation in their field (in Language A) ...

　　Can communicate (in Language B) the sense of what is said (in Language A) on subjects within their fields of interest ...

B1　Can communicate (in Language B) the main sense of what is said (in Language A) on subjects of personal interest ...

A2　Can communicate (in Language B) the main point of what is said (in Language A) in predictable everyday situations ...

A1　Can communicate (in Language B) other people's personal details and very simple, predictable information (in Language A) ... (Council of Europe, 2020: 238–239)

It can be seen from the above descriptors that plurilingualism in action involves moving between two (or more) languages to convey meaning. The conceptual framing of these can-do statements is strongly suggestive of the user/learner, *qua* mediator, engaging in the use of two languages as distinct and separate linguistic systems. So the characterization of plurilingualism in terms of switching from one language to another seems to be premised on keeping the language boundaries intact, hence the repeated reference to 'from Language A to Language B'. There is no question that the view here is that when interlocutors move from one language to another, they keep to one language at a time. However, this view of plurilingual language use seems to have sidestepped a good deal of the more recent research in the fields of English as lingua franca (ELF), flexible multilingualism and translanguaging (e.g. Blommaert, 2010; Canagarajah, 2011; Cenoz & Gorter, 2015; Creese & Blackledge, 2010; García & Li, 2014; García *et al.*, 2016; Jenkins, 2015; Kramsch & Whiteside, 2008; Leung & Valdés, 2019; Otheguy *et al.*, 2015, 2018; Seidlhofer, 2011; and others).

A relevant insight emerging from these fields of research, despite their many conceptual and epistemological differences, is that multilinguals do not necessarily move from one language to another in bounded language formations, i.e. whole utterances and passages of text expressed in one language at a time, e.g. from Language A (English) to Language B (Spanish). There is ample empirical data to show that multilinguals' language resources can be used in highly contingent ways, depending on the interlocutors, purposes and contexts. Perhaps an early example of flexible multilingualism in action from Kramsch and Whiteside would be apt here, as it foreshadows a good deal of the discussions in the relevant fields in recent times:

	Participants	Exchanges	English translation
1	Juan:	how much *panza* you want?	(tripe)
2	DF:	*voy a comprar cinco libras de panza mañana*	I'm going to buy 5 lb of tripe tomorrow
3	Juan:	OK *mañana*	
4	DF:	/\ma′ alob	good
5	Juan:	_/OK!	
6	DF:	\/Dios bo dik	thanks
7	Juan:	_/bo dik	
8	DF:	_/saama	tomorrow
9	Juan:	@@,	
10		@@	
11		_saama	
12	DF:	ah	

Transcription conventions: / rising tone; \ falling tone; _/ low to rising tone; V high-low-high; @@ laughs

(Kramsch & Whiteside, 2008: 648)

The above interaction took place in a grocery store in San Francisco. Juan was the store owner from Vietnam. Don Francisco (DF), from Yucatan, was a customer known to Juan. In this stretch of interaction three languages were involved: English and Spanish in turns 1, 2, 3, 5 and 12; Maya in turns 4, 6, 7, 8 and 11. The three languages were interwoven in the interaction; the linguistic resources were used dynamically to accomplish communication. Turns 1 and 3 are of particular interest because elements of English and Spanish were blended to create meaning, in a way often referred to as translanguaging in the more recent literature. The research literature in flexible multilingualism and specialist ELF data collections such as the ELFA and VOICE corpora[1] testify to this kind of fluid and contingent use of multilingual resources. Seen in this light, the statement that plurilingualism 'involves the ability to call flexibly upon an interrelated, uneven, plurilinguistic repertoire'

(Council of Europe, 2020: 30) has clearly been built on a view that languages are structurally bounded systems; there does not seem to be any provision for intra-utterance and intra-sentential translanguaging. How far such a view of language is compatible with the action-oriented approach is a moot point.

Language in Action: Accounting for Contingency and Fluidity

The discussion so far has pointed to some fundamental conceptual and operationalization issues related to mediation and plurilingualism. A key but unstated pre-requisite for mediation in the CEFR is that the user/learner is given space to think on their feet, to be prepared to follow their own feelings to gauge what other people may need, to make use of whatever linguistic and other resources are available to achieve communication. Given that it is virtually impossible to pre-judge what one's interlocutors may need in any real-life communication, the user/learner's fleet-footedness and readiness to act *in situ* are necessary attributes. The CEFR, with sound reasons, has connected these user/learner attributes with emotional intelligence. However, it is unclear how far this notion has been acknowledged properly in its operationalization, given its rather truncated and inconsistent inclusion in the can-do statements in the scales under mediation. One clue for this somewhat haphazard treatment may lie in the difficulties in developing and lining up sufficient descriptors for all the levels in the various scales. It is interesting to note that the following supplementary descriptors are included in Appendix 9 of the CEFR-CV:

ESTABLISHING A POSITIVE ATMOSPHERE

B2   Can create a positive atmosphere and encourage participation by giving both practical and emotional support. (Council of Europe, 2020: 261)

FACILITATING PLURICULTURAL COMMUNICATION

B2   Can establish a relationship with members of other cultures, showing interest and empathy through questioning, expressions of agreement and identification of emotional and practical needs. (Council of Europe, 2020: 263)

The reasons given for not including these descriptors in the formally presented illustrative descriptors are: 'it had not been possible to develop descriptors for a sufficient range of levels' and 'because of comments in the consultation phases' (Council of Europe, 2020: 259). These operationalization reasons point to a more fundamental conceptual problem. If emotional intelligence is needed for mediation, then, from a user/learner's perspective, it would be needed in much the same way, *ceteris paribus*, whether one is at A1 level or C2 level in the other aspects of proficiency. Granted that it may well be easier for a user/learner with linguistic competence at C2 level in Language B (the other language) to enact their emotional-intelligence related volition than someone at A1 level in terms of being able to express themselves (in Language B), but this ability to use the other language does not, in itself, say anything about the emotional intelligence of the individuals involved. Indeed, it may well be that a readiness to communicate would trigger the use of linguistic resources flexibly, as shown in the example involving English, Spanish and Maya, which raises further questions regarding the conceptual adequacies of plurilingualism.

From the cumulative research of the past 20 years or so, it is now quite clear that in flexible multilingual communication, or translanguaging, when speakers use one or other of their languages in response to the perceived needs of their interlocutors at any given moment in an exchange, they deploy their multilingual resources at word, phrase/clause, sentence and discourse levels contingently to facilitate expression and understanding. The kind of multi-level interweaving of multilingual resources, as exemplified by the grocery store encounter involving Juan and Don Francisco, is played out turn by turn contingently in context, and it does not always follow any pre-established norms. In turn, this situated variability in linguistic form makes it almost impossible to think of ranking the quality of a speaker's use of Language A or Language B separately. For this reason, some of the level descriptors can at best provide partial capture of what user/learners may do. For instance, the trajectory from A1 to C2 in the Acting as Intermediary in Informal Situations scale is in part premised on the assumption that the use of languages is progressively more sophisticated and wide-ranging but they are kept structurally separate:

A1   Can communicate (in Language B) other people's personal details and very simple, predictable information (in Language A) ...

C2   Can communicate in a clear, fluent, well-structured way (in Language B) the sense of what is said (in Language A) on a wide range of general and specialized topics, maintaining appropriate style and register, conveying finer shades of meaning ... (Council of Europe, 2020: 238–239)

The criteria such as 'fluent' and 'well-structured', construed from the perspective of languages as separate bounded entities, can become problematic. If the ultimate purpose of mediation is to enable effective communication, and the effective plurilingual is able to strategically deploy their linguistic repertoires in the moment, then it would be difficult to judge the quality of a piece of language use 'better' or 'worse' just on grounds of fluency and structural accuracy from a monolingual perspective. Is '*Cuanta panza* do you want' better than 'How much *panza* you want'?

Beyond the more technical concerns of ranking and rating plurilingual language use, it is important to acknowledge that plurilingual communication is not just about transmission of information. The flexible uses of plurilingual resources in on-the-spot co-construction is often accompanied by transcultural accommodation and interactional openness, which can trigger unanticipated follow-on interactions. Anyone who has tried to mediate highly socioculturally complex meanings residing in everyday terms such as 'middle class' plurilingually will appreciate the potential unpredictability. The conduit metaphor embedded in the 2020 CEFR-CV descriptors related to plurilingual mediation does not offer any possible pathway towards handling such contingencies (for a detailed discussion, see Leung & Jenkins, 2020).

This discussion has pointed to some of the conceptual and operationalization difficulties regarding emotional intelligence and plurilingualism. The following are some of the issues and questions that would benefit from further examination:

- If emotional intelligence and plurilingualism in mediation within an action-oriented approach cannot be calibrated on the basis of a pre-specified and enumerated body of knowledge and skills (e.g. lexicogrammar), how far would it be possible to construct an array of can-do statements in hierarchical scales?
- If emotional intelligence in mediation within an action-oriented approach is an emergent phenomenon reflecting user/learners' in-the-moment judgements of interlocutors' needs and the probability of achieving a satisfactory interactional outcome (however defined), it points to a multi-faceted construct. This construct will need to take account of, *inter alia*, the interaction between individual user/learners' volition *in situ*, highly variable contexts and purposes of language use, and diverse interlocutor needs. Many unpredictable moving parts are involved, so to speak. How far is it possible to have a unitary concept of emotional intelligence to cover all aspects and uses of mediation? Would it be possible to render emotional intelligence a general enabling attribute that permeates can-do statements at all levels in the different mediation scales?
- If mediation is about enabling communication, and plurilingualism is an inherently flexible linguistic resource that can promote effective communication, then there is no reason to maintain a strict one-language-at-a-time approach in plurilingual language use. However, there may well be an issue with the construct of linguistic competence. As it stands the CEFR framework as a whole has tended to construe language competence in monolingual terms. A more flexible approach to plurilingualism or multilingualism will require further explorations

into how to account for different types of language proficiency in contemporary contexts. How far would it be possible to develop language proficiency scales that can address flexible multilingualism in action?

Perhaps the rub is that applied language research is progressively showing that language in use can be an assemblage of resources from different named languages, and that the readiness to use multilingual resources in social interaction is contingently and dynamically enacted. It is becoming increasingly clear that an (indeed any) action-oriented approach to language proficiency, and by extension teaching and learning, would need to pay attention to the dynamic and fluid nature of language use in real-life language practices. Mediation and plurilingualism are two of the key components of the CEFR framework that are particularly well placed to begin the process of addressing these issues.

Note

(1) The ELFA corpus may be accessed at https://www.helsinki.fi/en/researchgroups/english-as-a-lingua-franca-in-academic-settings/research/elfa-corpus and the VOICE corpus at https://www.univie.ac.at/voice/page/what_is_voice

References

Blommaert, J. (2010) *The Sociolinguistics of Globalization*. Cambridge: Cambridge University Press.

Canagarajah, A.S. (2011) The plurilingual tradition and the English language in South Asia. *AILA Review* 22 (1), 5–22.

Cenoz, J. and Gorter, D. (2015) Translanguaging as a pedagogical tool in multilingual education. In J. Cenoz, D. Gorter and S. May (eds) *Language Awareness and Multilingualism. 3rd Edition* (pp. 309–321). *Encyclopedia of Language and Education* (10 vols, Series Editor: Stephen May). Cham: Springer.

Council of Europe (2001) *Common European Framework of Reference for Languages: Learning, Teaching, Assessment*. Cambridge: Cambridge University Press.

Council of Europe (2020) *Common European Framework of Reference for Languages: Learning, Teaching, Assessment – Companion Volume*. Strasbourg: Council of Europe.

Creese, A. and Blackledge, A. (2010) Translanguaging in the bilingual classroom: A pedagogy for learning and teaching? *Modern Language Journal* 94 (1), 103–115.

García, O., Johnson, S.I. and Selltzer, K. (2016) *The Translanguaging Classroom: Levering Student Bilingualism for Learning*. Philadelphia, PA: Caslon.

García, O. and Li Wei (2014) *Translanguaging: Language, Bilingualism and Education*. Basingstoke: Palgrave Macmillan.

Jenkins, J. (2015) Repositioning English and multilingualism in English as a lingua franca. *Englishes in Practice* 2 (3), 49–85.

Kramsch, C. and Whiteside, A. (2008) Language ecology in multilingual settings: Towards a theory of symbolic competence. *Applied Linguistics* 29 (4), 645–671.

Leung, C. and Valdés, G. (2019) Translanguaging and the transdisciplinary framework for language teaching and learning in a multilingual world. *The Modern Language Journal* 103 (2), 348–370.

Leung, C. and Jenkins, J. (2020) Mediating communication – ELF and flexible multilingualism perspectives on the *Common European Framework of Reference for Languages*. *Australian Review of Applied Linguistics* 3 (1), 26–41.

Otheguy, R., García, O. and Reid, W. (2015) Clarifying translanguaging and deconstructing named languages: A perspective from linguistics. *Applied Linguistics Review* 6 (3), 281–307.

Otheguy, R., García, O. and Reid, W. (2018) A translanguaging view of the linguistic system of bilinguals. *Applied Linguistics Review* 10 (4), 625–651. doi:https://doi.org/10.1515/applirev-2018-0020

Seidlhofer, B. (2011) *Understanding English as a Lingua Franca*. Oxford: Oxford University Press.

Part 3: Plurilingualism, Plurilingual Education and Mediation

Introduction to Part 3

David Little

The *Common European Framework of Reference for Languages* (CEFR) defines plurilingualism as follows:

> Plurilingualism differs from multilingualism, which is the knowledge of a number of languages, or the co-existence of different languages in a given society. … [T]he plurilingual approach emphasises the fact that as an individual person's experience of language in its cultural contexts expands, from the language of the home to that of society at large and then to the languages of other peoples (whether learnt at school or college, or by direct experience), he or she does not keep those languages and cultures in strictly separated mental compartments, but rather builds up a communicative competence to which all knowledge and experience of language contributes and in which languages interrelate and interact. (Council of Europe, 2001: 4)

Traditionally, the CEFR explains, the goal of language education has been to 'achieve "mastery" of one or two, or even three languages, each taken in isolation, with the "ideal native speaker" as the ultimate model' (Council of Europe, 2001: 5). By contrast, the plurilingual approach aims to develop an integrated communicative competence that is a close relative of Vivian Cook's concept of linguistic multicompetence as 'the compound state of a mind with two [or more] grammars' (Cook, 1991: 112). A plurilingual repertoire accommodates partial competences (Council of Europe, 2001: 2) and uneven proficiency profiles (Council of Europe, 2001: 133). However, it is unlikely to develop seamlessly – 'as an individual person's experience of language in its cultural contexts expands' – when curricula and teaching methods follow traditional paths..

Two learner profiles summarized by Ofelia García help to clarify the CEFR's distinction between 'multilingual' and 'plurilingual':

> Born in France to educated middle-class parents, Christine has spoken French since birth. In school she learned English, and then Spanish. Now 36, she considers French her L1, English her L2, and Spanish her L3. She is secure in her identity as a francophone and uses French personally and professionally in her daily life. She seldom uses English, although she often reads reports in English for work; she says that she likes Spanish

better than English, but uses it only to sing songs she loves. Christine considers only French as her own language. The others are simply 'gifts' which she borrows.

In contrast, Carlos was born and grew up in Peru and is now 43. In the home where he was raised, he spoke Spanish and Quechua. However, at school only Spanish was taught, although Quechua was frequently used. Carlos is a talented musician, and in Peru he was part of a bilingual musical group that sang songs in Quechua and Spanish. He considered himself a bilingual Peruvian, with neither language identified as L1 or L2. At the age of 38, because of economic hardship, Carlos migrated to Germany. When he first arrived, he took a German language 'integration' course. Two years ago, he married a German-speaking woman. He is required to use German as his everyday lived language, both at home and at the Peruvian restaurant where he works and sings in Spanish and Quechua. German is not his L2 or L3; it has become his own (although not his sole) everyday lived language. (García, 2017: 18)

García explains that Christine is a 'second' language learner who learns the language of 'the other', whereas Carlos must integrate new features of German into his own language repertoire for 'everyday lived use' (García, 2017: 18). In the CEFR's terms Christine is partially multilingual, whereas Carlos is plurilingual. The difference between them is captured in Figure P3.1. Christine's francophone identity is reflected in the largest of the three discs that represent her repertoire. The English disc is larger than the Spanish disc because she has a fuller command of English; on the other hand, more of the Spanish disc overlaps the French disc because of her emotional attachment to the language. In Carlos's repertoire, the alternating stripes indicate that Spanish and Quechua are equally his first language, while the German features he has acquired are fully integrated with the rest of his repertoire.

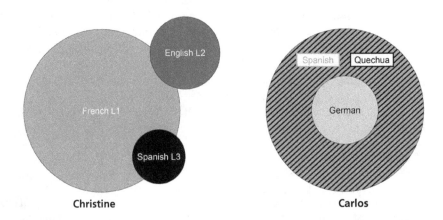

Figure P3.1 Christine's multilingual repertoire and Carlos's plurilingual repertoire

As the examples of Christine and Carlos underline, there is a clear *qualitative* difference between (individual) multilingualism and plurilingualism. So, how do we get from Christine to Carlos? How do we ensure that languages taught and learnt in formal educational contexts become part of learners' *everyday lived language*? Bearing in mind that language user/learners are 'individuals and ... social agents' (Council of Europe, 2001: 9), how do we ensure that each new language is integral to what they are and a channel of their agency? According to the authors of the discussion paper 'Plurilingual and intercultural education as a project', 'plurilingual and intercultural education is not to be thought of as a new methodology for the teaching of languages' but, rather, as 'a change of perspective' (Cavalli *et al.*, 2009: 7). This is surely misguided. The development of integrated plurilingual repertoires requires pedagogies that are grounded in language use, that engage learners' identities and agency, and use their existing linguistic repertoires to support the learning of new languages. Such pedagogies fulfil two of the Council of Europe's central aims as summarized by John Trim: to

- promote the personal development of the individual, with growing self-awareness, self-confidence and independence of thought and action combined with social responsibility as an active agent in a participatory, pluralist, democratic society;
- make the process of learning itself more democratic by providing the conceptual tools for the planning, construction, conduct and evaluation of courses closely geared to the needs, motivations and characteristics of the learners and enabling them so far as possible to assess, steer and control their own progress.

(Trim, 2012: 23)

Perhaps needless to say, these are not regular features of language teaching as it is practised in Council of Europe member states. They are to be found, however, in pedagogies that are shaped by the principle of learner autonomy (see, for example, Little *et al.*, 2017).

According to the CEFR, plurilingualism has to be seen in the context of pluriculturalism: plurilingual competence is one component of pluricultural competence (Council of Europe, 2001: 6). This seems to imply that learning a new language necessarily means acquiring a new culture, which common sense suggests is by no means always the case. For the most part the CEFR does not distinguish clearly between 'pluricultural' and 'intercultural': 'plurilingual' is combined sometimes with one and sometimes with the other term. A degree of clarification is provided, however, in Chapter 8:

Plurilingual and pluricultural competence refers to the ability to use languages for purposes of communication and to take part in intercultural interaction, where a person, viewed as a social agent has proficiency, of varying degrees, in several languages and experience of several cultures. (Council of Europe, 2001: 168)

There is a crucial difference here between 'proficiency', understood as a capacity for agentive language use, and 'experience', which may stop a long way short of participation.

A discussion paper that Michael Byram (2009) wrote for the Council of Europe's project 'Languages in Education, Languages for Education' helpfully distinguishes further between 'pluricultural' and 'intercultural'. Byram explains that pluriculturalism 'involves identifying with at least some of the values, beliefs and/or practices of two or more cultures, as well as acquiring the competences which are necessary for actively participating in those cultures' (Byram, 2009: 6). Pluriculturality, he continues, can be expressed in various ways: via 'multiple cultural allegiances irrespective of context'; via 'alternation', e.g. switching between the culture of the home and the prevailing peer culture; and via 'hybridity', 'the eclectic fusion of resources and elements drawn from multiple cultures' (Byram, 2009: 6). On the other hand, Byram defines 'interculturality' as the capacity 'to experience and analyse cultural otherness, and to use this experience to reflect on matters that are usually taken for granted within one's own culture and environment' (2009: 6). Interculturality involves 'being open to, interested in, curious about and empathetic towards people from other cultures'; 'using this heightened awareness of otherness to engage and interact with others and, potentially, to act together for common purposes'; 'evaluating one's own everyday patterns of perception, thought, feeling and behaviour in order to develop greater self-knowledge and self-understanding' (2009: 6). Interculturality is a defining goal of all language education programmes that truly reflect Council of Europe values.

The concept of plurilingualism as developed by the CEFR has two complementary implications for language education. First, when learners develop integrated communicative repertoires they are equipped to engage in various kinds of crosslinguistic mediation, as the CEFR itself points out:

In different situations, a person can call flexibly upon different parts of this [plurilingual] competence to achieve effective communication with a particular interlocutor. For instance, partners may switch from one language or dialect to another, exploiting the ability of each to express themselves in one language and to understand the other; or a person may call upon the knowledge of a number of languages to make sense of a text, written or even spoken, in a previously 'unknown' language, recognising words from a common international store in a new guise. Those with some knowledge, even slight, may use it to help those with none to communicate by mediating between individuals with no common language. (Council of Europe, 2001: 4)

These consequences of plurilingualism prompt two questions: How should curriculum languages be viewed in relation to one another? and Should crosslinguistic mediation be explicitly taught and formally assessed? Chapter 7, by Bessie Dendrinos, provides answers to these questions from the perspective of Greece's Integrated Foreign Languages Curriculum, which is underpinned by extensive and ongoing corpus linguistic research. The curriculum is supported by a languages profile that draws on a corpus of learner data collected from the national foreign language exams. An innovative feature of the curriculum is the inclusion of linguistic mediation descriptors that draw on empirical data from exams that have been testing oral and written mediation since 2003.

In Chapter 8, Peter Lenz offers some critical reflections on the testing of crosslinguistic mediation. He begins by pointing out that the CEFR *Companion Volume*'s (CEFR-CV) descriptive apparatus is so vast that it cannot yield a single overarching test construct for mediation. Turning his attention to the characteristic aim of mediation activities – building bridges between communication partners, constructing shared meaning – he argues that these should have consequences for the rating criteria applied to performances. He explores the nature of these consequences by analysing tasks from the Occupational English Test (OET) Speaking Sub-test and a draft task from a test for foreign-language teachers, and concludes that although reference frameworks such as the CEFR and the CEFR-CV can be extremely helpful, we must not expect them to provide one-size-fits-all solutions.

The second implication of the CEFR's concept of plurilingualism arises from the fact that the basis of any plurilingual repertoire is the language first acquired at home. From this it follows that we must find ways of including in the educational process the languages that pupils and students bring with them, even if those languages are unknown to their teachers and peers and are not part of the official curriculum. Chapter 9, by Déirdre Kirwan and David Little, describes an approach based on this principle, which is followed by an Irish primary school with an unusually diverse pupil cohort. The school encourages pupils from immigrant families to use their home languages for whatever reasons seem to them appropriate, inside as well as outside the classroom. This turns out to be highly motivating: pupils develop high levels of age-appropriate literacy in English (the principal language of schooling), Irish (the second language of the curriculum), French (in the last two primary grades), and (in the case of pupils from immigrant families) home languages – this last without benefit of explicit instruction. Pupils also acquire an unusually high degree of metalinguistic awareness and from an early age are motivated to undertake ambitious language learning projects on their own initiative. This version of the plurilingual approach fosters pupils' self-esteem and promotes social cohesion, converting linguistic diversity into educational and social capital.

References

Byram, M. (2009) Multilingual societies, pluricultural people and the project of intercultural education. Strasbourg: Council of Europe. Available at https://rm.coe.int/CoERMPublicCommonSearchServices/DisplayDCTMContent?documentId=09000016805a223c (accessed 26 August 2020).

Cavalli, M., Coste, D., Crişan, A. and van de Ven, P.-H. (2009) *Plurilingual and Intercultural Education as a Project*. Strasbourg: Council of Europe, Language Policy Division. Available at https://rm.coe.int/CoERMPublicCommonSearchServices/DisplayDCTMContent?documentId=09000016805a219f (accessed 26 August 2020).

Cook, V.J. (1991) The poverty-of-the-stimulus argument and multi-competence. *Second Language Research* 7 (2), 103–117.

Council of Europe (2001) *Common European Framework of Reference for Languages: Learning, Teaching, Assessment*. Cambridge: Cambridge University Press. https://rm.coe.int/1680459f97 (accessed 26 August 2020).

García, O. (2017) Problematizing linguistic integration of migrants: The role of translanguaging and language teachers. In J.-C. Beacco, H.-J. Krumm and D. Little (eds) *The Linguistic Integration of Adult Migrants: Lessons from Research/L'intégration linguistique des migrants adultes: Les enseignements de la recherche* (pp. 11–26). Berlin: De Gruyter Mouton.

Little, D., Dam, L. and Legenhausen, L. (2017) *Language Learner Autonomy: Theory, Practice and Research*. Bristol: Multilingual Matters.

Trim, J.L.M. (2012) The Common European Framework of Reference for Languages and its background: A case study of cultural politics and educational influences. In M. Byram and L. Parmenter (eds) *The Common European Framework of Reference: The Globalisation of Language Education Policy* (pp. 14–34). Bristol: Multilingual Matters.

7   A Data-driven Curriculum with Mediation Descriptors for Plurilingual Education

Bessie Dendrinos

This chapter presents research linked to the CEFR (2001) and the CEFR-CV (2018/2020) as part of a comprehensive project carried out in Greece, so as to create documents and instruments that permit context-sensitive use of these two Council of Europe tools. In describing our project, the intention is not merely to document our work for others but to seek collaboration for further research in ways that may support the contextually appropriate implementation of the two tools in different educational systems. The Greek project has resulted in a CEFR-based Integrated Foreign Languages Curriculum (IFLC) and a Language Curriculum Database (LCD) used to make IFLC descriptors, aligned to the CEFR levels, explicit in terms of linguistic data, hence documenting how learners might articulate the can-do statements at each level of proficiency. The development of the IFLC is supported by the (Greek) Languages Profile, using a corpus comprised of learner data from our national foreign language exams, in the context of what is known as the KPG (Kratiko Pistopiitiko Glossomathias) multilingual examination suite. An innovative aspect of the IFLC is the inclusion of linguistic mediation descriptors that draw upon empirical data from the KPG exams that have been testing oral and written mediation since 2003.

Developing a CEFR-based, Data-driven Curriculum

Since its publication in 2001, the *Common European Framework of Reference for Languages* (CEFR) has had a huge impact on foreign language teaching, testing and assessment in Europe and beyond. Undoubtedly it met the very real need for an explicit description of language proficiency at six-levels, which may 'facilitate mutual recognition of qualifications gained in different learning contexts' (Council of Europe, 2001: 1), useful in a globalized world and indispensable in Europe, where mobility for work and study is not only desirable but necessary.

Our own concern, which jump-started our multifaceted research project at the National and Kapodistrian University of Athens (NKUA),[1] was to use the CEFR constructively, keeping in mind that this useful tool was never created to replace curricula and testing content, nor to impose a 'one size fits all' language teaching and testing approach, nor to dictate a single language teaching methodology. It is the *Common European Framework of Reference for Languages*: a platform to be used as a foundation for developing applications. It was not meant to be implemented as is. As John Trim (2011) reminds us, it may 'stand as a central point of reference, itself always open to amendment and further development, in an interactive international system of co-operating institutions ... whose cumulative experience and expertise produces a solid structure of knowledge, understanding and practice shared by all' (Trim, 2011: xi).

Agreeing with Trim and concurring with scholars who believe that research is needed so as to situate the relevance of the CEFR in local contexts (cf. Alderson, 2007), I directed a team of 25 language teaching professionals in a foreign language curriculum reform project commissioned by the Ministry of Education. In 2011, we embarked on the intricate task of deliberating on, selecting, fine-tuning and aligning to the six-level scale of the CEFR, a set of can-do statements. Next, we aligned these to the descriptors contained in KPG specifications, which are supported by learner performance data and task analysis documentation, and we developed the final version of the Integrated Foreign Languages Curriculum (IFLC) descriptors which specify generic, functional criteria about how communicative competences are expected to develop across learning stages. Our goal was to treat all foreign languages taught in Greek state schools as a single discipline, with coherent aims from start to finish, based on systemic functional linguistic theory and a genre-based approach to the production of language.

When the curriculum had been designed, an RCeL team[2] began working on a sub-project whose purpose was to add, on an ongoing basis, linguistic details to the IFLC reference level descriptors so that the curriculum designates not only *what* a language learner should be able to do (with can-do statements) at each level of proficiency, but also *how* – that is, lexicogrammatically. To achieve this, we created the Language Curriculum Database (LCD) – a multilingual database, which contains detailed descriptions of elements approximating the communicative competences in foreign languages currently offered in state schools in Greece.

The LCD has been designed as the essential methodological apparatus for specifying benchmarks of language proficiency and furnishing comparable descriptions of communicative performance across languages. The task of documenting descriptors with empirical language data from different languages (English, French, German, Italian and Spanish) is ongoing work. Nonetheless, by the time the IFLC was adopted as the national foreign languages curriculum in 2016, it was finalized with the reference level descriptors accompanied by linguistic details that correspond to the language proficiency that students finishing compulsory education are likely to have in two out of the five languages offered in Greek schools. To date, this has been the first and only data-driven curriculum in the Greek educational system.

The details of the aforementioned project have been presented, discussed and illustrated in Dendrinos and Gotsoulia (2015). Nevertheless, it is perhaps appropriate to explain briefly here that the data of our multilingual database – the LCD – represent discrete types of language competences at each of the CEFR's six levels of language proficiency and they are drawn from a variety of sources (i.e. profiles of different languages, school textbooks, the KPG exam specifications, and the KPG Corpus). Language competences are represented in terms of a common metalanguage (i.e. a common ontological schema) *across languages*. This representation enables comparisons of data within and across languages, aimed at the description of each level in terms of objective criteria. It also allows for data links across languages for a genuinely multilingual curriculum. The LCD components include the reference level descriptors for all languages, whereas for each individual language at each CEFR level the following is documented for: language functions, grammatical features, lexical features, and text types. The representation of competences in terms of hierarchies of linguistic types is suitable for modelling the gradual development of linguistic knowledge, i.e. each type is associated with a CEFR level, and more abstract types are expected to develop fully at higher levels of proficiency. Comparisons and data links in this populated multilingual database are essential for documenting, evaluating and refining the IFLC descriptors, so that they capture communicative language competences in a precise, transparent, and consistent fashion across languages.

As mentioned earlier, the IFLC reference level descriptors are informed by those in the KPG specifications.[3] At this point, it is important to add that the KPG feeds into the IFLC in one more way. The IFLC database is fed by the (Greek) Languages Profile (GLP), a tool that draws from the KPG Corpus data, as described in detail by Gotsoulia and Dendrinos (2011). It has been developed to contain compilations of scripts produced by candidates for the KPG exams. Scripts have been marked using the KPG marking grids and are then classified and annotated. What distinguishes the GLP from related projects, such as the English Profile, is that the GLP makes systematic links between discrete types of competences, while also attempting to make descriptions of competences comparable *across* languages.

Using state-of-the-art tools for automated text analysis combined with manual inspection and correction, KPG scripts are coded with sets of lexical, semantic and grammatical features. Automatically acquired frame semantic structures are used to jointly capture lexical, semantic and grammatical features. Frames group together semantically related lexical items, associated with the syntactic patterns in which they appear (Baker *et al.*, 1998), and map words to events in the real world. As such, the research model created for the design of the IFLC provides a context for: (a) relating languages to one another; (b) attending to learners' plurilingual and intercultural competences; and (c) encouraging language teachers to work together on projects involving two or more languages.

The Mediation Construct for Plurilingual Education

It has sometimes been claimed that the CEFR promotes the outdated monolingual tradition in language didactics. Yet such an uninformed opinion has been created on account of how the CEFR has been put to use by language education policymakers and curriculum designers, and by how it has figured in teacher training programmes and foreign language textbooks, both of which have guided teaching practice. Despite the fact that CEFR descriptors were generated without reference to a specific language, so that they are applicable to any language, the CEFR has by and large been used as a basis for the design of single language curricula, syllabuses, assessment tools and proficiency testing. With few exceptions,[4] schools are still monolingual spaces whereby the language of schooling, i.e. the medium of instruction, is the national or official language(s) of the country, sustaining language loyalty and collective identity ideologies.

The publication of the CEFR 2001 by the Council of Europe coincided with the 2002 Barcelona decision of the European Union designating that European students are to learn two languages in addition to their mother tongue, which was followed by decision-implementation policies for foreign language learning advocated as a means to sustaining European multilingualism. However, as European Commission policymakers think of multilingualism as polyglossia, and language teaching as a means to learning the dominant languages of Europe, it was crucial that the CEFR introduced and defined the concept of plurilingualism, as well as the plurilingual approach to language education, foreshadowing pedagogical practices that do not keep languages apart from one another.

For those of us working on the KPG examinations in Greece, it was particularly important because the CEFR endorsed our understanding of the concept of plurilingualism (cf. Dendrinos & Mitsikopoulou, 2004), which fits into the theory of language on which we based both the KPG exams and the IFLC – a theory of language that does not see meaning as residing in language but as constructed with language (Dendrinos, 2020). Meaning for us was, and is, 'languaged' (in Halliday's terms), often through one or more languages, varieties of language and semiotic modes (visuals, sound, space, gesture) used together. We understand the plurilingually competent speaker/writer resorting to all verbal and nonverbal modes of communication that they have developed by participating in communicative events that frequently involve diversity, variability and hybridity in different contexts of interaction. As this understanding of communication was far from the beliefs that guided conventional monolingual language teaching, we were keen on progressively changing the widespread didactic paradigm.

Therefore, we welcomed the CEFR's introduction of the concept of linguistic mediation as an aspect of plurilingual competence, because it endorsed our aims for language teaching and learning. The problem was that the CEFR's description of mediation was unrefined: it designated only four acts of mediation (spoken interpretation, written translation, summarizing and paraphrasing texts in the same or a different language), and referred to mediation strategies but did not delineate them. Yet, the CEFR did empower those of us who had been arguing against the monolingual paradigm to introduce crosslinguistic mediation in language teaching and testing for a language didactics that does not keep languages separated from one another and does not consider the mixing of languages a grave transgression.

In 2002, shortly after the publication of the CEFR, a team of language professionals and scholars was appointed by the Ministry of Education to design the KPG multilingual examination suite. One of our bold decisions – given that all exam batteries we were familiar with were monolingual – was to test candidates for their ability to mediate across two languages, namely Greek (the common language of candidates in our glocal exam system) and the target language, from proficiency level B1 to level C2. Our decision was somewhat risky as we knew that our prospective candidates would not have been taught explicitly how to mediate.

Less daring was our decision to include in our exams what we called intralinguistic mediation – a term which also appeared many years later in the CEFR *Companion Volume* (CEFR-CV) – because we were rather certain that, in our context, schooled people such as our candidates are socially required to have the necessary literacy to *understand* (multimodal) texts in the language they use in school, at work and within the sphere of public service, as well as adequate awareness of the generic characteristics of the oral and written texts they deal with on a daily basis; awareness that is likely to facilitate text comprehension and help them answer questions regarding the generic features of texts in the target language. Therefore, the KPG test papers include intralinguistic items which test learners' language awareness, but also intralinguistic test tasks requiring candidates: (a) to relay (selected) information from a source text in the target language to another text in the same language, in a contextually appropriate manner, via a different channel of communication; (b) to relay messages from one source text to another of a different register, genre or style of speech than the original; and (c) to summarize, review, convey the main idea or give the gist of a source text in the same or a different language, in a context-specific manner (cf. Dendrinos, 2006: 21).

Our more daring decision to include crosslinguistic test tasks in our exams, even though we knew that our potential candidates had not been specifically trained to mediate across languages, was informed by research. Firstly, we considered research results showing that people build upon the knowledge and skills developed in and through their first language to learn other languages; and, secondly, we studied outcomes of crosslinguistic communication studies showing that learners of more than one language mediate across languages in their daily lives. Based on this information, we piloted 100 cross-linguistic oral and written test tasks with statistically significant samples of B- and C-level Greek learners of English, French, German and Italian. We discovered that they could all manage the task, and that the most competent language learners could outperform their peers, by mediating rather than producing a bad text translation. We also had indications, which were later confirmed by research findings, that (a) the source text in a different language regulates the target text and leads to hybrid linguistic output, and (b) the poorer the degree of language competence of candidates at the same proficiency the greater the hybridity in their linguistic production – sometimes resulting in unintelligible performance.[5] Actually, as Stathopoulou (2009) discovered, regulation of the target text may vary from weak to strong, and this variation depends on a series of factors, which she explores in her study. Therefore, finally, we included oral and written crosslinguistic mediation test tasks.[6] The sources in both are written texts in Greek but, whereas in their writing test candidates are required to produce a context-specific written text using the Greek text as their source of information or merely as a reference, in the speaking test they use the written text in Greek to extract information and use this in discussion or a short speech in the target language.

Obviously, because of our understanding of intralinguistic and crosslinguistic mediation, we did not include *written translation* and *oral interpretation* test tasks, as designated by the CEFR. Our understanding was (and still is) more similar to how linguistic mediation is presented in the CEFR-CV, which, through detailed descriptors of linguistic mediation, presents a different construct than that which was presented in the CEFR, which basically reduced mediation to interpretation, translation and text summary (cf. Piccardo & North, 2019).[7]

Unlike in Germany, where crosslinguistic mediation – adopted into its 2003 national educational standards and, subsequently, into many federal curricula (Kolb, forthcoming) – was viewed as 'the ability to transfer the meaning of coherent utterances and texts from one language to another' (Melo-Pfeifer & Helmchen, forthcoming), in Greece we viewed mediation as 'a form of everyday social practice involving meaning-making agents in acts that require negotiation of meaning, which is relayed across the same or different languages' (Dendrinos, 2006: 12). We also understood the mediator:

> [as] a social actor who monitors the process of interaction and acts when some type of intervention is required in order to help the communicative process and sometimes to influence its outcome; as a facilitator in social events during which two or more parties interacting are experiencing a communication breakdown or when there is a communication gap between them; as a meaning negotiator operating as a meaning-making agent especially when s/he intervenes in situations which require reconciliation, settlement or compromise of meanings. (Dendrinos, 2006: 11)

Finally, we believed that 'in order to play their role effectively, mediators are required to interpret and create meanings through speech or writing for listeners or readers of a different linguistic or cultural background. In this context, the mediator takes on an active role as an arbiter or arbitrator of meaning' (Dendrinos, 2006: 11) during 'social practices [which] are culturally bound', thereby making mediation a culturally encoded act (2006: 11).

It was on the basis of this understanding that we designed the KPG mediation test tasks and assessed the performance of B (B1–B2) and C (C1–C2) level candidates. The first couple of years of exam administration provided us with a limited set of learner data and a clump of mediation test tasks from Greek to English, French, German and Italian, which we analysed and discovered that, depending on the mediation task, whether this is intralinguistic or crosslinguistic, challenging demands are made on candidates as mediators, requiring that they have: (1) background knowledge and awareness;[8] (2) different types of literacy;[9] (3) communicative competences;[10] and (4) cognitive and social skills[11] (Dendrinos, 2006: 22).

Continued mediation test task analysis (from 2006 to 2008) showed that the higher the level of proficiency that the mediation tasks are meant to test, the higher their complexity and, therefore, the greater the demands made on the candidates for whom the tasks are designed. It also revealed that it is not only the language level of the candidates that is taken into consideration by test task designers, but also other factors such as age, school knowledge, etc. Finally, there were strong indications that the resources mediators use and the strategies they employ are *context specific* and *task specific*. These findings were confirmed by the results of another phase of our mediation test task research (2008–2010),[12] which set out to determine differentiated level performance and expected output of mediation test tasks, resulting in the creation of the KPG Task Database. Approximating an ontology, it was organized in terms of metadata concerning: the source text (e.g. topic, genre, register, communicative purpose), text environment (e.g. internet, newspaper, journal, brochure), addressor and addressee, dominant lexicogrammatical features, context of the target text, and dominant generic features of the target text (cf. Dendrinos, 2013).

The research questions we raised and attempted to answer were related to the most common characteristics of source and target texts used and the most common contextual features of the mediation test tasks at each proficiency level, which led later through another research project produced as a PhD thesis (Stathopoulou, 2013) to the creation of a typology of crosslinguistic (written) mediation test tasks with the intention of answering the research question: 'How do crosslinguistic mediation test tasks differ across proficiency levels?' The research conducted by Stathopoulou (2013) also led to an inventory of crosslinguistic written mediation test tasks, resulting in an understanding of the strategies that successful response to these tasks involves. Moreover, Stathopoulou's thesis – a revised version of which was published as a book (Stathopoulou, 2015) – later showed clearly that the strategies candidates as mediators use are categorically task dependent.[13]

Such understanding allowed us to develop task-related assessment criteria so that candidates are appraised both for their linguistic output in an oral or written text of a particular genre and discourse, and also for their mediation performance. So, for example, when we wish to ascertain if the learner/candidate 'Can relay (in Language B) specific information given in straightforward informational texts (e.g. leaflets, brochure entries, notices and letters or e-mails) in Language A' (Council of Europe, 2020: 94), we develop a task with contextual details (who, to whom and for what purpose) that figure in the assessment criteria.

By the time the IFLC was being finalized in 2015, our data, research outcomes, practical experience and resources allowed us to compose mediation descriptors for learning, teaching and assessment purposes. The descriptors were composed once we had decided what type of mediation activities Greek language learners in compulsory education should be trained to perform. The activities include:

- selecting and relaying information, ideas and messages from one language to another;
- presenting, explaining, clarifying, rationalizing and comparing or contrasting information, ideas and messages across languages or within the same language;

- recontextualizing information from texts of one type of discourse, genre, register, style or semiotic mode to another across languages or within the same language.

Conclusion

What has been presented in the two preceding sections demonstrates systematic efforts to 'implement' the CEFR and the CEFR-CV, in a contextually sensitive manner, in our foreign language teaching and testing programmes in Greece, via research, critical assessment and interpretation of outcomes.[14] I do not believe, and I still think it is wrong to put, the whole range of CEFR descriptors directly into teaching and testing practice. It may lead to the frustration of practitioners because it is extremely difficult if not inappropriate to do so. For each educational programme, in each pedagogical context, a different teaching and testing curriculum must be developed, *facilitated* by the CEFR descriptors. After all, as mentioned earlier, the CEFR is not a curriculum in itself but a *framework* for curricula and testing specifications.

This is true for the CEFR-CV as well. This new, useful tool, which has expanded on the notion of plurilingualism, elucidated the concept of mediation, concocted a wide array of descriptors for different social contexts, and named types of mediation – which nevertheless need to be investigated and appraised – can feed language curricula for courses in different educational contexts. Teaching, learning and assessing the ability to linguistically mediate cross- and intralinguistically may be a useful component of the school curriculum, but it could prove equally valuable in the language curricula of military academies, university language centres and university language departments, vocational colleges, and adult centres offering language courses for general or specific purposes. Of course, in each educational context there are different mediation needs and requirements, which must be investigated, so that a curriculum takes them into account. Certainly, the CEFR-CV will be of immense value. It offers a great variety of intralinguistic and crosslinguistic descriptors that can be *adopted* and *adapted* to cover the real mediation needs of language learners in different social encounters, and which have not been investigated up until now (cf. Dendrinos, forthcoming). However, primary research is needed into what people are really required to do, what and how they are expected to mediate in different contexts, for different social purposes, because though the descriptors of the CEFR-CV are wide-ranging, they are the result of surveys regarding what language professionals and language teaching experts *think* mediation involves, not what it actually *does* involve – much like the descriptors of the CEFR, which are also not derived from empirical data.

Notes

(1)   The research is conducted – at a pace that the funding secured allows – at the Research Centre for Language Teaching, Testing and Assessment (RCeL) of the NKUA (www.rcel.enl.uoa.gr).

(2)   Under my guidance as project director, Dr Voula Gotsoulia, computational linguist, worked as team leader for the development of a multilingual database, for providing metadata for our corpora, and counselling us on approaches to learner data analysis.

(3)   For information in English about the KPG exams – administered by the Greek Ministry of Education – visit the KPG website in English at https://rcel2.enl.uoa.gr/kpg/en_index.htm. For material related to KPG research see also Karavas & Mitsikopoulou (2018).

(4)   One notable exception is the language-friendly Irish school for girls whose programme is described in Chapter 9 of this volume, but it is important perhaps to mention the work of the Language Friendly School Network (https://language-friendlyschool.org/) and acknowledge recognition of the importance of multilingual schools by the European Commission (https://op.europa.eu/en/publication-detail/-/publication/c5673e19-c292-11e6-a6db-01aa75ed71a1).

(5)   During an in-house seminar at the RCeL in 2007, I had discussed the linguistic traces of the source in the target text as hybrid formations rather than as 'errors' and proposed the exploration of linguistic hybridity in mediated texts.

(6)   At this point we used the term 'interlinguistic' instead of crosslinguistic – the term adopted later partly because of its use in the CEFR-CV.

(7)   Yet, Piccardo and North (2019: 6–7) criticize such implementation: 'Many people appear to associate mediation in the CEFR solely as cross-linguistic mediation – usually conveying the information given in a text, and to reduce it to some form of (more or less professional) translation and interpretation,'

(8)   That is, lifeworld knowledge, as this develops with experience and social participation; language awareness of how two languages operate at the level of discourse, genre and register, as well as at sentence or utterance and word level; awareness of the grammar of visual design; and intercultural awareness.

(9)   That is, school literacy, social literacy, practical literacy, and test-taking literacy.

(10)   That is, linguistic competence, sociolinguistic competence, discourse competence, and strategic competence.

(11)   That is, receptive skills, operational skills, productive skills, and interactive skills.

(12)   It was part of a larger project, conducted at the RCeL, aimed at the description and analysis of all tasks in the test papers of the KPG exams.

(13)   In the abstract of her PhD thesis, entitled 'Task-Dependent Interlinguistic Performance as Translanguaging Practice: The Use of KPG Data for an Empirically Based Study', Stathopoulou explains that her research, which has used data from the KPG Task Repository and the KPG English Corpus, 'both of which have been compiled with tasks and scripts, views mediation as inextricably linked to the tasks which instigate and thus affect performance', and 'attempts a systematic linguistic description of KPG mediation test tasks by level, which leads to the construction of a task taxonomy, organized in terms of task characteristics'. And she continues: 'Task-dependent performance exploration follows. It is empirically investigated through the textual analysis of scripts, with a view to finding task-dependent mediation strategies used for successful communication at different levels of proficiency. The KPG task and learner data are analysed using both top-down and bottom-up methodologies.'

(14)   The inclusion of linguistic mediation in the curriculum is assumed to have led to teachers incorporating mediation activities in their classroom practices. However, no research has been authorized by the Ministry of Education and it is not clear to

us how teachers deal with this aspect of the IFLC curriculum. Research is urgently needed so that findings may feed initial teacher-training and professional development programmes.

References

Alderson, J.C. (2007) The CEFR and the need for more research. *The Modern Language Journal* 91 (4), 659–663.

Baker, C.F., Fillmore, C.J. and Lowe, J.B. (1998) The Berkeley FrameNet Project. In *Proceedings of the 36th Annual Meeting of the Association for Computational Linguistics and 17th International Conference on Computational Linguistics (COLING-ACL)*. Montreal, Canada. Morgan Kaufmann Publishers/ACL.

Council of Europe (2001) *Common European Framework of Reference for Languages: Learning, Teaching, Assessment*. Cambridge: Cambridge University Press.

Council of Europe (2020) *Common European Framework of Reference for Languages: Learning, Teaching, Assessment. Companion Volume*. Strasbourg: Council of Europe.

Dendrinos, B. (2006) Mediation in communication, language teaching and testing. *Journal of Applied Linguistics* (Greek Applied Linguistics Association) 22.

Dendrinos, B. (2013) Teaching and testing mediation. *Directions in Language Teaching and Testing*. http://rcel.enl.uoa.gr/directions/issue1_1f.htm (accessed 19 October 2020).

Dendrinos, B. (2020) The magic of language and language teaching. In T. Tinnefeld (ed.) *The Magic of Language: Productivity in Linguistics and Language Teaching* (pp. 13–46). Saarbrücken Series on Linguistics and Language Methodology (SSLLM), Volume 11 (Saarbrücker Schriften zu Linguistik und Fremdsprachendidaktik). Saarbrücken: htw saar.

Dendrinos, B. (ed.) (forthcoming) *Mediation as Linguistic and Cultural Negotiation in Plurilingual Education*. London: Routledge.

Dendrinos, B. and Mitsikopoulou, B. (eds) (2004) *Policies of Linguistic Pluralism and the Teaching of Languages in Europe*. Athens: Metaixmio Publications and NKUA.

Dendrinos, B. and Gotsoulia, V. (2015) Setting standards for multilingual curricula to teach and test foreign languages. In B. Spolsky, O. Inbar-Lourie and M. Tannenbaum (eds) *Challenges for Language Education and Policy: Making Space for People*. New York: Routledge.

Gotsoulia, V. and Dendrinos, B. (2011) Towards a corpus-based approach to modelling language production of foreign language learners in communicative contexts. In G. Angelova, K. Bontcheva, R. Mitkov and N. Nikolov (eds) *Proceedings of the 8th International Conference on Recent Advances in Natural Language Processing* (pp. 357–361). Stroudsburg, PA: Association for Computational Linguistics (http://lml.bas.bg/ranlp2011/proceedings.php).

Karavas, E. and Mitsikopoulou, B. (eds) (2018) *Developments in Glocal Testing. The Case of the Greek National Foreign Language Exam System*. Oxford: Peter Lang.

Kolb, E. (forthcoming) Mediation as a test format in German high-stakes school-leaving exams. In B. Dendrinos (ed.) *Mediation as Linguistic and Cultural Negotiation in Plurilingual Education*. London: Routledge.

Melo-Pfeifer, S. and Helmchen, C. (forthcoming) Representations of mediation in foreign language education: An explorative case-study with different stakeholders in Hamburg. In B. North, E. Piccardo, T. Goodier, D. Fasoglio, R. Margonis and B. Rüschoff (eds) *Enriching 21st Century Language Education: The CEFR Companion Volume, Examples from Practice*. Strasbourg: Council of Europe.

Piccardo, E. and North, B. (2019) *The Action-oriented Approach: A Dynamic Vision of Language Education*. Bristol: Multilingual Matters.

Stathopoulou, M. (2009) Written mediation in the KPG exams: Source text regulation resulting in hybrid formations. MA dissertation, National and Kapodistrian University of Athens.

Stathopoulou, M. (2013) Task-dependent interlinguistic performance as translanguaging practice: The use of KPG data for an empirically based study. PhD thesis, National and Kapodistrian University of Athens.

Stathopoulou, M. (2015) *Cross-Language Mediation in Foreign Language Teaching and Testing*. Bristol: Multilingual Matters.

Trim, J.L.M. (2011) Preface. In A. Green, *Language Functions Revisited: Theoretical and Empirical Bases for Language Construct Definition across the Ability Range* (pp. xxi–xli). Cambridge: Cambridge University Press.

8 Some Thoughts about the Testing of Mediation

Peter Lenz

This chapter deals with questions that have arisen from my recent practice. It first gives some general thought to the testing of mediation, now that the concept of mediation is as broad as the CEFR Companion Volume defines it (CEFR-CV; Council of Europe, 2020). The vast descriptive system in the CEFR-CV quickly makes it clear that an overarching test construct and a corresponding 'test of mediation' are inconceivable. The second part of the chapter discusses the impression that the characteristic aim of mediation activities – building bridges between communication partners, constructing shared meaning – should have consequences for the rating criteria applied to performances. An analysis of tasks from the Occupational English Test (OET) Speaking Sub-test and a draft task from a test for foreign language teachers confirm the need for specific functional (action-oriented) and linguistic criteria in order to do justice to the relevant aspects of performances. One of the findings is that linguistic scales favouring more complex, more sophisticated and more fluent language are inadequate for some task settings. I argue that we should take as our starting point the tasks and success criteria found in actual communicative practice and we should use reference frameworks such as the CEFR and the CEFR-CV as expert tools that can be extremely useful but must not be expected to provide one-size-fits-all solutions.

Mediation and its Testing

The additional scales of illustrative descriptors contained in the recently published *Common European Framework of Reference for Languages: Learning, Teaching, Assessment. Companion Volume* (CEFR-CV; Council of Europe, 2020) were long awaited. For mediation alone, 26 descriptor scales illustrating mediation activities and mediation strategies are now available for use (for a simplified overview see Council of Europe, 2020: 90). The activities scales are subdivided into three categories:

(1) 'Mediating a text' (e.g. explaining data; translating a text);
(2) 'Mediating concepts' (sub-categories: 'Collaborating in a group'; 'Leading group work');
(3) 'Mediating communication' (e.g. acting as an intermediary).

The strategies scales are subdivided into two categories:

(1) 'Strategies to explain a new concept' (e.g. linking to previous knowledge);
(2) 'Strategies to simplify a text' (e.g. streamlining a text).

In the *Common European Framework of Reference for Languages* (CEFR; Council of Europe, 2001) mediation was part of the descriptive scheme; however, scales and descriptors were missing, which reduced the visibility of this mode of communication compared to the other, more familiar ones – reception, production and interaction. Also, the scope of the notion of mediation was more limited in the CEFR compared to the CEFR-CV. The earlier version of the concept can be adequately described as comprising language activities in which a language user acts as an intermediary when translation or interpretation is needed to establish understanding between other language users who do not sufficiently understand each other's language or language variety (cf. Council of Europe, 2001: 14). The CEFR-CV describes its 'broader view of mediation' as follows:

> In mediation, the user/learner acts as *a social agent who creates bridges and helps to construct or convey meaning*, sometimes within the same language, sometimes across modalities (e.g. from spoken to signed or vice versa, in cross-modal communication) and sometimes from one language to another (cross-linguistic mediation). The focus is on the role of language in processes like *creating the space and conditions* for communicating and/or learning, *collaborating to construct* new meaning, *encouraging others to construct or understand* new meaning, and *passing on new information in an appropriate form*. The context can be social, pedagogic, cultural, linguistic or professional. (Council of Europe, 2020: 90; italics added)

The phrases in italics show immediately how much the concept and related activities (and strategies) have evolved. They clearly surpass – but still include – the formerly prototypical interpreting and translating. Considering the variety of parameters present in the new concept, it would be foolhardy to assume that we could have a single test of, say, 'B2 Mediation', as some have called for. The 'focus … on the role of language' that is obviously meant to reduce the scope of mediation, still leaves a great number of sometimes vastly different types of mediation activities. The fact that mediation activities may combine reception, production and interaction not only within one language but also across different languages, makes this quite obvious. Drawing a representative sample of tasks and performances across the full range of the concept would never be achieved in a real-world test – neither would there be a realistic need for an overarching, hard-to-define mediation certificate. (In the case of the traditional 'skills' of listening, reading, speaking and writing, general-level tests are in great demand. I often have my doubts, however, as to how validly they test proficiency at the level they claim to test, especially from B2 upwards. My suspicion is based on the observation that test specifications often exclude contexts, topics, activities, etc., that appear 'too specific' – although language ability at the highest CEFR levels is precisely defined by successful language use in dealing with increasingly less familiar and more complex tasks and topics.)

For teaching and learning, we would not attempt to tackle immediately the huge range of learning objectives contained in the structure of the new mediation concept and tentatively illustrated through the scales and descriptors, because it is not feasible. The same should be true for language proficiency tests. To specify a test that is not (yet) specifically linked to an existing syllabus, we should start with a principled selection and concretization of objectives, primarily based on the communicative needs of a definable target group and additionally guided by scales and descriptors. 'Working backwards from what the users/learners need to be able to do in the language' (Council of Europe, 2020: 28), i.e. starting from needs analysis, is an approach that is intrinsically linked to the ideas of action-orientation and individual proficiency profiles that underlie the CEFR and are therefore particularly highlighted in Chapter 2 of the CEFR-CV, which chapter outlines the key aspects of the CEFR.

In sum, with the arrival of the CEFR-CV we now have at our disposal an abundance of scales and descriptors characterizing a new and enhanced concept of mediation. They illustrate and point to a wide range of potentially worthwhile objectives for language learning and therefore language assessment and testing. Good test craftsmanship suggests that we define a test construct (Bachman & Palmer, 2010: Chapter 3) that is underpinned by an analysis that takes account of the language needs of the test-taker population and limits itself to test objectives that can realistically be achieved through a given test. No single test can be advertised as testing mediation in its entirety at a specific level: a more precise description is needed.

Language Quality in Mediation Tasks

As the above quotation from the CEFR-CV (Council of Europe, 2020: 90) states, in mediation the mediators' main task is to use language to create bridges and to help construct and convey meaning. Generally in communication, the communication partners and/or recipients of a message cannot be ignored, but in mediation they clearly gain importance as a factor determining the criteria by which the appropriacy and suitability of the (supportive) actions taken and the language used can be judged. For example, a mediator's most elaborate vocabulary cannot be rated highly if it does not help overcome the communicative challenge at hand because it isn't understood. Taking into consideration many mediation tasks and settings, I suspect that the common aspects of language quality – e.g. (high) complexity and (high) fluency in the case of spoken language – may conflict with task-internal criteria gleaned from real-world judgements of the quality of task performance. Also, I doubt that 'the focus ... on the role of language' captures the decisive features of successful performance on many mediation tasks in which the language ability of the communication partner is much inferior to the speaker's, or in which a high degree of professional or interpersonal skills are a *conditio sine qua non*.

In order to explore these considerations, I shall take a closer look at (1) the Speaking Sub-test of the Occupational English Test (OET) and (2) a draft task from an oral teaching skills test for foreign language teachers.

The rating criteria of the OET Speaking Sub-test

The Speaking Sub-test of the OET (OET, 2020) tests the oral communication skills of healthcare professionals who are non-native speakers of English. The tasks consist of two role-play interactions between a test candidate and an actor. For physicians, the partners are a patient in the first role-play and a carer – e.g. a patient's parent – in the second role-play. The OET tasks are not explicitly labelled mediation tasks, and there is no single scale in the CEFR-CV that would directly apply to the OET tasks. However, the role of the medical professional in these tasks is predominantly that of a facilitator 'who creates bridges and helps to construct or convey meaning'. Also, the type and number of 'clinical communication criteria' applied to the test performances clearly point in that direction.

Clinical communication criteria

- *Relationship-building*: The impact of your choice of opening to the conversation and demonstration of empathy and respect on your listener's comfort
- *Understanding and incorporating the patient's perspective*: The impact of how fully you involve the patient in the conversation on your listener's understanding and comfort
- *Providing structure*: The impact of how you organize the information you provide and introduce new topics for discussion on your listener's understanding

- *Information-gathering*: The impact of the type of questions you ask and how you listen to the responses on your listener's understanding
- *Information-giving*: The impact of how you provide information and check this information is being understood on your listener's comfort and understanding

(OET, 2018: Taking the Speaking Sub-test)

These criteria make clear that the focus is on the quality of the facilitative behaviour in the selected types of professional interaction. For each of these five categories, an assessment grid provides from three to five 'indicators' elaborating the criterion (OET, 2018). For the criterion 'Providing structure', for example, these are: *C1 sequencing the interview purposefully and logically*; *C2 signposting changes in topic*; and *C3 using organising techniques in explanations*. The overall degree of attainment is expressed using four categories, ranging from *adept use* to *inefficient use*. While it is undoubtedly crucial for the candidates to have sufficient linguistic means at their disposal, it is obvious that highly competent users of English who lack specific training in clinical communication might fail on these five criteria. It is only the additional four linguistic criteria applied to the performances that clearly identify the OET as a test for learners of English. Interestingly, the brief characterization provided as an overview seems to be in line with the communication criteria:

Linguistic criteria

- *Intelligibility*: The impact of your pronunciation, intonation and accent on how clearly your listener can hear and understand what you're saying
- *Fluency*: The impact of the speed and smoothness of your speech on your listener's understanding
- *Appropriateness of language*: The impact of your language, tone and professionalism on your listener's understanding and comfort
- *Resources of grammar and expression*: The impact of your level of grammatical accuracy and vocabulary choices on your listener's understanding.

(OET, 2018: Taking the Speaking Sub-test)

These criteria leave the possibility open that an unfamiliar native accent, rapid speech, or sophisticated language entail negative ratings because many potential patients or carers might have difficulty following what is being said. In the more detailed rating grid for these criteria, indicators such as the ones for the highest level of *Resources of grammar and expression* set the tone: 'rich and flexible'; 'wide range of grammar and vocabulary used accurately and flexibly'; 'confident use of idiomatic speech'. It seems that a common 'faster, higher, stronger' – in other words 'complex, accurate, fluent' – paradigm has been adopted for the specialized OET and its mediation-type tasks. This is likely due to the primary purpose of the test, which is to establish a sufficient level of English language proficiency in medical professionals with a limited English language background. Nevertheless, it appears strange that the linguistic criteria scales suggest that demonstrating impressively good language according to general standards correlates in a straightforward manner with real-life success on the kinds of task represented in the OET Speaking Sub-test. Such tasks require language use that not only performs the necessary functions – adequately reflected by the Clinical Communication Criteria – but that is also well adapted to the communication partners. The latter appears not to be well reflected in the Linguistic Criteria.

Scales and levels applied to a speaking task from a language test for foreign language teachers

In my second example, I am going to discuss the challenges a team of task developers encountered when trying to apply ideas of progression underlying the mediation and linguistic scales from the CEFR-CV to a concrete test task. The (draft) task in question was meant to be an element of a specific-purpose speaking test for future foreign language teachers in primary school (teaching learners aged 8–12 on the way to level A1). In brief, the task assignment was to tell (or rather 'facilitate') a story taken from a children's picture book to a class, and thereby to activate the class, i.e. to actively involve the pupils. The main part of the simulated teaching activity consists in an interactive introduction of the cover picture and the protagonists of the story. The activity ends with the lively telling of part of the story. This makes it an enhanced text-to-speech task set in a very special context.

The most important defining feature of the task is arguably the very elementary language level of most of the pupils, which requires precise accommodation of the English language used as well as frequent integration of pupils' utterances made in German, the language of schooling. The primary target group for the test is future primary school teachers (generalists teaching one or two foreign languages), who are expected to reach CEFR level C1 by the end of their education in every language they will teach. Arguably, the main reason for the C1 requirement is a progression logic within the school system: better than the B2 expected at the end of the academic track of secondary education. In practice, some future teachers do not actually reach that level, especially in the Swiss national languages learned as 'foreign' languages. Often an internal examination focusing on the professionally most relevant tasks gives these students the chance to attain a 'specialized C1'. The task I am concerned with here was proposed as part of such an examination.

Carrying out the task involves a variety of mediation activities relatable to at least three mediation scales – Processing Text in Speech and Sign; Managing Interaction; Encouraging Conceptual Talk. Part of the task at hand roughly corresponds to the mediation sub-category of processing text to speech (Council of Europe, 2020: 98–101). The best matching descriptors can be found at levels A2 and B1, for example: *Can report in simple sentences (in Language B) the information contained in clearly structured, short, simple texts (in Language A) that have illustrations or tables* (A2). The CEFR-CV (Council of Europe, 2020: 101) characterizes the principles of progression up this scale with regard to the following features of an activity: cognitive and linguistic demands, variety of text types, text complexity, abstraction of topics and sophistication of the vocabulary. The Managing Interaction scale appears relevant with regard to the task instruction to activate and involve the pupils. According to the CEFR-CV, at B1 language users *Can give clear instructions, allocate turns, and bring participants in a group back to the task*, while by C1 they *Can organize a varied and balanced sequence of plenary, group and individual work, ensuring smooth transitions between the phases, intervening diplomatically in order to redirect discussion, to prevent one person dominating or to confront disruptive behaviour* (Council of Europe, 2020: 112). The third scale, Encouraging Conceptual Talk, illustrates level A2 with the descriptor *Can ask what somebody thinks of a certain idea*, and level C1 with the descriptor *Can ask a series of open questions that build on different contributions in order to stimulate logical reasoning (e.g. hypothesising, inferring, analysing, justifying and predicting)* (Council of Europe, 2020: 112–113).

The above allows for interesting observations concerning the usefulness of selected mediation scales to a (draft) test task set in a very specific professional context. The categories of the progression underlying the Processing Text in Speech scale, such as text complexity and abstraction, seem to have little relevance to our example when it comes to distinguishing between stronger and weaker candidate performances. What we expect of a good performance is 'doing an excellent job' on an A2 or B1 mediation task geared to A1 listeners. Special vocabulary (e.g. plants and animals) in the input text may be demanding, but in practice a teacher can look up infrequent words when preparing the lesson.

In the case of the Managing Interaction scale, we cannot easily discard the C1 descriptor cited. It would be good to see the kind of classroom language described, even in a beginners' class. When a can-do descriptor appears at C1, we expect the activity to be performed at a quality level that corresponds to our general understanding of C1. But what does this mean in a mediation context where the priority is to retain the engagement of communication partners who may not have reached A1?

In the case of our last scale, Encouraging Conceptual Talk, the descriptor for C1 outlines a broader functional range than the descriptor for A2. The question is: what are the linguistic realizations of these functions when they are performed in our classroom setting? They may boil down to little more than we expect from the simple A2 descriptor. Adding the flexibility and independence in language use that comes with B1 (Council of Europe, 2020: 173) seems preferable because it would better meet real-world expectations. If, however, we look at the CEFR-CV Appendix 3, Qualitative Features of Spoken Language (Council of Europe, 2020: 183–185), we are likely to come to the conclusion that we cannot be satisfied with a teacher's language if it contains systematic basic mistakes (A2) and in which pauses, false starts, reformulations and/or repair (A2/B1) are very evident. The descriptions for the C levels undoubtedly appear much more appealing. However, we should not forget that the expectations regarding the quality of language at the C levels extend to performance on a wide range of demanding tasks also associated with these levels. What we wish for in the test performances of our primary school foreign language teachers is likely a performance within a functional range expected for up to B1, as well as a formal gloss that reminds us of what we know from users at the C levels but which does not need to extend to C-level tasks – what I'm suggesting here is rather a hypothesis than a final statement. However, what we can safely say after analysing task examples from two testing contexts is that the definition of adequate rating criteria for mediation tasks, and their relationship to the reference scales and levels, is anything but straightforward. In that respect, the initial impression has been confirmed.

Conclusion

In light of my discussion of the OET Speaking Sub-test and the oral teaching task for primary school teachers, it may seem that the CEFR and the CEFR-CV have little to contribute to mediation test tasks like these. In my opinion, however, this conclusion would be premature. The CEFR and the CEFR-CV are both tools for language professionals who need to make informed choices. Both works are much more than collections of scales and descriptors – and these are presented as 'illustrative', not imperative. At their core, the CEFR and the CEFR-CV are meant as empowerment tools that support informed decisions on the part of their readers and users. Nothing reflects this better than the recurring text boxes in the CEFR, starting with 'Users of the Framework may wish to consider and where appropriate state: ...'. Chapter 2 of the CEFR-CV, on action-orientation, needs analysis, individual profiles and the selective use of scales and descriptors, points in the same direction. Starting from the actual learning and assessment needs of real people, analysing real-world communication tasks using appropriate categories, for example from the CEFR, helps prevent uncritical adherence to a supposedly given system of scales. As both examples discussed above show, real or potential limitations of the communication partner who needs mediational behaviour must be reflected also in the linguistic performance requirements and the rating scales. Very complex and fluent language will be overwhelming instead of 'excellent' for many patients with limitations, and certainly for pupils striving to reach level A1 in a foreign language. In these and many other cases, it is the language professional's responsibility to adapt or substitute ideas of progression inherent in common scales, replacing them by features carefully derived from the observation of communication in real-world settings – just as the CEFR's needs-based and action-oriented approach suggests.

References

Bachman, L.F. and Palmer, A.S. (2010) *Language Assessment in Practice: Developing Language Assessments and Justifying their Use in the Real World*. Oxford: Oxford University Press.

Council of Europe (2001) *Common European Framework of Reference for Languages: Learning, Teaching, Assessment*. Cambridge: Cambridge University Press.

Council of Europe (2020) *Common European Framework of Reference for Languages: Learning, Teaching, Assessment. Companion Volume*. Strasbourg: Council of Europe.

OET (2018) Occupational English Test. Speaking assessment criteria and level descriptors (from September 2018) (public version). https://prod-wp-content. occupationalenglishtest.org/resources/uploads/2018/08/22102547/speaking-assessment-criteria-updated-2018.pdf (accessed 3 November 2020).

OET (2020) Taking the Speaking Sub-Test. https://www.occupationalenglishtest.org/test-information/speaking/ (accessed 3 November 2020).

9 Implementing Plurilingual Education: The Experience of an Irish Primary School

Déirdre Kirwan and David Little

This chapter describes the plurilingual approach to education developed and implemented by Scoil Bhríde (Cailíní) (SBC; St Brigid's School for Girls), a linguistically diverse primary school of which Déirdre Kirwan was principal from 1987 to 2015. The goal of SBC's approach is to ensure that immigrant pupils gain maximum benefit from their primary schooling, and its essential feature is the inclusion of home languages in classroom communication. The development of SBC's policy and practice was influenced by the CEFR's action-oriented approach to the description of language proficiency, its view of the language user/learner as an autonomous social agent, and the concept of plurilingualism; the school found its own way to plurilingual teaching and learning. SBC's pupils develop high levels of age-appropriate literacy in English (the principal language of schooling), Irish (the second language of the curriculum), French (learnt in the last two primary grades) and (in the case of pupils from immigrant families) home languages – this last without benefit of explicit instruction. Pupils also acquire an unusually high degree of language awareness and from an early age are motivated to undertake ambitious language learning projects on their own initiative. SBC's version of plurilingual education fosters pupils' self-esteem and promotes social cohesion, converting linguistic diversity into educational and social capital.

Introduction

Since the mid-1990s, Ireland has experienced unprecedented levels of immigration, which has transformed the linguistic profile of the school-going population. In 1994, the first non-native speaker of English, a refugee from the war in Bosnia, was enrolled in Scoil Bhríde (Cailíní) (SBC; St Brigid's School for Girls), Blanchardstown, Dublin. This was a new experience for the entire school community – pupils, parents and staff. By 2014, almost 80% of the school's 322 pupils spoke a language other than English at home, and the school had identified 51 home languages (HLs). This chapter describes the plurilingual approach to education that was SBC's response to the increasing linguistic diversity of its pupil cohort. We begin by explaining how the school first encountered three of the CEFR's key concepts: its action-oriented approach (Council of Europe, 2001: 9), its view of the language user/ learner as an autonomous social agent (2001: 1), and plurilingualism. Next we summarize the evolution of the school's all-inclusive language policy, starting from its decision not only to welcome the use of HLs on the school premises but to include them in classroom communication. After that we describe SBC's plurilingual approach in practice, focusing in turn on classroom discourse, language awareness and the development of plurilingual literacy. Finally, we consider the general educational benefits of the approach: high levels of pupil self-awareness and self-esteem, and a strong sense of social justice and social cohesion.

Primary schooling in Ireland comprises two preparatory years, Junior and Senior Infants, and six Classes; pupils start school when they are 4½+ and move on to post-primary school when they are 12½+. SBC receives no additional resources apart from those allocated to all schools for the provision of English language support for pupils from immigrant families. The chapter draws on a corpus of qualitative data that Déirdre Kirwan collected over a number of years: video recordings of classroom interactions, examples of pupils' written work, teachers' work plans and monthly reports, accounts of particularly illuminating classroom episodes, interviews with pupils and teachers.

Laying the Foundations

At the end of the 1990s, the Irish government responded to unprecedented immigration and rapidly increasing linguistic diversity in schools by funding two years of English language support for primary pupils and post-primary students whose HL was neither English nor Irish. This allowed for the appointment of language support teachers. In addition, Integrate Ireland Language and Training (IILT), a not-for-profit campus company of Trinity College Dublin, was funded to provide in-service seminars and resources for teachers (Little & Lazenby Simpson, 2009), many of whom were struggling to meet new educational demands.

To guide the planning and delivery of English language support, IILT developed *English Language Proficiency Benchmarks* (Integrate Ireland Language and Training, 2003). Based on the CEFR's first three proficiency levels (A1, A2, B1), the *Benchmarks* comprised a series of grids modelled on the so-called self-assessment grid (Council of Europe, 2001: 26–27): language activities on the vertical axis and proficiency levels on the horizontal axis. Altogether there were 15 grids: global benchmarks of communicative proficiency, global scales of underlying linguistic competence, and 13 grids devoted to recurrent curriculum themes.

The *Benchmarks* introduced SBC's teachers to the action-oriented approach, which views language use as a matter of performing actions for a specific purpose in a particular social context. This encouraged them to think of EAL (English as an Additional Language) pupils' English language development in terms of their participation in classroom activities. The *Benchmarks* also encouraged teachers to think of classroom discourse and curriculum content as a close-textured weave of reception, interaction and production and to recognize the interdependence of speaking and writing in the development of pupils' literacy skills in English, Irish, French and HLs. As one teacher put it:

> While a number of years ago I would have said, 'Oh, written work, no. The oral is the most important', I think that if they form their thoughts with pen and paper first, it gives them the confidence to go and speak … they then have that bank of ideas … and the speaking is done without any reference to any written word. I do think that reading and writing is a great bedrock and it does give confidence.

As a companion piece to the *Benchmarks*, IILT developed a version of the European Language Portfolio (ELP; see also pp. 5–6 above), conceived by the Council of Europe as a means of mediating the CEFR's underlying ethos to language learners. The ELP has three obligatory components and three pedagogical purposes. The components are: a language passport, which summarizes the owner's experience of language learning and language use; a language biography, which provides a reflective accompaniment to teaching and learning; and a dossier, in which the owner collects work in progress and evidence of language learning achievement. The ELP's pedagogical purposes are to support learner autonomy, promote plurilingualism and foster intercultural awareness (Council of Europe, 2011). The language passport contains the CEFR's self-assessment grid or an equivalent (in the case of IILT's ELP, an abbreviated version of the global benchmarks of communicative proficiency), while the language biography includes checklists of 'I can' descriptors (in the case of IILT's ELP, derived from the thirteen *Benchmarks* grids that focus on recurrent curriculum themes). With the help of their teachers, learners use the checklist descriptors to identify learning targets and assess learning outcomes; at regular intervals they summarize their progress in the language passport.

IILT designed its ELP not only to encourage the reflective teaching and learning of English, but also to allow EAL pupils to record the other languages they knew and the contexts in which they used them.

Working with the ELP familiarized SBC's teachers with the concept of learner autonomy supported by self-assessment and introduced them to plurilingualism as 'a communicative competence to which all knowledge and experience of language contributes and in which languages interrelate and interact' (Council of Europe, 2001: 4).

The Evolution of a Plurilingual Approach to Primary Education

When linguistic diversity first became a challenge for Irish schools, the central concern was to find ways of developing EAL pupils' proficiency in English as quickly and efficiently as possible. To this end some schools advised immigrant parents to speak English with their children at home, even though in many cases the parents' English was rudimentary. By contrast, IILT's in-service seminars emphasized the importance of maintaining HLs, partly because they were central to EAL pupils' identity and partly because they provided a link to family members in their parents' countries of origin. But, although the ELP helped pupils to capture their own plurilingual profile, IILT's remit was EAL and it did not consider ways of giving HLs a role in EAL pupils' schooling.

SBC responded to the increasing linguistic diversity of its pupil cohort by welcoming HLs, but from an early stage the principal and teachers recognized that it was not enough simply to include HLs in classroom displays, exhibitions and special events. One of the chief aims of the Primary School Curriculum is to enable children to realize their full potential as unique individuals (Government of Ireland, 1999: 7). The curriculum recognizes that 'the child's existing knowledge and experience form the basis for learning' (1999: 8); that language 'helps the child to clarify and interpret experience, to acquire new concepts, and to add depth to the concepts already grasped' (1999: 15); and that 'the life of the home is the most potent factor in [the child's] development during the primary school years' (1999: 24). If SBC was to be true to these principles, it must include EAL pupils' HLs in classroom communication, even though those languages were mostly unknown to the teachers and other pupils.

In taking this policy decision the school was prompted in part by history: in 19th-century Ireland children attending national schools were forbidden to use Irish (their first language), and this contributed to language loss (Ó Ceallaigh & Ní Dhonnabháin, 2015: 182). SBC was determined not to replicate this process with pupils from immigrant families in the 21st century. In retrospect it became clear that to exclude HLs from EAL pupils' schooling would have been contrary to the human rights perspective of the Council of Europe's concept of plurilingual education (Beacco & Byram, 2007). After all, the language the child has acquired at home is central to her identity and self-concept, so to suppress its use in school is to suppress the child. Such suppression is in any case likely to be counter-productive, because the child's first language is her primary cognitive tool, the default medium of her discursive thinking, and thus the indispensable basis of effective intentional learning. Attempts to suppress HLs are moreover doomed to failure, because HLs inevitably persist in the never-ending but unspoken stream of EAL pupils' consciousness (Little *et al.*, 2017: 202).

As SBC's plurilingual approach to primary education evolved through the 2000s it became clear that using HLs in the classroom was contributing positively to the education of *all* pupils. Déirdre Kirwan used her PhD research (2004–2009; Kirwan, 2009) to inform the ongoing professional development of teachers and ancillary school staff, and in 2010 the school's approach was enshrined in a policy document (see Little & Kirwan, 2019: 174–178) that was endorsed by the Board of Management and shared with parents. Regularly reviewed and updated, the document is based on four principles:

- The cultivation of an inclusive ethos that welcomes the diversity of SBC's pupil population, acknowledging the contribution that each learner can make to her own education.
- No restrictions on pupils' use of HLs at school, whether inside or outside the classroom.
- A strong emphasis on developing language awareness, which means treating HLs as a resource for all learners.
- A strong emphasis on the development of literacy skills in English, Irish, French and HLs, recognizing that writing and speaking support one another in many different ways.

From the beginning, the policy of acknowledging, valuing and *using* all languages present in the classroom elicited a very positive response from learners. Encouraging pupils from immigrant families to share their HL and their linguistic intuitions with the rest of the class coincided with the curricular principle that children are active agents in their own learning (Government of Ireland, 1999: 8) and fostered the development of learner autonomy (Little, 1991; Little *et al.*, 2017). Using their HLs allowed pupils to express themselves more fully, giving them the motivation and the means to undertake work on their own initiative. The inclusion of collaborative learning (Government of Ireland, 1999: 9) in the approach helped to ensure that the plurilingual capital of the classroom benefited all learners.

When immigrant parents enrolled their daughter in the school, the principal explained SBC's plurilingual approach. Some parents expressed reservations, believing that their daughter should spend as much time as possible using and therefore learning English. But they usually changed their minds when they saw the impact the approach had on their daughter's motivation and involvement in the life of the classroom and the school. For other parents, especially those who were not fluent in English, SBC's plurilingual approach came as a great relief. A Ukrainian parent, for example, said that 'a weight was lifted off my shoulders when I heard that it was alright to speak my language at home'. An Indian parent was also happy with 'the school's interest in our language. Before, my daughter was ashamed to hear us speaking Malayalam. Now she wants to read and write in it.' And an Italian parent commented that 'finding the similarities between your own home native language and English and Irish and French, it definitely speeds up the learning of English.'

When SBC was contemplating the inclusion of HLs in classroom communication, some teachers wondered whether this would have an adverse impact on the Irish language, already under pressure from English. As the first official language of the state, Irish is the obligatory second language of the curriculum from the beginning to the end of schooling. Although learning outcomes are generally disappointing, SBC has a strong tradition in teaching and learning Irish, and the high levels of proficiency achieved by SBC's pupils have been acknowledged by Department of Education inspectors (Department of Education and Skills, 2014). In the presence of so many HLs, teachers redoubled their efforts to use Irish in lessons dealing with other areas of the curriculum and to interact in Irish with one another and with pupils outside the classroom. At the same time, hearing their EAL classmates explain: 'In my language we say …', motivated English-speaking pupils to think of Irish as the 'other' language in which they could express themselves. Interviewed for a local radio programme, an Irish parent thought that being in a multilingual environment was increasing Irish pupils' motivation to learn Irish: 'I think it makes them want to speak the Irish more at home. I think it spurs them on.'[1] All this had the effect of raising the status of Irish not only among teachers and pupils but also among ancillary staff. In addition, the Parents' Association, whose members included both indigenous Irish and immigrants, asked the school to help them set up Irish language classes for themselves.

Plurilingual Education in Practice

Dealing with a large number of languages in the classroom certainly presented challenges in the early stages, especially as most of those languages were unknown to the teachers (the potential exceptions were the foreign languages of the Irish post-primary curriculum: French, German, Italian and Spanish). Teachers quickly came to realize, however, that the inclusion of HLs in classroom communication enhanced learning in a multitude of ways.

Broadly speaking, when the teacher herself does not speak them, HLs can fulfil three roles in classroom discourse. First, they can be used in reciprocal communication between two or more pupils who have the same or a closely related HL. This happens quite naturally in Junior Infants classes in the time devoted to free play at the beginning of the school day. In due course it can also occur during pair and group work: pupils solve a maths problem in their HL, for example, then use English to explain to the teacher and the rest of the class how they arrived at their solution.

Second, HLs can be used for non-reciprocal purposes of display: 'This is what we say in my language.' From their first days in school, EAL pupils are encouraged to use their HLs in the activities typical of junior classrooms. For example, they learn to count from one to five in English, then in Irish, and then they show their classmates how they count in their HL. The same technique is used when playing action games and working with shapes and colours. In this way, HLs help to reinforce the learning of English and Irish, and autochthonous Irish pupils grow accustomed to experiencing the classroom as a multilingual environment. Also, the fact that HLs are continuously in play helps to ensure that they are fully activated in their speakers' minds. From these simple beginnings, pupils gradually acquire the habit of transferring concepts and skills between languages, which is decisive in developing high levels of age-appropriate literacy in English, Irish, French and HLs.

Third, HLs are a rich source of linguistic intuition and insight that EAL pupils can share with the rest of the class. As they progress through the school, pupils are able to discuss increasingly complex issues of vocabulary, syntax and idiom, and this enriches the presentation and processing of curriculum content for all learners (for further discussion see Kirwan, 2014; Little & Kirwan, 2019).

Use of HLs in the classroom encourages the early emergence of language awareness. For example, a Chinese pupil in First Class (6½+) recognized and was able to translate a number of words in a children's publication from China; however, she referred to *gate* as *door*. When asked about this she acknowledged her mistake and explained that in 'her language', *door* is used to describe a means of entry both indoors and outdoors, while in English two different words are needed to take account of the different locations. A pupil in Third Class (8½+) showed how language awareness is relevant across the curriculum. Introducing fractions to her class, the teacher associated *fraction* with *fracture* and elicited synonyms (*break*, *split*) and words for *break* in other languages. A Romanian pupil offered *rupt*, which pupils quickly linked to the *eruption* of a volcano, *interruption* and *disruption*. Besides being only 8 or 9 years old, most of these pupils were not native speakers of English.

Pupils make crosslinguistic semantic connections, too. Having listened to a Filipino pupil reading versions of the same story in Irish, English and Tagalog, a pupil of Russian/Nigerian heritage said that she now knew that the word for hedgehog in Tagalog was *parkupino*. She worked this out 'because it was almost at the end of the story and the spikes [of the hedgehog] reminds me of porcupine's'. A further example of the impact of crosslinguistic comparison on pupils' English vocabulary was reported by a teacher of Fourth Class (9½+). In a maths lesson she asked: 'What is an oblique line?' A Romanian pupil suggested it was like *oblig* in her language, which meant *something you must do*. The teacher explained the difference between *oblique* and *oblige*. An Irish pupil noted that *obligatory* is like Romanian *oblig*, while a Filipino pupil offered *obligate*. Answering the teacher's original question, a Lithuanian pupil said: 'There's an oblique line on the end of the letter q.'

Pupils enjoy responding to new languages and are proud of their ability to understand fragments of languages they neither know nor have been taught. An Irish pupil in Fifth Class (10½+) whose parents had been on holiday in Italy, brought an Italian newspaper to school that contained a report on a rugby match between Italy and Ireland. The Special Needs Assistant, who was Italian, read part of the article aloud to the class. The pupils were thrilled to discover that they were able to understand many words in the article – *verde y bianchi, azzurra, stadio olympico a Roma, ovale, prendo corragio* – even though they had not learnt Italian.

The development of plurilingual literacy skills is central to the school's mission because literacy is essential to educational achievement in any language. Clearly, it would be impracticable to provide formal instruction in more than 50 HLs; and any attempt to do so would be likely to fragment the process of schooling beyond repair. Some immigrant communities organize weekend schools in order to develop their children's HL literacy skills, but this kind of support is not available to all SBC's EAL pupils. The approach adopted by SBC seeks to develop high levels of age-appropriate literacy in English and Irish in all pupils; encourages EAL pupils, with help from their parents and older siblings, to transfer their emerging literacy skills in English and Irish to their HLs; and, in Fifth and Sixth Class, grounds the learning of French in pupils' existing plurilingual repertoires. Plurilingual writing activities typically begin with the collaborative production of a story in Irish or English that the teacher writes on the whiteboard and which pupils copy into their copybooks.

In Senior Infants (5½+), teachers provide worksheets that can be completed in English and Irish/HLs (Figure 9.1). In First Class (6½+) pupils produce simple identity texts in English and their HL and rewrite well known stories in two languages: for example, 'Goldilocks and the Three Bears' in English and Congolese French. In Second Class (7½+) and Third Class (8½+) dual language texts become more elaborate – pupils describe themselves, the school, hobbies, etc. In Third Class some

Figure 9.1 Worksheets completed in English, Irish and home languages by Senior Infants pupils (5½+ years old)

pupils begin to write texts in English, Irish and their HL – Hungarian in the case of the text reproduced in Figure 9.2. In Fourth Class (9½+) a Romanian pupil filled six pages of her copybook with a story in English in which several of the characters speak Romanian. In Fifth Class (10½+) French is added to English, Irish and HLs, as in the following example, which records the weather in four languages:

Au nord il pleut
Sa tuaisceart tá sé fliuch
In [the] north it is raining
In nord ploua.

A l'ouest il y a du vent
San iarthar ta sé gaofar
In [the]west it is windy
In vest este vent

Au sud il fait beau
Sa deisceart tá an ghrian ag taithneamh
In [the]south it is sunny and cloudy
In sud este inorat cu soare

A l'est [il]est nuggeux
San oir-thear ta sé ag scamallach.

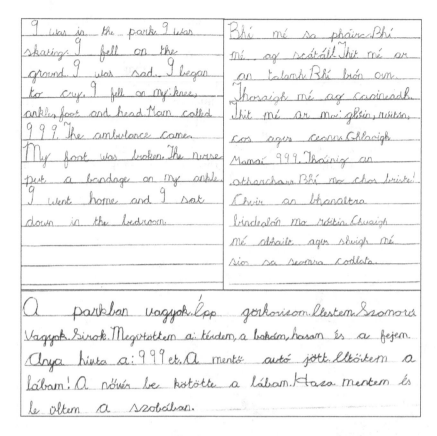

Figure 9.2 Parallel texts in English, Irish and Hungarian written unaided by a Third Class pupil (8½+ years old)

In Sixth Class (11½ +) pupils write confidently in English, Irish, French and their HL. Sometimes they give themselves the challenge of writing a coherent text in four languages, as in the following account that a speaker of Tagalog wrote of a visit to her prospective post-primary school:

Cuairt ar an Meánscoil

Chuaigh mé agus mo chlann go dtí Pobal Scoil Mhin. Talagang yumao sa gabi. Nous avons vu beaucoup filles e garcons. Thosaigh an phríomhoide ag caint. The whole room started to quiet down. We were told that all the sixth class children were to make their way to the door. Ensuite, une fille a amenée nous dans une piece. Thosaigh said ag scoilt ar na páistí. Si Rabia, si Duska, at si Ana at ako nag paghati-hatiin sa isang grupo. We went into one of the English Classes and we did a Volcano Quiz. Une femme a demandé une question difficile et facile a propos de volcan sur le tableau. We also saw a bit of Romeo and Juliet. Four of my neighbours were part of the play.

By the time they are in Sixth Class, pupils are very familiar with the practice of comparing words from different languages, and this allows them to engage in sophisticated language play – for example, setting themselves the task of writing a text in English that contains as many words of French origin as possible (for examples, see Little & Kirwan, 2019: 116–117). At the end of their final year in the school, one Sixth Class asked their teacher if they could organize a fashion show. She said that they could but imposed two conditions: all the languages present in the class must be included in the show, and each pupil must invent a model and describe her in three or more languages. The four texts reproduced in Figure 9.3 describe Marceline in English, Irish, French and Mandarin.

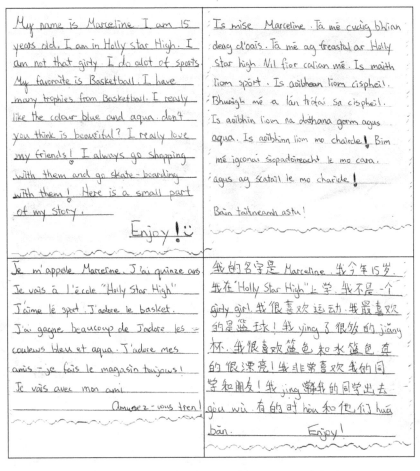

Figure 9.3 'Marceline' in English, Irish, French and Mandarin (Sixth Class, 11½+ years old)

General Educational Benefits

SBC's plurilingual approach to education succeeds at the level of language. When pupils move on to post-primary education, they take with them integrated plurilingual repertoires each of whose components represents significant educational capital. They can produce fluent and mostly accurate written text in English, Irish, French and (in the case of EAL pupils) HLs. As we have tried to show in the limited space available to us, SBC's pupils develop 'a communicative competence to which all knowledge and experience of language contributes and in which languages interrelate and interact' (Council of Europe, 2001: 4). But SBC's plurilingual approach also promotes pupils' self-awareness. For example, an English-speaking pupil told Déirdre Kirwan: 'When we learn a language it's easier to learn other ones; sometimes it's not really about which language you're learning it's, like, how to learn a language.' And pupils' enthusiasm for all things linguistic motivates them to work autonomously on projects that explore their own language and the languages of others simply because they are interested in finding out for themselves. Further benefits include increased pupil motivation to engage in classroom discourse, pride in HLs and the cultural heritage they embody, and delight in the ability to live in more than one language. As for the situation of Irish, a Polish pupil remarked that she sometimes felt as if Irish was her 'first language because we speak it all the time in our school and it's very good, it's nice and it's interesting'.

SBC's plurilingual education also addresses issues of identity and social cohesion. When asked about the inclusion of HLs in classroom communication, a Kurdish speaker said: '[It helps pupils to get] personal into each other's cultures and languages [and] is very useful for friendship, for knowledge, so in many ways we're all expanding ... it makes you feel closer because you have a perspective on that person's point of view.' A speaker of Yoruba expressed the view that 'when two people speak the same language there's a kind of a bond between both of them'. Pupils' views regarding the exclusion of HLs in other schools provide a stark contrast. Another speaker of Yoruba felt that 'a child without a language is a child without a soul'; and a German speaker said: 'Don't hide away from your own language, because it's what makes you **you**, and it's special and it's ... like having an arm or a leg, you can't take it away from you.'

Conclusion

In this chapter we have sought to show how the CEFR's action-oriented approach, its view of the language user/learner as an autonomous social agent, and its advocacy of plurilingualism inspired an approach to primary education whose outcomes have been transformative. Not only has SBC found a way of helping its pupils to develop fully integrated and literate plurilingual repertoires: the approach adopted also enhances pupils' self-awareness and self-esteem and promotes social cohesion in the school as a whole. It is important to acknowledge that SBC's approach evolved in response to an unusually high level of linguistic diversity: in retrospect it is difficult to imagine how the school could have responded otherwise while remaining faithful to its educational mission. It is also important to note the role played by Irish as the obligatory second language of the curriculum. Because the language is new to all SBC's pupils, whether they come from Irish or immigrant families, it provides them with an equal challenge, acting as a bridge between English and HLs. Arguably, without this bridge the inclusion of EAL pupils' HLs in classroom communication would be much more difficult to maintain. These considerations notwithstanding, SBC's experience prompts three questions. Has SBC discovered a model of plurilingual education that could be replicated by other schools with a similarly diverse pupil cohort? How would the model need to be adapted by schools that have fewer minority-language pupils and/or HLs? And, finally: Does the model have implications for language teaching in primary schools more generally? With regard to this last question, it is worth noting that, in 2019, a new Primary Language Curriculum was introduced in Ireland that aims to integrate 'English and Irish and includes all children and the language knowledge and experiences that they bring to the classroom' (Department of Education and Skills, 2019: 4; see also Little & Kirwan, 2021).

Note

(1) *Language Jewels*, a three-part radio series documenting the experience of Scoil Bhríde (Cailíní), available at http://nearfm.ie/podcast/?cat=30

References

Beacco, J-C. and Byram, M. (2007) *From Linguistic Diversity to Plurilingual Education: Guide for the Development of Language Education Policies in Europe*. Strasbourg: Council of Europe. https://rm.coe.int/CoERMPublicCommonSearchServices/DisplayDCTMContent?documentId=09000016802fc1c4 (accessed 15 May 2020).

Council of Europe (2001) *Common European Framework of Reference for Languages: Learning, Teaching, Assessment*. Cambridge: Cambridge University Press. https://rm.coe.int/1680459f97 (accessed 7 August 2020).

Council of Europe (2011) *European Language Portfolio (ELP) Principles and Guidelines, with added explanatory notes*. Strasbourg: Council of Europe. https://rm.coe.int/CoERMPublicCommonSearchServices/DisplayDCTMContent?documentId=09000016804586ba (accessed 22 October 2020).

Department of Education and Skills (2014) Whole School Evaluation Report – Scoil Bhríde (Cailíní), Blanchardstown, Dublin 15. Dublin: Department of Education and Skills. https://www.gov.ie/en/school-reports/?school_roll_number=18047C (accessed 19 November 2021).

Department of Education and Skills (2019) *Primary Language Curriculum/Curaclam Teanga na Bunscoile*. Dublin: Department of Education and Skills. https://curriculumonline. ie/getmedia/2a6e5f79-6f29-4d68-b850-379510805656/PLC-Document_English.pdf (accessed 23 July 2020).

Government of Ireland (1999) *Primary School Curriculum: Introduction*. Dublin: Stationery Office. https://curriculumonline.ie/getmedia/93de2707-f25e-4bee-9035-92b00613492e/ Introduction-to-primary-curriculum.pdf (accessed 30 July 2020).

Integrate Ireland Language and Training (2003) *English Language Proficiency Benchmarks for non-English-speaking Pupils at Primary Level*. Dublin: Integrate Ireland Language and Training. https://ncca.ie/media/2064/english_language_proficiency_benchmarks. pdf (accessed 7 August 2020).

Kirwan, D. (2009) English language support for newcomer learners in Irish primary schools: A review and a case study. PhD thesis, University of Dublin, Trinity College.

Kirwan, D. (2014) From English language support to plurilingual awareness. In D. Little, C. Leung and P. Van Avermaet (eds) *Managing Diversity in Education: Languages, Policies, Pedagogies* (pp. 189–203). Bristol: Multilingual Matters.

Little, D. (1991) *Learner Autonomy 1: Definitions, Issues and Problems*. Dublin: Authentik.

Little, D. and Kirwan, D. (2019) *Engaging with Linguistic Diversity: A Study of Educational Inclusion in an Irish Primary School*. London: Bloomsbury Academic.

Little, D. and Kirwan, D. (2021) *Language and Languages in the Primary School: Some Guidelines for Teachers*. Dublin: Post-Primary Languages Ireland. https://ppli.ie/ teaching-and-learning/supporting-multilingual-classrooms/?gresource=ppli-primary-guidelines/ (accessed 23 December 2021).

Little, D. and Lazenby Simpson, B. (2009) Teaching immigrants the language of the host community: Two object lessons in the need for continuous policy development. In J.C. Alderson (ed.) *The Politics of Language Education: Individuals and Institutions* (pp. 104–124). Bristol: Multilingual Matters.

Little, D., Dam, L. and Legenhausen, L. (2017) *Language Learner Autonomy: Theory, Practice and Research*. Bristol: Multilingual Matters.

Ó Ceallaigh, T.J. and Ní Dhonnabháin, Á. (2015) Reawakening the Irish Language through the Irish education system: Challenges and priorities. *International Electronic Journal of Elementary Education* 8 (2), 179–198. https://files.eric.ed.gov/fulltext/EJ1085869. pdf (accessed 28 September 2020).

Part 4: Descriptors, Scales and Constructive Alignment

Introduction to Part 4

David Little

The CEFR's use of can-do descriptors allows us to bring curriculum, teaching/learning and assessment into closer interaction with one another than has traditionally been the case: each descriptor can be used simultaneously to specify a learning outcome, provide a teaching/ learning focus and imply an assessment task. This makes the CEFR an instrument of 'constructive alignment'. The concept of constructive alignment was first proposed by John Biggs, who has summarized its two dimensions as follows:

> The 'constructive' aspect refers to the idea that students *construct meaning* through relevant learning activities. That is, meaning is not something imparted or transmitted from teacher to learner but is something learners have to create for themselves. Teaching is simply a catalyst for learning. ...

> The 'alignment' aspect refers to what the teacher does, which is to set up a learning environment that supports the learning activities appropriate to achieving the desired learning outcomes. The key is that the components in the teaching system, especially the teaching methods used and the assessment tasks, are *aligned* with the learning activities assumed in the learning outcomes. The learner is in a sense 'trapped', and finds it difficult to escape without learning what he or she is intended to learn. (Biggs, no date; italics in original)

Biggs's 'constructive' aspect sits comfortably with the implication of the CEFR's action-oriented approach that learners 'construct' their proficiency by performing communicative tasks and monitoring task performance and the progress of their learning (cf. Biggs, no date: 49–50). The 'alignment' aspect requires that each step in the design of the curriculum, teaching/learning procedures and assessment is carried out with detailed reference to the CEFR and the CEFR-CV.

The first step in a process of constructive alignment based on the CEFR/CEFR-CV is to define the knowledge that learners are required to engage with and master, and the skills they are required to develop while doing so. Then the levels and illustrative scales in the CEFR-CV are used to determine the language activities learners should be able to perform by the end of the programme and the linguistic competences they will need to develop. The CEFR-CV provides a useful diagrammatic illustration of the results of this process when applied to the development of a curriculum for lower secondary CLIL (Content and Language Integrated Learning); an important feature of this example is that learners are not expected to achieve the same level in all activities (Council of Europe, 2020: 38). On the basis of such a curriculum it is possible to elaborate a programme of teaching and learning, bearing in mind the status of the learners as individuals and as social agents, the action-oriented approach and its pedagogical implications, the descriptive taxonomy in Chapters 4 and 5 of the CEFR, the discussion of learning and teaching in Chapter 6 and the discussion of tasks in Chapter 7. The final step is to design assessment instruments that are fully aligned with the learning activities defined by the curriculum, with reference to Chapter 9 of the CEFR and the guide to CEFR-inspired test development (Council of Europe, 2011). A further step might be to provide learners with a version of the European Language Portfolio to help them manage and document their learning. The inclusion of checklists of 'I can' descriptors, used to identify learning targets and to self-assess progress, would establish firm links with the curriculum on the one hand and teacher and institutional/external assessment on the other, drawing learners themselves into the process of constructive alignment. The mediation scales in the CEFR-CV provide teachers with a useful stimulus to reflect on the dynamics of classroom discourse and the role they and their learners should play in shaping it.

The relation between the CEFR's six proficiency levels is captured in Figure P4.1, which reminds us of three things: each level above A1 incorporates the level(s) below it; the levels become progressively more substantial, and thus require more learning time as we move up the scale; and the growth of proficiency is 'horizontal' as well as 'vertical', a matter of applying steadily expanding linguistic competences to the performance of an ever-wider range of tasks.

As Figure P4.2 shows, there is a significant shift in the focus of language use as one moves up through the levels. A1 is mostly concerned with physical and social survival. A2 and the lower part of B1 are concerned with social interaction and getting things done, but already in B1 there is a shift towards using the target language for academic and professional purposes. This is illustrated in the descriptors for overall spoken interaction included in Figure P4.2 and it raises an issue that to my knowledge has rarely been addressed: the extent to which it is possible to teach B1, B2, C1 and C2 in the traditional sense of the verb 'teach'. Current theories differ in their view of the cognitive mechanisms that produce L2 development, but they agree that the essential dynamic is spontaneous, interactive language use (for a recent summary, see Truscott & Sharwood Smith,

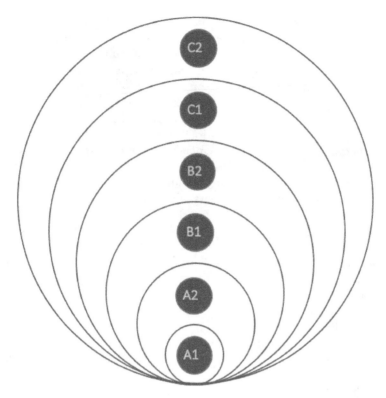

Figure P4.1 Relation between the CEFR's proficiency levels

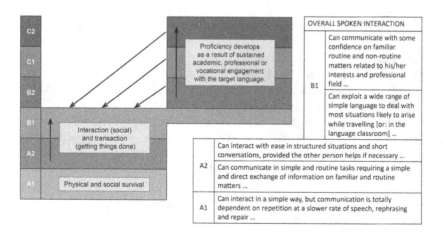

Figure P4.2 A shifting focus of language use

2019). Now, learners need to engage in a great deal more spontaneous, interactive (target) language use than occurs in traditionally organized classrooms if they are to develop the communicative proficiency specified for B1, for example: 'I can enter unprepared into conversation on topics that are familiar, of personal interest or pertinent to everyday life' (CEFR; Council of Europe, 2001: 26). This is where mediation has an enhanced role to play. In contexts of formal L2 learning, interactive language use is framed by mediation – teacher to learner(s), learner(s) to learner(s). It is important to remember, moreover, that mediation as it is presented in the CEFR-CV is both intra- and inter-linguistic: as we have seen, the plurilingual approach entails, among other things, that in learning a new language, learners draw on *all* the linguistic resources available to them.

The three chapters that follow explore issues and challenges that arise when aligning teaching/learning, curricula and assessment with the CEFR and the CEFR-CV. Armin Berger begins Chapter 10 by pointing out that whereas the two documents provide ample support for the horizontal alignment of teaching in terms of communicative activities, strategies and competences, teachers must rely on their intuition if they wish to refine the reference levels vertically by subdividing them for particular classroom purposes. As a solution to this problem, Berger proposes the development of 'local reference points': empirically supported benchmarks that help teachers to refine vertical progression in a coherent way. Based on local assessment instruments and keyword analysis of calibrated CEFR descriptors, the reference points he describes define sublevels of C1 and C2 and function as benchmarks for curriculum design, lesson sequencing, task selection, formative assessment, rating scale development, and other purposes for which the broad distinction between C1 and C2 is insufficient. The chapter points the way to further research into the vertical dimension of the CEFR.

In Chapter 11, Elaine Boyd focuses on the challenge of aligning curricula with the CEFR and CEFR-CV. She argues that to date there have been three approaches to alignment: a retrofit model, which maps an existing curriculum to the CEFR; an assessment-driven model, which defines curriculum content in terms of test constructs already aligned to the CEFR; and a coursebook model, which uses coursebook content to define the curriculum. Boyd argues that if we wish to develop alignment procedures that allow reliable and transparent comparison between curricula, we must take account of these existing practices. Recognizing that many users will be overwhelmed by the number of descriptors in the CEFR-CV, she suggests that effective alignment may be a matter of developing widely accepted procedures for choosing and priori-tizing a manageable set of descriptors and agreeing, as a community, on the evidence needed to demonstrate alignment. She concludes that a precondition for the widespread alignment of curricula with the

CEFR/CEFR-CV is that agreed procedures can be managed and evidence collected and interpreted by non-expert users.

Chapter 12, by Elif Kantarcıoğlu, focuses on the mediation descriptors introduced by the CEFR-CV. Kantarcıoğlu welcomes the mediation scales on the ground that they offer to make assessment in academic contexts more meaningful, introducing new dimensions to the definition of test specifications, the elaboration of marking schemes and the provision of feedback to test takers. At the same time, however, the complexity of mediation skills challenges assessment and standard-setting practices at the level of construct definition and feedback to learners, and the alignment of examinations to the CEFR is made more complex by overlaps between interaction and mediation activities. Kantarcıoğlu explores these issues with close reference to evolving assessment practices in her own institution, Bilkent University.

References

Biggs, J. (no date) Aligning teaching for constructing learning. London, York and Edinburgh: Higher Education Academy (UK). Available at https://www.heacademy.ac.uk/sites/default/files/resources/id477_aligning_teaching_for_constructing_learning.pdf (accessed 27 August 2020).

Council of Europe (2001) *Common European Framework of Reference for Languages: Learning, Teaching, Assessment*. Cambridge: Cambridge University Press. https://rm.coe.int/1680459f97.

Council of Europe (2011) *Manual for Language Test Development and Examining, for Use with the CEFR*. Produced by ALTE on behalf of the Language Policy Division of the Council of Europe. Strasbourg: Council of Europe. Available at https://rm.coe.int/CoERMPublicCommonSearchServices/DisplayDCTMContent?documentId=0900001680667a2b (accessed 20 August 2020).

Council of Europe (2020) *Common European Framework of Reference for Languages: Learning, Teaching, Assessment. Companion Volume*. Strasbourg: Council of Europe. Available at https://rm.coe.int/common-european-framework-of-reference-for-languages-learning-teaching/16809ea0d4 (accessed 25 August 2020).

Truscott, J. and M. Sharwood Smith (2019) Theoretical frameworks in L2 acquisition. In J.W. Schwieter and A. Benati (eds) *The Cambridge Handbook of Language Learning* (pp. 84–107). Cambridge: Cambridge University Press.

10 Refining the Vertical Axis of the CEFR for Classroom Purposes: Local Reference Points

Armin Berger

The Common European Framework of Reference for Languages *(CEFR)* *and its* Companion Volume *(CEFR-CV)* *provide a rich resource for teachers to align their teaching horizontally in terms of communicative activities, strategies and competences. However, if practitioners wish to refine the reference levels vertically in terms of further subdivisions for specific classroom purposes, they have to rely heavily on their intuition. In this chapter, I present a practical approach to this problem in the context of a university language programme: local reference points, i.e. empirically supported benchmarks intended to help teachers refine progression in a coherent way. Based on local assessment instruments and keyword analyses of calibrated CEFR descriptors, these reference points characterize different sublevels at C1 and C2. They function as benchmarks for curriculum design, lesson sequencing, task selection, formative assessment, rating scale development, and other educational purposes for which the basic distinction between C1 and C2 is not granular enough. More generally, the local reference points have contributed towards implementing the CEFR in the local university context. This chapter describes the development, characteristics and uses of local reference points and concludes by evaluating the concept and calling for further research and development in relation to the vertical dimension of the CEFR.*

Introduction

While the CEFR's descriptive scheme covers a range of general and communicative language competences, communicative language activities and strategies, domains of language use, and different parameters shaping language use (the *horizontal* axis), the common reference levels describe a proficiency continuum from pre-A1 to C2 (the *vertical* axis) (Council of Europe, 2020: 36). These reference levels are probably the best known and most widely used part of the CEFR. In fact, in many teaching contexts where curricula are associated with the CEFR, the illustrative descriptors characterizing the reference levels act as the *de facto* framework, to the extent that users have become oblivious to the illustrative nature of the descriptors, which are designed to offer a heuristic as opposed to a normative scheme (North, 2014: 23). As a result, content that is covered by the descriptors is often taught and assessed in the classroom, whereas content not explicitly covered is not. While this runs counter to the conceptual density and open-ended nature of the CEFR (Piccardo & North, 2019), it reflects the great need for standardized proficiency levels for language teaching and assessment purposes.

More specifically, the level descriptors are intended to 'facilitate the provision of transparent and coherent alignment between curriculum, teaching and assessment, particularly teacher assessment' (Council of Europe, 2020: 44). They provide a resource for defining learning aims in relation to real-world language use, for signposting learning pathways in a transparent way, for negotiating learning priorities, for designing classroom tasks, and for promoting criterion-referenced assessment (Council of Europe, 2020: 42). To meet the needs of the local classroom context, teachers can adapt the descriptors by adding missing details and merging them with existing educational aims. If teachers wish to measure and report even small gains in learning, which is necessary for many classroom purposes, subdivision of the broad levels into narrower bands is required. However, while the CEFR's branching scheme is designed to be flexible enough to allow for such modifications (Council of Europe, 2001: 31–33), there is not sufficient guidance on how to subdivide the levels meaningfully, and teachers often resort to intuitive, abstract and circular formulations rather than real and concrete distinctions based on empirical evidence to describe subtler proficiency levels.

One practical answer to this problem is the concept of *local reference points*, i.e. locally developed, empirically supported benchmarks designed to help teachers define CEFR-related progressions for classroom purposes. This chapter explains and illustrates this concept, which grew out of a pedagogical need in the context of a tertiary-level language programme – namely the English Language Competence (ELC) programme at the Department of English and American Studies at the University of Vienna – to define progression *within* the C levels in a more nuanced way. Teachers were faced with the practical task of establishing course objectives, syllabi, lesson aims and assessment criteria for several new language competence courses (see Berger *et al.*, forthcoming), some with similar yet divergent aims but all reflecting progression within C1 and C2. While the illustrative descriptors for these levels provided useful signposts, they were not fine-grained enough to capture the typically slow-paced vertical progression of advanced language learners. The team solved this dilemma by creating local reference points: sets of salient features representing progressions that are more precise than the CEFR's reference levels but not too specific to be deprived of their referential nature. These 'user- and constructor-oriented' (Alderson, 1991) level specifications provide design benchmarks for teachers, allowing them to create or select learning and teaching objectives, lesson plans, materials, and assessment instruments at the right level while at the same time referring back to a framework linked to the CEFR.

The next section begins by discussing the need to refine the vertical axis of the CEFR for classroom purposes. An example is then given of how such a set of local reference points was developed in relation to text mediation. After that I elaborate on the characteristic features of the local reference points. I go on to give an account of how the reference points can be used in practice. Finally, the chapter concludes by evaluating the concept of local reference points and by calling for further research and development relating to the vertical axis of the CEFR.

The Horizontal and Vertical Axes of the CEFR

It is well known that the CEFR has a horizontal and a vertical axis (Council of Europe, 2001: 16; Council of Europe, 2020: 36). The horizontal axis refers to the CEFR's descriptive scheme for characterizing what is involved in language use and language learning. It comprises different categories for describing aspects of communicative activity and competence, including four modes of language use (reception, production, interaction, and mediation) and related strategies, general competences, and communicative language competences. This scheme is horizontal in that it provides a taxonomy of knowledge and skills in a non-hierarchical way. The vertical axis, on the other hand, is defined by a number of can-do statements representing progress in the above-mentioned categories. This part of the CEFR is vertical in that these statements are calibrated into a series of six proficiency levels grouped into three broader bands: Basic User (A1 and A2), Independent User (B1 and B2), and Proficient User (C1 and C2). The presentation of an ascending sequence of levels allows language users to deal with relevant categories in a progressive way. Progress in language learning takes place along both dimensions, with advancing learners being able to engage in a continually increasing number of communicative activities in progressively sophisticated ways.

The CEFR *Companion Volume* (CEFR-CV; Council of Europe, 2020) has expanded the scope of the CEFR both laterally and vertically.

The horizontal axis has been extended considerably by several additional subcategories, most notably in relation to mediation. The vertical dimension has been extended in that new descriptors characterizing a level halfway towards A1 have been added. This level, termed 'Pre-A1', represents proficiency that is not yet generative but reliant on isolated words and formulaic expressions. However, what the CEFR-CV does not provide, and is not intended to provide, is additional information on how to make narrower subdivisions *within* the levels. Although the so-called 'plus levels', representing a very strong competence at the level concerned, have been more fully defined in the CEFR-CV, there is no further guidance on how to make narrower subdivisions within the levels.

Such finer level distinctions are a great desideratum in learning contexts where even slow progress and small advances need to be captured. For several reasons, this is particularly the case in *advanced* second language education. To begin with, the C levels are the least clearly defined levels in the original version of the CEFR (Green, 2012: 2). Although the CEFR-CV provides more extensive coverage at the upper levels, partly rebalancing the level descriptions, C1 and C2 continue to have the smallest number of functional descriptors (de Jong, 2018). A number of projects have attempted to add detail to the C levels. Notably, in relation to English, projects associated with the English Profile Programme have begun to extract so-called *criterial features*, i.e. 'features from all aspects of language which can distinguish CEFR levels from one another and thus serve as a basis for the estimation of a learner's proficiency level' (Salamoura & Saville, 2010: 101). For example, analysing instructional and assessment materials linked to the CEFR, Green (2012) identifies criterial language functions at levels C1 and C2; Hawkins and Filipović (2012) offer an overview of lexical and syntactic criterial features established thus far; and O'Keeffe and Mark (2017) profile learner language in relation to grammatical competence. Also, a number of other, usually corpus-based, studies have investigated learner language linked to the CEFR levels with a view to specifying what distinguishes higher-rated texts from lower-rated ones (e.g. Chen & Baker, 2016; Thewissen, 2013; Treffers-Daller *et al.*, 2018). Although such studies have great potential when it comes to enhancing our understanding of the CEFR levels, they are a long way from providing a coherent picture (Wisniewski, 2017).

While the CEFR-CV and research projects of the 'criterial feature' type have gone to great lengths to specify the C levels more fully, another issue persists. Vertical under-specification at advanced levels is a problem because progress tends to be slower and less tangible as compared to lower levels. Citing evidence from Finnish projects, North (2014: 98) illustrates the non-linearity of progress: Finnish learners usually need about 800–900 hours of study to reach level B2, whereas the study time required for level C1 increases exponentially to an estimated 3000 hours. It can be conjectured that the progress curve continues to flatten from C1 to C2. Problematic as such estimates may be, they suggest that without further specification of the proficiency continuum, progress can be described mainly horizontally in terms of an ever-growing number of competences a learner develops but not vertically in terms of how learners move up the proficiency continuum. In other words, vertical progress is difficult to capture at the higher proficiency levels, and possible repercussions for the learning process range from a false sense of stagnation to the impression that learning goals are unattainable ideals, along with a loss of motivation on the learners' part. Attempts to improve the vertical dimension in the sense of providing more fine-grained distinctions are rare. One exception is Pearson's Global Scale of English,[1] which offers can-do descriptors on a scale from 10 to 90, describing language proficiency in a more granular way than the CEFR (de Jong et al., 2016). The local reference points described here can be seen as an attempt to refine the vertical axis of the CEFR for classroom purposes. Before the characteristic features and practical uses of local reference points are elaborated upon, the following section explains how they were developed.

Developing Local Reference Points: A Practical Example

This example illustrates the development of local reference points in the context of teaching mediation skills in the ELC programme. The reference points were developed by synthesizing salient features extracted from a five-point analytic rating scale, embracing C1 and C2, for the assessment of text transformations with the findings from a number of keyword analyses of CEFR descriptors. The rating scale is used operationally in English in a Professional Context (EPCO), a two-course module in the ELC programme following a largely text-based approach with a focus on text analysis and mediation. Amongst other things, students learn to mediate texts to suit different target groups and purposes: for example, by transforming specialist texts from the fields of business, law, medicine, or technology into texts for non-specialist audiences. As such, the course is closely related to the concept of processing text, one of the central mediation activities presented in the CEFR-CV (Council of Europe, 2020: 98–101).

While the EPCO rating scale was developed intuitively, the local reference points are supported empirically by a series of keyword analyses of CEFR descriptors. Keyword analysis is a common procedure in discourse and genre analysis to ascertain the 'aboutness' or style of a text by comparing it with a reference corpus (Baker, 2004: 347). The main benefit of a keyword analysis is that it allows us to identify salient concepts in a text with less researcher bias. It identifies words that are proportionally more frequent in the focus text than in the reference corpus, as indicated by a keyness factor, in this case generated by the program KeyWords Extractor (Cobb, 2020) based on a 10-million token mixed written–spoken US–UK corpus (Nation, 2018). In the present example, the focus texts comprised all calibrated C1 and C2 descriptors from the CEFR, divided into five equidistant bands according to their logit values on the scale underlying the CEFR levels (North, 2020). The analysis was conducted for each of the five bands separately, first using *all* calibrated C1 and C2 descriptors ($n = 178$; 4016 tokens) and then the calibrated C1 and C2 descriptors for mediation activities and strategies specifically ($n = 77$; 1947 tokens). As the purpose of the keyword analyses was to identify salient features of the five proficiency bands, the main interest lay in those keywords that are unique to a particular band. Table 10.1 provides an overview of the band-specific keywords. Band 1 represents the top level, whereas band 5 is the bottom level.

While Table 10.1 lists keywords based on *all* calibrated C1 and C2 descriptors in the CEFR, Table 10.2 presents the relevant keywords based on C1 and C2 descriptors for *mediation*.

The keywords seem to reveal a few significant differences between the bands, reflecting a systematic progression. A detailed discussion of the keywords would go beyond the scope of this chapter, but a cursory glance should suffice to see the progression. For ease of interpretation, the keywords can be grouped into typical component elements of can-do statements, such as operations, the object of the operation, and qualities (see Green, 2012). Operations, for example, seem to advance from *summarizing* (band 5) to *commenting* and *evaluating* (band 4) to *discussing* (band 3). Similarly, qualities reflect a discernible progression: *original*, *technical* (band 5), *professional* (band 4), *appropriate*, *effective*, *special* (band 3), *fluent*, *wide*, *range* (band 2). The interpretation of the keywords, needless to say, depends on the surrounding text. For this reason, the descriptors were also converted into a full concordance index for every word, and the concordance lines were inspected qualitatively to interpret the keywords more accurately. The EPCO rating scale, the keyword lists, and the concordance tables provided the basis for the local reference points for text mediation as presented in Table 10.3.

As can be seen, the local reference points show a clear progression in relation to text mediation. At band 5, students can extract relevant ideas from the source text and transfer them to another text; however, they may still rely (too) heavily on the original so that the transformation remains somewhat superficial, and the genre of the target text may not always be clear. At band 4, students have sufficient language and mediation skills to cope with different genres and genre conventions, particularly in relation to professional and technical texts. They can use essential mediation strategies appropriately, and their transformations

Table 10.1 Keywords with a keyness factor >25, ranked in descending order (all C1 and C2 descriptors)

Band 1	Band 2 keywords		Band 3 keywords		Band 4 keywords		Band 5 keywords	
	Keyness factor	Keyword	Keyness factor	Keyword	Keyness factor	Keyword	Keyness factor	Keyword
Not enough calibrated descriptors to generate band-specific keywords	58,252.00	situation	10,917.00	sociolinguistic	31,192.00	relation	1,314.00	subsidiary
	1,532.95	consecutive	2,183.40	nuance	668.39	intelligible	239.18	expand
	448.09	implicit	2,183.40	colloquial	266.60	usage	194.94	relevant
	413.14	convey	1,819.50	mediation	220.18	genre	114.70	length
	320.07	simultaneous	545.85	differentiate	165.91	literary	52.35	argue
	238.25	shade	330.82	spontaneous	123.12	discourse	44.15	point
	118.64	implication	321.09	ambiguity	121.72	elaborate	42.39	example
	87.47	range	222.80	collaborate	100.21	narrate	36.79	support
	79.06	aware	152.69	abstract	97.98	clarify	26.60	develop
	74.72	express	74.52	overcome	72.33	original		
	60.59	wide	55.56	translate	69.94	integrate		
	32.45	structure	55.56	persuade	60.92	evaluate		
	28.32	fine	48.85	virtually	57.34	technical		
			44.74	emphasis	46.35	convention		
			44.56	audience	43.32	conclusion		
					41.96	joke		
					40.91	instruction		
					40.68	detail		
					38.91	interact		
					37.69	variety		
					37.41	emotional		
					37.38	describe		
					28.84	adjust		
					26.05	cultural		
					25.50	difference		

Table 10.2 Keywords with a keyness factor >25, ranked in descending order (C1 and C2 descriptors for mediation)

Band 1 keywords		Band 2 keywords		Band 3 keywords		Band 4 keywords		Band 5 keywords	
Keyness factor	Keyword	Keyness factor	Keyword	Keyness factor	Keyword	Keyness factor	Keyword	Keyness factor	Keyword
149.25	register	3,447.47	consecutive	117.64	accessible	47,923.00	professional	235.66	original
109.65	style	3,447.47	fluent	95.90	appropriate	130.40	audience	112.09	technical
		719.80	simultaneous	49.78	special	93.60	evaluate	106.05	summarize
		98.35	range	45.77	discuss	61.84	target	76.99	communicate
		68.12	wide	35.05	effective	40.07	comment	68.36	joke
						33.37	source	44.19	detail

Table 10.3 Local reference points for text mediation at C1–C2

Bands	Local reference points	
1	Full Academic	• successful challenging of genre conventions (if appropriate) • skilful use of creative elements (if appropriate) • a high degree of flexibility in language use • virtual absence of errors
2	Advanced Academic	• managing a wide range of texts, topics, and devices • effective use of transformation/mediation strategies • precision in finer shades of meaning • managing implications and implicit meaning • a good command of idiomatic expressions and colloquialisms
3	General Academic	• abstract, specialist, and specialized texts/topics (also outside own field) • effective persuasion • nuances and differentiation • managing ambiguity • effective language use • common idiomatic expressions
4	Full Operational	• professional and technical texts/topics • managing different genres and genre conventions • awareness of target audience and context • appropriate use of essential transformation/mediation strategies • effective evaluation • appropriate language use • few lapses in linguistic control; little need for compensatory strategies
5	Effective Operational	• relevant ideas • (over)emphasis on original (source text) • summation and argumentation • adequate support by subsidiary points, examples, and details

show sufficient awareness of the target audience and context. At band 3, this extends to abstract, highly specialized and specialist texts, even outside their own field of specialization. The students' functional repertoire includes effective persuasion, differentiation and managing ambiguity; the reader has no difficulty identifying the target text type. By the time students have reached band 2, they can manage a wide range of texts, topics and devices, making effective use of mediation strategies such as breaking down, simplifying, amplifying and streamlining. They can also manage complex information that is not explicitly stated, both receptively and productively, and transfer subtle nuances of meaning with great precision. At band 1, finally, students can, if appropriate, also challenge established genre conventions and use other creative elements effectively, such as irony, allusive or figurative language. A similar set of local reference points, relating to academic speaking, is described in Berger (2020).

A Local Instrument Complementing a Common Framework

As the example above shows, the local reference points are characterized by several features:

- First and foremost, they subdivide the broad level descriptions of C1 and C2 into narrower, more practical bands, thereby refining the vertical dimension of the Common Framework for classroom purposes. The salient features characterizing performance at different points along the proficiency continuum help practitioners to better capture small gains in proficiency and slow learning progress.
- Secondly, although they define progression in a way that is more detailed than the common reference levels, they are not so specific that they forfeit their referential nature. The level of granularity is somewhere between the common reference levels and specific rating scale descriptors. As such, the local reference points provide a link between the CEFR and locally developed instruments, which allows users to relate other descriptors back to a common system.
- Thirdly, the local reference points are empirically supported. They are not just intuitive subdivisions of the CEFR's reference levels in the sense that experienced teachers decide on a plausible progression, but, unlike many other locally developed tools, the reference points are informed by empirical methods. While the example given above involved empirically-scaled teacher interpretations of descriptors along with keyword analysis, a range of other empirical methods could be used as well to extract salient reference points.
- Fourthly, the local reference points refer to real and concrete – as opposed to abstract – performance features dependent on semantic qualifiers. They represent something definite, typical, and indicative of the level concerned which has stand-alone integrity and whose interpretation does not depend on the way in which other descriptors are formulated. In this sense, the local reference points are in line with the CEFR's general principle of *definiteness* underlying the formulation of the illustrative descriptors (Council of Europe, 2001: 206).
- Fifthly, the local reference points are locally developed but not confined to the local context from which they originate. Although they have been created in a particular setting and for a particular purpose, they could also be useful beyond the local context. Much as these reference points are based on specific descriptors, they are abstract enough to serve as criterial features in similar settings.
- Finally, as far as their primary purpose is concerned, the local reference points could be characterized as 'user- and constructor-oriented' instruments, according to Alderson's (1991) well-known classification of scales. While user-oriented scales provide users, including teachers and learners, with information about typical or likely behaviour at a given level, constructor-oriented scales are designed to help teachers and testers to elicit an adequate sample of performance which demonstrates the features specified in the scale.

Applying Local Reference Points in Practice

Based on the experience in the ELC programme, there would seem to be at least five practical uses for such local reference points in classroom contexts. One area of application is curriculum design and the formulation of learning and teaching objectives. While the CEFR's reference levels usually form the basis for the definition of broad normative outcomes at the end of a formal teaching period, local reference points can help teachers and course designers to break the general goals down into more specific objectives, not just horizontally but vertically, tracing students' development in relation to the overall goals from basic to successively more advanced levels. Teachers can use them to establish clearer, more transparent, and attainable objectives reflecting an incremental view of ability and, by the same token, make progress more visible, which in turn profoundly affects learner motivation.

Secondly, in a related sense, the local reference points provide a framework for lesson sequencing that is not just intuitively appealing but empirically informed and more consistent with the order in which students are likely to benefit from instruction. For example, in EPCO, texts are selected in accordance with the local reference points, a typical order being technical and professional texts about concrete topics, specialized texts from the students' own field, specialized texts from a field that is not their own, abstract texts, and texts that convey a great deal of implied meaning. Organizing teaching units in accordance with the local reference points has facilitated a certain degree of standardization in a context where teachers have traditionally designed their courses largely independently, and such standardization is felt to be a desirable change in a language programme that offers a number of parallel courses each semester.

A third area in which local reference points can be of great practical use is formative assessment, a core activity in any classroom context. Assessment is formative in that it is designed to influence learners' language development through continuous monitoring of the learning process and subsequent adaptation of teaching to meet the most immediate needs (Heritage, 2013). Eliciting, interpreting and using evidence about a learner's current status is at the heart of this process (Black & Wiliam, 2009). Similar to learning progressions (Bailey & Heritage, 2014), the local reference points offer a framework for collecting and interpreting such evidence with a view to directing or redirecting teaching and learning to improve learner achievement. They can provide the basis for reflective tools to help teachers, as well as students, to draw reasonable inferences about the current level of ability and to give learning-oriented feedback in relation to the paths learners should follow if they want to improve attainment.

Fourthly, local reference points can be a useful tool for summative assessment purposes. For example, the local reference points for mediation have helped the course coordinators to extend and adapt the existing rating scale for a new course titled Mediation and Genre Analysis for English Teachers. Whereas the existing scale operationalizes a construct for general professional and academic purposes, the new scale is complementary in that it reflects the specific text mediation skills needed by teachers in a classroom context. The local reference points served as benchmark criteria, which allowed the course coordinators to develop the new rating scale descriptors in a coherent and transparent way.

Finally, on a general level, the common reference points have facilitated implementation of CEFR-related ideas and principles in ELC classrooms. It has been pointed out multiple times that while the impact of the CEFR has been strongest in formal, large-scale testing, the impact on the language classroom has been relatively small, particularly in the university sector (Little, 2011). To evaluate the impact the CEFR has had on classrooms, it may be helpful to distinguish between 'strong' and 'weak' implementation. Implementation in a strong sense would involve a holistic approach to the CEFR, with a deliberate alignment between all relevant areas of pedagogy, curriculum design, and assessment at both the micro and the macro levels, with the CEFR's principles put into action. Implementation in a weak sense, on the other hand, would reflect an atomistic approach to the CEFR in isolated areas, with the core ideas and principles being espoused rather than enacted. Arguably, the local reference points have contributed to stronger implementation of the CEFR in a programme that has, until recently, been virtually untouched by CEFR-related ideas.

Conclusion

This chapter has described the concept, development and uses of local reference points, a tool designed in a bottom-up adaptation of the common reference levels to refine the vertical axis of the CEFR for classroom purposes. Extracted from specific descriptors in various ways, the local reference points, in essence, represent a coherent set of meaningful and concrete sublevel specifications at the upper end of the proficiency range. Probably the greatest practical advantage of such subdivisions is that student achievement and progress can be conceptualized, reported and rewarded more effectively than is possible with broad level specifications. The local reference points can thus provide a sound basis for a range of educational purposes that need more granular subdivisions than the basic distinction between C1 and C2. On a more general level, the local reference points can contribute towards implementing the CEFR in language classrooms in the local context.

Of course, the local reference points have some limitations. They have been extracted from specific rating-scale descriptors and calibrated teacher interpretations of descriptors by exploiting the benefits of keyword analysis, and, as such, they represent an empirically informed progression but not a developmentally determined or inevitable trajectory. It is important to emphasize that learning does not happen in a lockstep fashion, nor is the learning path exactly the same for everyone. What can be asserted is that the reference points represent expected tendencies, informed by empirical research, in relation to the steps learners may follow as they become more proficient; in this sense, they offer a productive, but not prescriptive, tool for classroom purposes. From a methodological point of view, keyword analysis is quite sensitive to text length and may over-attend to lexical similarity while at the same time underestimating functional or semantic similarity. Therefore, the approach may provide an incomplete picture as some level characteristics remain obscure. Future research and development could usefully combine the procedures described here with complementary approaches – for example, learner corpus-based analyses.

Notwithstanding the limitations, to the extent that teaching, learning and assessment in the classroom rely on clear, transparent and attainable objectives, we need empirically based instruments that are sensitive enough to capture also slight gains in learning. In other words, as teachers we need a better understanding of the vertical axis of the CEFR, especially at higher levels, where progress tends to be slower and less evident than at lower levels. Empirically informed local reference points intermediate between the CEFR's reference levels, and specific rating scale descriptors may have potential in this respect. Such tools can help us to localize language learning, teaching and assessment. At the same time, they facilitate comparability across contexts as teachers can use them for their own purposes and yet refer back to a common framework. The work presented here is a practical example of the research and development needed to flesh out the CEFR descriptors for classroom purposes. Beyond the small-scale empirical work done here, however, more research is clearly needed to understand progression within and across the levels. Future research and development work will have to continue investigating the vertical dimension of the CEFR to enhance our understanding of how language learning progresses and to develop further tools that are of practical use in the classroom.

Note

(1) https://www.pearson.com/english/about/gse.html

References

Alderson, C. (1991) Bands and scores. In C. Alderson and B. North (eds) *Language Testing in the 1990s: The Communicative Legacy* (pp. 71–94). London: Macmillan.

Bailey, A. and Heritage, M. (2014) The role of language learning progressions in improved instruction and assessment of English language learners. *TESOL Quarterly* 48 (3), 480–506. doi: 10.1002/tesq.176.

Baker, P. (2004) Querying keywords: Questions of difference, frequency, and sense in keywords analysis. *Journal of English Linguistics* 32 (4), 346–359. doi: 10.1177/0075424204269894.

Berger, A. (2020) Specifying progression in academic speaking: A keyword analysis of CEFR-based proficiency descriptors. *Language Assessment Quarterly* 17 (1), 85–99. doi: 10.1080/15434303.2019.1689981.

Berger, A., Heaney, H., Resnik, P., Rieder-Bünemann, A. and Savukova, G. (eds) (forthcoming) *Developing Advanced English Language Competence: A Research-informed Approach at Tertiary Level*. Cham: Springer.

Black, P. and Wiliam, D. (2009) Developing the theory of formative assessment. *Educational Assessment, Evaluation and Accountability* 21 (1), 5–31. doi: 10.1007/s11092-008-9068-5.

Chen, Y.-H. and Baker, P. (2016) Investigating criterial discourse features across second language development: Lexical bundles in rated learner essays, CEFR B1, B2 and C1. *Applied Linguistics* 37 (6), 849–880. doi: 10.1093/applin/amu065.

Cobb, T. (2020) KeyWords Extractor (Version 2.2) [Software], accessed 4 September 2020. https://www.lextutor.ca/key/.

Council of Europe (2001) *Common European Framework of Reference for Languages: Learning, Teaching, Assessment*. Cambridge: Cambridge University Press.

Council of Europe (2020) *Common European Framework of Reference for Languages: Learning, Teaching, Assessment. Companion Volume*. Accessed 5 November 2020. https://rm.coe.int/common-european-framework-of-reference-for-languages-learning-teaching/16809ea0d4.

de Jong, J. (2018) Updates to the CEFR. In D. Little, *The CEFR Companion Volume with New Descriptors: Uses and Implications for Language Testing and Assessment*. Report on the 6th EALTA CEFR SIG, Trinity College Dublin, Ireland, 27 January (pp. 3–5). European Association for Language Testing and Assessment. http://www.ealta.eu.org/events/Report%20on%20VIth%20EALTA%20CEFR%20SIG%20rev%2023.02.18.pdf (accessed 19 December 2021).

de Jong, J., Mayor, M. and Hayes, C. (2016) *Developing Global Scale of English Learning Objectives Aligned to the Common European Framework*, Global Scale of English Research Series, London: Pearson. Accessed 14 September 2020. https://online.flippingbook.com/view/894261/2/.

Green, A. (2012) *Language Functions Revisited: Theoretical and Empirical Bases for Language Construct Definition Across the Ability Range*. Cambridge: Cambridge University Press.

Hawkins, J. and Filipović, L. (2012) *Criterial Features in L2 English: Specifying the Reference Levels of the Common European Framework*. Cambridge: Cambridge University Press.

Heritage, M. (2013) *Formative Assessment in Practice: A Process of Inquiry and Action*. Cambridge, MA: Harvard Education Press.

Little, D. (2011) The *Common European Framework of Reference for Languages*, the European Language Portfolio, and language learning in higher education. *Language Learning in Higher Education* 1 (1), 1–21. doi: 10.1515/cercles-2011-0001.

Nation, P. (2018) The BNC/COCA word family lists. Accessed 14 September 2020. https://www.victoria.ac.nz/__data/assets/pdf_file/0004/1689349/Information-on-the-BNC_COCA-word-family-lists-20180705.pdf.

North, B. (2014) *The CEFR in Practice*. Cambridge: Cambridge University Press.

North, B. (2020) The CEFR illustrative descriptors: Validation reference paper for researchers [Unpublished manuscript]. Council of Europe, Strasbourg.

O'Keeffe, A. and Mark, G. (2017) The English grammar profile of learner competence: Methodology and key findings. *International Journal of Corpus Linguistics* 22 (4), 457–489. doi: 10.1075/ijcl.14086.oke.

Piccardo, E. and North, B. (2019) *The Action-oriented Approach: A Dynamic Vision of Language Education*. Bristol: Multilingual Matters.

Salamoura, A. and Saville, N. (2010) Exemplifying the CEFR: Criterial features of written learner English from the English Profile Programme. In I. Bartning, M. Martin and I. Vedder (eds) *Communicative Proficiency and Linguistic Development: Intersections between SLA and Language Testing Research* (pp. 101–132). EuroSLA Monographs Series 1. European Second Language Association. Accessed 14 September 2020. http://eurosla.org/monographs/EM01/101-132Salamoura_Saville.pdf.

Thewissen, J. (2013) Capturing L2 accuracy developmental patterns: Insights from an error-tagged EFL learner corpus. *The Modern Language Journal* 97 (S1), 77–101. doi: 10.1111/j.1540-4781.2012.01422.x.

Treffers-Daller, J., Parslow, P. and Williams, S. (2018) Back to basics: How measures of lexical diversity can help discriminate between CEFR levels. *Applied Linguistics* 39 (3), 302–327. doi: 10.1093/applin/amw009.

Wisniewski, K. (2017) Empirical learner language and the levels of the Common European Framework of Reference. *Language Learning* 67 (S1), 232–253. doi: 10.1111/lang.12223.

11 Commonality versus Localization in Curricula

Elaine Boyd

When looking at the future of how curricula might be developed with some degree of alignment across language communities with differing needs and a variety of educational policies, it is useful to consider how the Common European Framework of Reference for Languages *(CEFR; Council of Europe, 2001) has been used prior to the publication of the* Companion Volume *(CEFR-CV; Council of Europe, 2020) in order to establish what issues emerge that might threaten a coherent alignment process. Three models seem to generally represent the different contexts in which a CEFR-based curriculum appears to exist: a retrofit model, which maps an existing curriculum to the CEFR; an assessment-driven model, which limits a curriculum to test constructs; and a coursebook model, where a curriculum has been defined based on what is covered in a coursebook. In developing alignment procedures that allow reliable and transparent comparison, we need to take account of these existing usages as well as recognizing that the number of descriptors in the CEFR-CV is potentially overwhelming to users. The challenges in developing the procedures are likely to rest in defining a process for choosing and prioritizing a manageable set of descriptors and agreeing, as a community, on the evidence needed for any alignment such that this can be reasonably operationalized by non-expert users. Given these parameters, this chapter considers how far we should be investigating the notion that less is more in terms of requirements. It argues for a model that would encourage a tightly tailored but richer picture for specifications working with standardization procedures that are rooted in the overarching descriptors in the CEFR.*

Introduction

In discussing how curricula can be developed, managed and adapted it is first worth considering the relationship between a curriculum and a syllabus and where the CEFR-CV (Council of Europe, 2020) descriptors might fit in. In an overview, Richards (2013: 6) defines a curriculum as 'the overall plan or design for a course and how the content for a course is transformed into a blueprint for teaching and learning which enables the desired learning outcomes to be achieved'. A syllabus is one step below this in the hierarchy; it fleshes out the curriculum to meet specific needs, e.g. by being localized, or adapted to suit a particular age group. A curriculum is a specification of planned and guided knowledge to be achieved (Kelly, 1999; Smith, 1996, 2000) whereas a syllabus is a concise statement of contents much more connected to specific courses. A syllabus, in describing the order of teaching, often logical (Kelly, 1999), sits under the hierarchy of a curriculum and is a manifestation of the curriculum. Despite resistance to the idea, it could be argued that should one wish to cover everything it contains, then the CEFR is a curriculum – and the CEFR-CV has significantly expanded this curriculum. In terms of practical application, however, a curriculum would be extracted from the CEFR-CV by selecting the objectives to create a planned and guided learning programme. However, in looking at how curricula can be developed from, or aligned with, the CEFR-CV, we are concerned with the broadest defined level here – not with the order of learning or precise statements that describe the sub-factors in that learning, but with the general description of knowledge.

In our increasingly interactive global community, languages have posed a problem for creating and understanding standards across communities because the focus has been on content: for example, what grammar or vocabulary a learner knows. This is unlike other subject areas, where the approach tends to focus on process and the acquired cognitive skills or the evidencing of broad competences. This has resulted in many language curricula reflecting a subject-centred rather than a learner-centred design. Contemporary pedagogy in ELT would favour the latter, and the expanded CEFR-CV can facilitate this shift, with the inclusion of the mediation scales placing a greater emphasis on communication and interaction. The very purpose of the CEFR has been to help the language learning community recognize and align to standards. These are critical for ministries, who need a measurement of where their young population sits in global comparison, and equally for teachers, who need to be able to define expectations for their learners. Oates (2014), who advocates a return to standardized and stable curricula, cites Schmidt and Prawat (2006) in stressing the importance of consistency across development pathways, the coherence of all elements of a curriculum, and the fact that a curriculum must be based on an understood and agreed learning model if it is to be successful. In language learning, different models have emerged of how that consistency is achieved and it has been famously hard to truly compare standards, even across assessments, which are by their nature standardized. However, the introduction of an updated version of the CEFR in 2020, which describes much broader and more flexible approaches to communication, offers a more robust foundation to develop curricula that can be aligned to communicative competences in much the same way that credit-bearing courses in tertiary education, both nationally and across borders, are aligned with one another via generic cognitive skills.

In revisiting how we can help users to understand and operationalize the relationship between curricula and the CEFR-CV, the challenge is threefold:

(1) How do we support typical users (e.g. teachers, ministries, publishers) in utilizing the CEFR-CV to develop a curriculum for their learners?
(2) How do we help users with the alignment of existing curricula?
(3) For (1) and (2), how do we create a process of alignment procedures that allows for flexibility across communities without weakening standardization?

The overarching challenge is in finding a balance between giving users sufficient guidance to enable them to make robust decisions and stifling the flexibility required for localization by over-specification.

The Story So Far

The CEFR is already used by many language communities as a basis for curriculum alignment so we need to review and assess what exists to date in order to consider what is effective, what adaptations might be necessary, and what gaps or dissatisfactions exist. There are some common threads, all of which can help inform the creation of a more standardized and accessible process – or processes. The following three typical models are potentially each a manifestation of a localized model.

The retrofit model

Very commonly, any mapping of a set of curriculum standards to the CEFR is a retrofit, where some elements in an existing curriculum are more or less randomly linked to the CEFR, while others (which may in some way conflict with the CEFR) remain unchanged. While understandable as a process, this can lead to messy and non-standardized alignments based on needs-must, especially when seeking to cross-reference across languages or different communities within the same language. It can also result in gaps in competences if there is no option to adjust the curriculum model that is the starting point. A related issue, when this retrofit occurs within a single community, is that this type of alignment may be very roughly described and may not securely represent the full construct of the level. Üstünlüoğlu *et al.* (2012: 115) identify this issue in a Turkish setting where 'it is not currently common practice in Turkey either to develop language teaching programmes based on the Common European Framework as a reference, or to introduce improvements in these programmes based on an evaluation of their effectiveness', and this is common to many language communities. Having said that, there is nothing in principle wrong with retrofitting. Richards (2013) illustrates how retrofitting can be managed in a principled way (what he refers to as backward design; Richards, 2013: 28), and the key issue here is to ensure that there is a model for the retrofit. Micallef (2016) describes one such model in her workshop notes, so there is evidence that communities of practice are seeking to shape this. This model would ensure that different communities not only follow the same process, which can then provide points of comparison, but also that there is a transparent framework for identifying gaps and differences. In the interests of retaining flexibility, the model would not enforce the need for any gaps to be filled or differences corrected as these may well be a matter of localization. However, it would offer a principled and consistent approach that would make any differences or similarities visible and reportable, in the same way that assessments can be compared while retaining difference.

The assessment-driven model

Many users will be familiar with the option and process of aligning assessments to the CEFR. There has been a strong focus on using the descriptors to develop test constructs, especially as the global language teaching community has, as a whole, become more literate in assessment principles. However, the formal alignment process described in the manual for relating exams to the CEFR (Council of Europe, 2009) can be expensive and time-consuming if fully completed. Although the manual offers users a choice, the rigour of both specification and standardization is so burdensome that the process cannot be invested in equally across communities, and some users are tempted to take short cuts or to do 'rough' or partial alignments. This inevitably leads to a variation in the accuracy of the alignments, and rather than insisting on such an excessive process, it might favour better (albeit broader) standardization to recognize the challenges in time, resources and finances that users face and develop a model which allows different entry points depending on the context.

A separate point is that the assessment-driven model of developing a curriculum often starts with a syllabus, consisting of the precise cherry-picked constructs and content of the test, which in turn feeds backwards into a curriculum. In other words, if the test is taken as the learning objectives, which are then constructed into a syllabus (and perhaps back again into the curriculum), the outcome is that the learning points are then limited by the test content. Hence there are examples of language learning courses where the teaching content is entirely constructed around an assessment. While this often market-driven focus is understandable and arguably a useful driver for desired competences, it is not ideal as it magnifies the test constructs and skills to the exclusion of a broader set of language competences. It can limit the broader and deeper learning that is an especially important tool for students who are still in primary or secondary education. The attraction of the assessment-driven model is that, unlike the retrofit model, it is much easier to achieve a standard across learning communities. However, as a test cannot possibly cover every construct that may be required by a specific language learning community, it can end up being a checklist of language elements rather than a true curriculum.

The coursebook model

Although there is a lot of variation in how international publishers align their products to a market (e.g. by test or national curricula), the major publishers have been in the ELT market for a long time and there is an element of 'chicken or egg' about how curricula are agreed upon. This seems to be represented by a cline that stretches from a very traditional top-down approach, where the publishers were seen as the experts, to a more collaborative present, where publishers engage with teachers and learners to address their needs. The most worrying end of this cline is the top-down approach where, in the past, when native-speaker publishers were seen as part of a pool of experts on English language, they were, despite local collaborations, the touchstone for what was included both for curricula and the order of learning, i.e. the syllabus. These publishers were thus often able to drive curricula, sometimes informed by the testing ambitions of the market.

As the CEFR became a more widely referenced document there was often a clumsy retrofitting of coursebooks to broad levels within the CEFR. In the middle of the cline is where a publisher of English language coursebooks in, for example, Spain may have ensured, at the developmental stage of that course, that the proposed content aligned with any national or local curriculum. However, rather than triangulating the alignment at the outset – by pooling the curriculum, the CEFR, and the learner needs – a publisher may *post hoc* aim to align the course to the CEFR and will fit this backwards to the scope and sequence of the syllabus. This can result in an uncomfortable match that is localized to the specific market for which the book or course is intended but which cannot be aligned with similar courses across communities or geographies.

At the more contemporary end of the cline, we see that international publishers not only now seem to be more sensitive to local needs but also that many local publishers have emerged who produce courses that perhaps better fit the needs of their context or market. These publishers inevitably know the very precise needs of their market, but it is unclear if their success is due to this knowledge or simply that small publishers have had the business opportunity to emerge as players in the market. So again, the approach within this specific community is inconsistent, and there is an issue with legacy publications. This is where a successful coursebook (and there have been many for the English language) undergoes several revisions and new editions focusing on new topics and content, but where the overarching curriculum is never reviewed or revisited. This means that the objectives captured in that curriculum remain unchallenged as to whether they meet the current needs of the learners. This, for example, leads to tasks such as 'going shopping' always appearing at a certain point in a graded course regardless of whether the target learning group, such as Spanish youngsters, would ever need to go into an English-speaking shop.

Sometimes, the foundation of the courses is not updated to encompass contemporary pedagogies, such as communication skills or critical thinking, and leaves the 'curriculum' being driven by a grammatical approach that is at odds with the communicative approach of the CEFR generally and is certainly not reflective of the CEFR-CV. Despite a greater confidence in expertise and ownership of English in L2 or non-English-speaking communities, there are still many contexts where the native speaker is seen as the reference point and international publications seen as a reliable resource. In recognizing that this perceived expertise is a responsibility, it is important not to underplay the importance of coursebooks and their role in driving syllabi and, via that, curricula in some contexts. This is especially important in the light of a currently defined trend, which argues that coursebooks are becoming more – not less – core to learning (Sherrington, 2020).

Summary

In summary, these versions of how a curriculum might be aligned with the CEFR represent how this process can be operationalized on a practical level in different stakeholder communities. The problems created by the various models can mean that any so-called alignments potentially become more and more superficial and take us further and further away from the standards that the CEFR-CV seeks to support. Perhaps for this reason, there has been a tendency by researchers presenting at conferences, and professionals engaging in discussion lists, to highlight where processes are being followed incorrectly or incompletely, in the hope of reinforcing adherence to these processes.

However, it would be more fruitful to acknowledge the tensions and needs in different sectors or geographies and to ensure that any process accommodates these differences in a useful and accessible format.

Challenges To Be Addressed

In designing any alignment procedures, not only do we need to make sure we capture the issues identified in current models of alignment as described in the previous section, but we also need to recognize the impact of the several updates and additions to the CEFR now in the CEFR-CV. The extent of the CEFR already seems to have caused burdensome issues for users when one looks at studies such as Arslan and Özenici (2017). The number of descriptors is now potentially overwhelming, especially when we see there are already problematic shortcuts identified in the assessment-driven approach described above. In an already crowded and increasingly burdened curriculum, how can it be realistic to have added more to the fold? Teachers may well be concerned that there are now more competences, more skills to teach or achieve. On the other hand, the expansion allows users in different contexts to refine their selection of objectives better, so that any curriculum is a much closer match to their learners' needs.

Within this extended framework, the challenges for curriculum developers are likely to be:

- *Establishing the extent to which they require 'doing' versus 'knowing' as a standard.* In other words, will the objectives they set for learners in a curriculum reflect an expectation that the learner has the necessary language competence to perform something – or that they can actually *perform* it? This first challenge is at the heart of any curriculum and has to be resolved clearly before any further steps can be taken, otherwise what follows will become problematic.
- *How to choose and prioritize a manageable set of descriptors.* It is important that any developer can select descriptors appropriate to their learners' needs and purposes. However, this is not straightforward when set within the context of learning, e.g. is deep learning more important than surface learning? Pedagogically the teaching of languages, especially with younger learners, is exploring shifts that accommodate, e.g. emotional and cognitive learning models that support deeper learning with a focus on transferable skills rather than a wide range of objectives.
- *How to evidence any alignment.* This is where we, as a whole community, need to agree on what types of evidence are acceptable. As noted above, this has to be accompanied by a process for gathering evidence that is user-friendly and accessible to non-experts but robust enough to support transparent reporting and thus reliable comparisons.

In order to help users manage these challenges, there are further challenges in developing a readily accessible process for alignment:

- We need to take account of the different approaches to curriculum and syllabus development outlined in the previous section, so that these can be accommodated rather than penalized.
- We need to recognize that the desire for alignment can lead to a self-locking cycle where any existing curricula are simply mapped to identifiable CEFR descriptors without consideration of what might need revising. Additionally, this can lead to users offering 'common practice' as evidence rather than following standard procedures. In this context, users will need guidance on how to manage these issues.
- The CEFR-CV allows more precise descriptors on which to build a curriculum, but we live in a very imprecise world where rough fit is often seen as good enough. In the light of this, how far do we want to press for precision?
- How important is the content of a curriculum versus the process of development? Do we suggest a system that encourages users to dig deep into the constructs to make sure they are well defined? Or do we favour a process which, in its rigour, skews users' attention to defining this process rather than specifying learner or educational needs? Where is the balance? The CEFR-CV (Council of Europe, 2020: 43) usefully explains how users can 'flesh out' constructs but it stops short of saying how this might be managed as a whole or across a set of descriptors.
- Comparability is the key challenge that runs throughout. Following on from the point above, we may need to consider whether this challenge is caused by domain issues of the content in which the language will be used rather than linguistic issues of, for example, grammar or skills points. Arguably, distinctions in curricula are most evident in what skills might be required, what level of mediation competence is required, or how communicative a curriculum is – as opposed to linguistic features such as grammar, which might be more easily matched across levels.

Inevitably these challenges will have to be resolved through compromises and I suggest that, while encouraging careful consideration of the precise CEFR descriptors a curriculum might require, any process will have to draw comparisons at the broadest level.

Developing a Blueprint for Curriculum Development

We have to recognize that users will face practical challenges when preparing or operationalizing any alignment of a curriculum, whether new or via a retrofit. In most educational settings, whether in publishing, at education ministry level or in the classroom, most potential users will be constrained by time, money and access to expertise. In the light of this, any supporting processes or documents for using the CEFR-CV have to offer a set of routes that allow the various users to develop an alignment that is both acceptable in terms of consistency and also easy to implement and flexible enough to account for a variety of differing needs and resources. If not, users will likely continue to take non-standard short cuts, which will further undermine any coherent cross-referencing of standards. The routes or processes proposed have to suit different purposes but with enough core similarities to make an argument for alignment, even if that has some blurred boundaries. We need to find the common thread(s) running down the middle of what happens in the alignment process so that we can all agree on what the achievable standards are while allowing room for individual or local differences. An interesting model was reported by the OECD (2018) when it produced a favourable review on curriculum strategy in Portugal. This strategy had been implemented to support schools in effectively exercising autonomy and greater flexibility by designing their own curricula which nevertheless had to meet standard specified goals. The project's aim was:

> to ensure a mastery of core disciplinary subjects, while at the same time allowing space for interdisciplinary learning built on core subject mastery. ... It aimed to ameliorate curriculum overload, while supporting better and deeper learning for all students. (OECD, 2018: 9)

The review does not underestimate the challenges but certainly demonstrates what is possible and concludes that flexibility is a strength and not a limitation.

In order to capture accessibility and do-ability, the following issues could be considered:

Focus on the purpose or intention of a curriculum

Users who wish to use the CEFR to develop a curriculum should be encouraged to focus on this aspect first. What are the outcomes that are both essential and desirable? Guidance could be provided on how to identify these for the learner group and thus narrow down the set of descriptors required for a particular setting. Again, the CEFR-CV (Council of Europe, 2020: 43) makes reference to this slimming down, but a clearer process for making these decisions would be helpful. This support should include reassurance and a rationale for 'leaving things out' being positive rather than negative. For example, if learners need English for employability but will never leave their home country, which aspects of the descriptors in the CEFR-CV would be prioritized? If a purpose is defined, then it means standards can be compared more fairly and usefully across similar communities. This flexibility does not limit learning, but in fact can promote deeper learning by allowing learners to explore the competences they really need to the fullest degree, giving them more confidence that they can manipulate the tools and strategies they are likely to actually use.

We also need to take on board the increasing focus on autonomous learning and self-regulation and the pedagogical implications of the action-oriented approach, which seems to have received insufficient attention since 2001. The Portuguese model described above (OECD, 2018) could be a helpful starting point. There is an emerging transformation in *how* students learn but not necessarily *what* they learn, so they and their teachers need to be working with curricula that identify a smaller set of competences that can be elaborated more fully. The focus on deeper learning means learning less in quantitative terms but more in qualitative terms, which anticipates that part of the learning will include transferring skills, knowledge and competences. This would be a shift away from teachers being seen as in charge of learning content and more towards a pedagogy that allows them to facilitate the development of these transferable skills.

Developing support networks

Although the much wider understanding of assessment literacy has helped curriculum developers to see how assessment can fit into a broader cycle of learning objectives, there probably needs to be a much better understanding of how evidence to support any curricula decisions is collected and reported. It is also important that teachers, who are at the sharp end of this, are not additionally burdened with a process they may see as intrusive to their focus on teaching by, for example, being asked to trial curricula or having curricula imposed on them. The processes of staging and collaboration, of seeking multiple inputs and piloting and review, that are embedded in the assessment alignment process could perhaps be adapted in a more accessible way to curriculum development. This would mean that, although curricula may look very different across communities, the procedures for validating each curriculum would be consistent. The processes could include examples of different routes to meet the varied requirements and resources outlined in the first part of this chapter.

Trusting that less is more

The most generic level in the CEFR-CV is the overall scale for each activity (Council of Europe, 2020: 48, 54, 62, 66, 72, 82, 91) and the expanded self-assessment grid (2020: 177), and it may be that the only fair route to alignment is to require mapping to these with supporting evidence. In aiming to achieve the consistency that Schmidt and Prawat (2006) argue for, the route may be to come up to this overall level in each competence in the CEFR and ask for evidence that shows alignment of the broadest communicative skills described in the overall scale. As outlined previously, this example is used by universities, which ask for generic cognitive skills such as the ability to analyse and apply knowledge regardless of subject area, in order to show alignment between credit bearing courses.

In summary, a blueprint would need to capture a process that allows intersectional flexibility but addresses the core aspirations of a curriculum, which is to answer questions of capability (What do you know? What can you do?) and strength (How well do you know? How far can you go?). This surely argues for a model that would guide and encourage users to develop detailed underpinnings in a narrow and precisely tailored set of specifications together with a comparison and standardization structure that would be married to the overarching universal descriptors.

The advent of an updated and expanded CEFR-CV has inevitably prompted a reconsideration of how the descriptors are used. Unsurprisingly, there are models which historically or otherwise are not only a rougher fit than might be desirable but which have often been created in a professional or commercial vacuum, making any standardization impossible. The result is that it has become very hard to compare learning communities. Now we have an opportunity to revisit how we suggest alignment or standardization can be operationalized but what is vital is that the issues evident in the current models are accommodated within this and not ignored as aberrant. Given the substantial differences of context and domain, the most prudent proposal might be to position any alignment at the overall scales in the CEFR and allow individual communities to elaborate the detail as best suits their learners' needs.

References

Arslan, A. and Özenici, S. (2017) A CEFR-based curriculum design for tertiary education level. *International Journal of Languages' Education & Teaching* 5 (3), 12–36.

Council of Europe (2001) *Common European Framework of Reference for Languages: Learning, Teaching, Assessment*. Cambridge: Cambridge University Press.

Council of Europe (2009) *Relating Language Examinations to the Common European Framework of Reference for Languages: Learning, Teaching, Assessment. A Manual*. Strasbourg: Council of Europe, Language Policy Division. https://rm.coe.int/CoERMPublicCommonSearchServices/DisplayDCTMContent?documentId=0900001680667a2d (accessed 9 November 2020).

Council of Europe (2020) *Common European Framework of Reference for Languages: Learning, Teaching, Assessment. Companion Volume*. Strasbourg: Council of Europe. https://rm.coe.int/common-european-framework-of-reference-for-languages-learning-teaching/16809ea0d4 (accessed 5 November 2020).

Kelly, A.V. (1999) *The Curriculum: Theory and Practice* (6th edn). London: Sage.

Micallef, A. (2016) Relating foreign language curricula to the CEFR in the Maltese context. European Centre for Modern Languages colloquium, Graz, 7 December 2016. https://www.youtube.com/watch?v=NyOWi_Ku1tA (accessed 22 November 2021).

Oates, T. (2014) Why textbooks count. A policy paper. Cambridge: Cambridge Assessment. https://www.cambridgeassessment.org.uk/Images/181744-why-textbooks-count-tim-oates.pdf (accessed 16 December 2020).

OECD (2018) *Curriculum Flexibility and Autonomy in Portugal – an OECD Review*. Paris: Directorate for Education and Skills, OECD. https://www.oecd.org/education/2030/Curriculum-Flexibility-and-Autonomy-in-Portugal-an-OECD-Review.pdf (accessed 9 November 2020).

Richards, J. (2013) Curriculum approaches in language teaching: Forward, central, and backward design. *RELC Journal* 44 (1), 5–33.

Schmidt, W. and Prawat, R.S. (2006) Curriculum coherence and national control of education: Issue or non-issue? *Journal of Curriculum Studies* 38 (6), 641–658.

Sherrington, T. (2020) The next edu-revolution*: Textbooks! Post on teacherhead, 20 April 2020. https://teacherhead.com/2020/04/20/the-next-edu-revolution-textbooks/ (accessed 9 November 2020).

Smith, M.K. (1996, 2000) Curriculum theory and practice. In *The Encyclopedia of Pedagogy and Informal Education*. http://www.fnbaldeo.com/EDCI%20547%20-%20March%202018/Resource%20Materials/Curriculum%20Theory%20and%20Practice.pdf (accessed 16 December 2020).

Üstünlüoğlu, E., Zazaoğlu, K.F.A., Keskin, M.N., Sarayköylü, B and Akdoğan, G. (2012) Developing a CEF based curriculum: A case study. *International Journal of Instruction* 5 (1), 115–128.

12 The CEFR *Companion Volume* and Mediation: An Assessment Perspective

Elif Kantarcıoğlu

The contribution of the CEFR to the field of assessment has increased considerably with the introduction of the Companion Volume. *The introduction of the mediation descriptors in particular has shed new light on the academic context and made assessment in academic contexts more meaningful. The new descriptors facilitate the test design process by helping to further define test specifications, marking schemes and feedback to test takers. However, they also come with some challenges. The complexity of mediation skills, for instance, has brought challenges to assessment and standard-setting practices in terms of construct definitions and learner feedback. It also brings about challenges for judges in aligning examinations to the CEFR, particularly due to the overlaps between interaction and mediation activities. This chapter aims to explore these issues surrounding the concept of mediation and how it is defined and presented in the* CEFR Companion Volume.

Introduction

The *Common European Framework of Reference for Languages: Learning, Teaching, Assessment* (CEFR; Council of Europe, 2001) has had a significant impact on language assessment since its publication in 2001. Many institutions have aligned their exams to the CEFR following the steps outlined in the manual for relating language examinations to the CEFR (Council of Europe, 2009), resulting in growing expertise in this area. The CEFR's contribution to the field of assessment has increased considerably with the publication of the *Companion Volume* (CEFR-CV; Council of Europe, 2020). New descriptors make it possible to further define levels such as C1, C2 and A1, where descriptors were either not available or insufficient in the 2001 publication. For instance, the 2001 version of the scale for Sustained Monologue: Putting a Case did not include any descriptors for C2, C1, A2 and A1, whereas the 2020 version has descriptors for C1 and A2. In addition, while the plus levels have been strengthened, some new scales have been added, e.g. for Online Interaction and for Phonological Control.

It is, however, the introduction of the mediation descriptors that has brought a new perspective to the assessment of integrated skills and enriched construct definitions of such tasks. The CEFR-CV has also brought new challenges for teachers and testers. In particular, the mediation descriptors, while adding great richness to the educational domain, raise a number of questions that need to be addressed. The 6th EALTA CEFR SIG held in Dublin in January 2018 explored many of these issues (Little, 2018). One challenge is operationalizing the mediation descriptors; another is deciding whether aspects of language should be specified for online interaction since it also involves digital literacy. These are just two examples. The CEFR-CV has so many illustrative descriptors that they need to be mediated to teachers, and research is needed to determine how teachers can establish mediation in the classroom. In addition, some of the descriptors are very long, so there is the danger that users will neglect parts of them, which might distort their meaning.

Despite the challenges they pose, the development of mediation descriptors has shed light on the educational – particularly the academic – domain. Activities and strategies characteristic of this domain have come into sharper focus: the CEFR-CV provides us with tools to clearly define academic skills and help us to gain an in-depth understanding of what assessing these skills entails. In this respect, the mediation descriptors allow us to define test specifications more fully, capture more detailed requirements in marking schemes, and provide more satisfactory learner profiles based on exam scores.

This chapter will first explore the concept of mediation and then consider some of the challenges it poses for assessment and alignment with the CEFR. It will conclude by trying to shed light on the distinctions among the four modes of communication as presented by the CEFR.

The Concept of Mediation in the CEFR

The CEFR introduces mediation as one of four modes of language use together with reception, production and interaction, and defines it as follows:

In both the receptive and productive modes, the written and/or oral activities of *mediation* make communication possible between persons who are unable, for whatever reason, to communicate with each other directly. Translation or interpretation, a paraphrase, summary or record, provides for a third party a (re)formulation of a source text to which this third party does not have direct access. Mediation language activities – (re)processing an existing text – occupy an important place in the normal linguistic functioning of our societies. (Council of Europe, 2001: 14)

This definition suggests that mediation activities are a matter of facilitating communication between two people (or groups) who cannot communicate with each other directly. Section 4.4.4 of the CEFR (Council of Europe, 2001: 87) emphasizes interpretation and translation, as the CEFR-CV acknowledges (Council of Europe, 2020: 34). The CEFR-CV expands the concept to embrace cultural, social and pedagogic mediation but still presents issues in terms of the parties involved. A close examination of how mediation activities are explained in the CEFR-CV shows the existence of a second or third party. Here are the key phrases in the CEFR-CV's relevant definitions:

'Mediating a text' involves passing on to another person the content of a text to which they do not have access ...

'Mediating concepts' refers to the process of facilitating access to knowledge and concepts for others ...

'Mediating communication' aims to facilitate understanding and shape successful communication between users/learners ...
(Council of Europe, 2020: 91)

The question that arises here is: What if there is no other party involved and one is mediating for oneself? In that case the text being mediated is one of the parties involved and the mediator is the other. Mediation activities do not all require a third party. Illustrative scales, such as Listening and Note-taking and Processing Text in Writing, are text-to-text activities and categorized under mediation. In the academic context, university students engage in such mediation activities to help them with their studies, not necessarily to convey meaning to somebody else. They listen to lectures and take notes for themselves for future use, which involves only two persons; the mediator and the recipient are the same person. Similarly, university students summarize articles for further study. The act of summarizing is also a text-to-text activity and hence regarded as mediation; the mediator here is also the recipient. This type of mediation would be categorized under 'linguistic mediation' with a focus on the individual and 'interior mediation' as explained by North and Piccardo (2016).

Another possible confusion arises from the CEFR-CV's definition of mediation:

The focus [of mediation] is on the role of language in processes like creating the space and conditions for communicating and/or learning, collaborating to construct new meaning, encouraging others to construct or understand new meaning, and passing on new information in an appropriate form. (Council of Europe, 2020: 90)

Based on this definition, 'construction of new meaning' seems to be the key element of any mediation activity. But the CEFR-CV defines interaction as 'two or more parties co-constructing discourse' (Council of Europe, 2020: 70), which makes one wonder whether there is an essential difference between interaction and mediation. This matter is clarified by Piccardo and her colleagues thus:

> Whereas production is concerned with self-expression, and interaction involves the joint construction of discourse to reach mutual understanding, mediation introduces an additional element: the construction of new meaning, in the sense of new understanding, new knowledge, new concepts. Mediation usually involves reception and production – and often interaction. However, in mediation, in contrast to production and interaction, language is not just a means of expression; it is primarily a vehicle to access the 'other', the new, the unknown – or to help other people to do so. (Piccardo et al., 2019: 20–21)

This definition clarifies the issue mentioned earlier about mediation activities taking place at the individual level when accessing 'the new, the unknown'. However, accessing such important information through different sources apart from the CEFR or the CEFR-CV presents practicality issues for users.

The question about the difference between mediation and interaction also applies to mediation and integrated skills. By definition, mediation requires integration of skills. This raises two questions. Does the CEFR-CV's emphasis on mediation mean that the concept of 'integrated skills', which is used commonly not only in assessment but also in teaching, has become redundant? Or is there a difference between 'mediation' and 'integrated skills'? By their nature, some speaking activities, such as goal-oriented cooperation, require integration of skills (listening and speaking in this case) and are categorized not under mediation but under interaction. Although 'integrated skills' in its traditional meaning differs from mediation, it will continue to be widely used in the field of language assessment for some time to come.

Another issue raised by the CEFR-CV's treatment of mediation concerns the concept of 'emotional intelligence'. According to the CEFR-CV, 'A person who engages in mediation activity needs to have a well-developed emotional intelligence, or an openness to develop it, in order to have sufficient empathy for the viewpoints and emotional states of other participants in the communicative situation' (Council of Europe, 2020: 91). Interpretation of scales becomes more challenging and complicated when descriptors include factors that are not usually considered part of language use.

The issues raised here will be further explored in the following sections in relation to assessment, standard setting, and aligning exams with the CEFR-CV.

Designing Assessment Tasks for Mediation

In designing assessment tasks, one needs to consider both the input text and the level of reception required as well as the level of processing and production (Bachman & Palmer, 1996; Brindley & Slayter, 2002; O'Sullivan, 2011). The CEFR-CV provides guidance on how the mediation descriptors should be interpreted, as mediation entails integration of reception and production:

> All the descriptors for mediating a text involve integrated skills, a mixture of reception and production. The focus is not on reception, for which CEFR scales already exist. The level at which descriptors are calibrated reflects the level of processing and production required. (Council of Europe, 2020: 250)

However, the interaction among the components of an assessment task poses a challenge to the assessment of mediation. For instance, designing an assessment task that targets Relaying Specific Information in Writing (Council of Europe, 2020: 94–95), such as the sample in Figure 12.1, would necessitate the use of relevant ideas from an input text in responding to a writing task, which is commonly known as 'reading-into-writing'. Such a task would also rely on two assumptions: that the test taker, or the reader, can comprehend the input text at a certain level and that they know how to write reports and essays for an audience, the recipient of the written text.

WRITING PART 1

In the following text, the writer refers to a concern regarding artificial intelligence. In your opinion, is this concern justified? Write a paragraph of approximately 150 words.

Clearly identify what the concern is and write to your lecturer what you think about it by referring to the relevant arguments in the text and expanding upon these arguments.

Your paragraph will be assessed on task completion, organization, grammar and vocabulary. Copying sentences or chunks from the text is not acceptable and will be penalized.

The concept of artificial intelligence is that computer systems can be used to perform tasks that would normally require a human. Broadly speaking, anything can be considered artificial intelligence if it involves a program doing something that we would normally think would rely on the intelligence of a human. There are plenty of statements being thrown around about artificial intelligence – from a threat to our jobs to a threat to the human race. So is this all exaggeration or are the fears actually based on some facts? ....

Figure 12.1 A sample PAE Writing Part 1 prompt

The following example (Figure 12.1), taken from the Bilkent University Proficiency in Academic English (PAE) exam, illustrates the challenge.

The task in Figure 12.1 requires test takers to do the following:

- Activity 1 – identify the concern raised by the author and its justifications
- Activity 2 – write in response to the task whether this is a valid concern by giving their opinions
- Activity 3 – support their opinions in writing with ideas from the input text

Activity 1 corresponds to the Reading for Information and Argument scale, Activity 2 is in line with the Writing Reports and Essays scale, while Activity 3 is a matter of Relaying Specific Information in Writing. Unless the learner/test taker can comprehend the input text and write reports and essays, they cannot process the text and complete a task like the one in Activity 3, which is described in the following B2 level descriptor: *Can relay in writing (in Language B) the relevant point(s) contained in an article (written in Language A) from an academic or professional journal* (Council of Europe, 2020: 94).

Figure 12.2 shows the interaction between the different aspects involved in this mediation task. Testers would need to refer to the Reading for Information and Argument scale (Council of Europe, 2001: 70; Council of Europe, 2020: 56–57) to define the parameters of the input text, then to the Writing Reports and Essays scale (Council of Europe, 2001: 62; Council of Europe, 2020: 68) to define the parameters of the expected output. They would then need to define the processes

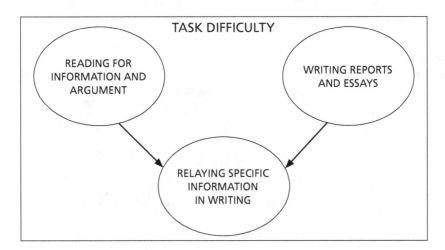

Figure 12.2 Assessing reading-into-writing / relaying specific information in writing

involved in completing the given mediation task. The interaction among all these three activities/skills or scales would determine task difficulty and the construct.

Looking at the sample mediation task provided in Figure 12.1 from the perspective of reporting scores and providing feedback, testers would find it difficult to identify which of the three activities described above a learner is struggling with and thereby failing to complete the mediation task. There may not be a performance problem in mediation (Relaying Specific Information in Writing), but one in comprehension (Reading for Information and Argument) or writing (Writing Reports and Essays). Teachers might be in a better position to point learners in the right direction because they would have the opportunity to go over the task with their students, identifying the areas that present problems and providing further practice opportunities.

The graphic representation of task difficulty in a sample mediation task (Figure 12.2), however, does not include the role of Language A and Language B as specified in the sample CEFR B2 level descriptor used above: *Can relay in writing (in Language B) the relevant point(s) contained in an article (written in Language A) from an academic or professional journal.* As far as the communicative activities involved are concerned, completion of a task in Language A and Language B may require similar communicative competence levels (Celce-Murcia *et al.*, 1995); however, they may impose different linguistic demands on the learner, which creates further challenges for testers in terms of construct. In addition, when exploring mediating communication, Leung and Jenkins (2020: 32) emphasize that 'it is impossible to think of assessing the quality of a speaker's use of Language A or Language B separately', and that 'it is the communicative effectiveness of their total mediation in the combination of whichever language(s) they select that constitutes the only factor which can be evaluated'. They conclude that the concept of mediation should be enriched by taking into consideration 'participant perception, values and practices in respect of discourse sensibilities, multilingualism and communication effectiveness' (Leung & Jenkins, 2020: 40). The idea surrounding communicative effectiveness as a result of a joint effort of the parties involved is relevant to mediating concepts and mediating communication, whereas it may not always be relevant to mediating a text since, as explained above, such mediation may not always take place among different parties but only at an individual level.

Another factor that influences mediation task difficulty is 'emotional intelligence'. As defined in the CEFR-CV (Council of Europe, 2020), 'emotional intelligence' seems to play a significant role in the success of mediation activities. This suggests that some mediation tasks measure far more than linguistic competence because emotional intelligence is commonly described as a 'predisposition' (Bocchino, 1999) or a 'personality trait' (Petrides, 2009). Like the complexity of integrating different scales or activities to determine task difficulty and define learner performance, the assumptions about 'emotional intelligence' in mediation raise issues to be resolved in the interest of 'developing, using and evaluating valid student grading procedures, and communicating assessment results to students' (Tsagari, 2018: 16). These are matters that threaten the construct validity of some, if not all, mediation tasks. If a learner's emotional intelligence interferes with their ability to complete a mediation task, the resulting performance score may be misleading and exam scores may be misinterpreted.

These issues present challenges for teachers as well as testers. Teachers play a key role in making assessment results meaningful for learners. They pinpoint learners' weak areas and help them to improve their language skills. However, the complexity of mediation tasks in terms of construct makes it difficult for teachers to determine the areas in which their students need remedial work. For instance, if we go back to the example of relaying specific information in writing, at the end of an assessment, looking at the results, teachers should be able to say whether learners struggle to understand the input text or have weaknesses in writing, or in fact lack mediation skills, i.e. relaying specific information in writing.

In many regards – the assumptions behind mediation, the competences involved in translanguaging, the difficulty of grading individual mediation performances given that mediation requires a joint effort – there is a need for empirical research to gain a better insight into mediation. Such research could include eye-tracking and stimulated-recall studies as well as think-aloud protocols and questionnaires investigating the cognitive processes taking place during the act of mediating. Findings would contribute to learning and teaching practices as well as to assessment.

Mediation and Aligning Examinations to the CEFR-CV

The manual for relating examinations to the CEFR (Council of Europe, 2009) proposes four stages in linking examinations to the CEFR: familiarization, specification, standardization and empirical validation. In the specification stage, the manual requires certain forms to be completed in order to support claims about an examination's link to the CEFR at specification level. Taken from the manual, Figure 12.3 shows the combination of skills that could be integrated in exams. It can be seen that spoken interaction or written interaction do not appear in these combinations. Such hints in the CEFR help us better understand the distinction between interaction and integrated skills, at least for assessment purposes. However, the CEFR itself is not clear about this distinction. In addition, the integrated skills combinations listed in Figure 12.3 are now categorized under mediation, which by definition, requires integration of skills.

A3.4   Integrated Skills

What combinations of skills occur in the examination subtests?
Indicate in Form A15 and then complete a copy of Form A16 for each combination

Integrated Skills Combinations		Subtest it occurs in
1 Listening and Note-taking	☐	
2 Listening and Spoken Production	☐	
3 Listening and Written Production	☐	
4 Reading and Note-taking	☐	
5 Reading and Spoken Production	☐	
6 Reading and Written Production	☐	
7 Listening and Reading, plus Note-taking	☐	
8 Listening and Reading, plus Spoken Production	☐	
9 Listening and Reading, plus Written Production	☐	

Form A15: Integrated Skills Combinations

Figure 12.3 Integrated skills form, taken from *Relating Language Examinations to the Common European Framework of Reference for Languages (CEFR). A Manual* (Council of Europe, 2009: 139)

The manual also suggests the use of the CEFR Content Analysis Grids (Council of Europe, 2009: 153–179) when mapping exams onto the CEFR scales. Grids exist for listening, reading, writing, and speaking; they 'offer the possibility to work at the more detailed level of individual test tasks, classifying them by standard criteria' (Council of Europe, 2009: 28). However, the grids not only let the CEFR down by not reflecting its approach to language learning: they also do not take account of interaction and, particularly, mediation. The grids are designed with a focus on skills, not on modes of communication. Although users of the manual have found the grids more effective than the specification forms (Council of Europe, 2009: 29) and they have served their purpose until now, they need to be revised to reflect the CEFR's approach to language learning, and grids for interaction and mediation need to be created.

The standardization stage involves choosing a standard setting method and implementing it to set cut scores on an exam in relation to the CEFR level(s). Standard setting is defined as 'the proper following of a prescribed, rational system of rules or procedures resulting in the assignment of a number to differentiate between two or more states or degrees of performance' (Cizek, 1993: 100), which results in the determination of a cut score. 'A cut score is simply the score that serves to classify the students whose score is below the cut score into one level and the students whose score is at or above the cut score into the next and higher level' (Bejar, 2008: 1). The cut scores set for an exam 'divide the distribution of examinees' test performances into two or more CEFR levels' (Council of Europe, 2009: 7).

In CEFR-based standard setting, if for instance the aim is to determine the cut score for a B2 level performance on an exam, a group of experts or judges examines items or sample performances at the relevant CEFR level (this procedure might change depending on the chosen standard-setting method). Following the related procedures, a cut score corresponding to the B2 level performance is calculated.

The complexity of the mediation activities and strategies defined in the CEFR-CV also poses new challenges for standard-setting practices. The standardization stage of aligning examinations to the CEFR requires a group of judges to use the descriptors in a scale that reflects the skills or competences measured by a task and to assign a level to individual items or performances. Although judges may be asked to refer to the relevant mediation scale when making decisions about the level of a task or the outputs, experience in aligning the Bilkent University PAE exam to the CEFR shows that they need all three scales – Relaying Specific Information in Writing, Reading for Information and Argument, Writing Reports and Essays, – to make solid decisions.

When certain mediation scales are closely examined in relation to some of the production scales, confusion in terms of categorization can be observed. For instance, in the Reports and Essays scale, categorized under production, mediation skills mainly from Relaying Specific Information in Writing, categorized under mediation, are referred to. The B1 descriptor in Reports and Essays states: *Can summarize, report and give their opinion about accumulated factual information on familiar routine and non-routine matters within their field with some confidence* (Council of Europe, 2020: 68). On the other hand, the B1 descriptor in Processing Text in Writing reads: *Can summarize in writing (in Language B) the main points made in straightforward, informational texts (in Language A) on subjects that are of personal or current interest, provided oral texts are clearly articulated* (Council of Europe, 2020: 101). While it is important to resolve the confusion over categorization, it should also be noted that summarizing as in the B1 and synthesizing as in the B2 descriptor of the Reports and Essays scale, are an integral part of writing reports and essays, particularly in an academic context.

As highlighted above, there is definitely a need to further investigate tasks that involve mediation and to carry out construct validation studies to clarify this type of task not only for testers and potential judges in alignment projects but also for teachers. The issues and challenges examined so far concern assessment and CEFR alignment projects. What follows is an attempt to clarify further these issues and offer some guidance.

An Attempt to Clarify the Distinctions among the Modes of Communication

In the preceding sections, some overlaps between the modes of communication have been discussed. The aim in pinpointing these overlaps is not to criticize the CEFR-CV but to point to areas that make it difficult for some users to understand the concept of mediation and how it differs from interaction or production, especially when they deal with scales such as Co-operating. Whereas there are inevitable and entirely natural overlaps among many linguistic features and modes of communication, such ambiguity seems to cause challenges for teachers and testers. The CEFR alignment projects carried out at Bilkent University English Language Preparatory Program involved teachers and testers in the alignment process in order to form a common understanding across the programme in relation to the level of the exams and what is required of students. As the project proceeded, testers and teachers came to the conclusion that users of the CEFR-CV should be open to the idea that there may not be clear-cut distinctions such as they would hope to find between mediation and the modes of communication or concepts such as integrated skills, between the modes of communication or concepts such as integrated skills, which users might start using interchangeably.

I have thus far attempted to highlight some of the challenges that users of the CEFR-CV, at least in my institution, have experienced with the mediation descriptors, in particular, and in linking exams with tasks that require mediation or interaction, partly due to the fact that crucial information to form a clear distinction must be derived from a number of documents. Table 12.1 may help to distinguish between production, interaction and mediation. Reception, though not presented as an issue in this chapter, is also included to provide a full picture.

As Table 12.1 shows, there seem to be three main features that help distinguish between the modes of communication: the number of social agents involved, the activities carried out, and the nature of the outcome. In terms of the number of social agents taking part in the different modes of communication, while there is a single person in reception and production, interaction requires at least two people and mediation one or more. To be more specific, mediating a text might take place at the level of the individual and mediating concepts and mediating communication requires at least two people. Reception and production are straightforward modes of communication as they encompass a single

Table 12.1 Clarification regarding distinctions among modes of communication

Modes of communication	Social agent(s) involved	Activity	Outcome
Reception	1 person	Reception	Comprehend a message
Production	1 person	Production	Communicate a message
Interaction	2 or more persons	Reception + production	Communicate a message
Mediation	1 or more persons	Reception + production + (frequently) interaction	Facilitate a message

activity. Interaction takes place as a result of two activities, namely reception and production. Mediation is similar to interaction in that it is generally a combination of reception and production activities, and frequently requires a third type of activity – interaction – to achieve the outcome. As regards the third feature distinguishing the modes of communication, the outcomes can be categorized as comprehending, communicating or facilitating a message.

It seems that the term 'integrated skills', which was discussed in comparison with mediation and interaction, has in fact become redundant. The integration of skills, covered through modes of communication in the CEFR, defines the very nature of mediation, and interaction in some cases, as presented in Table 12.1. However, in assessment terminology, I believe 'integrated skills' will continue to exist, at least for some time to come, until mediation is better understood and defined.

Conclusion

As it stands, the CEFR-CV has opened doors to a new enlightened world of languages, further defining concepts like mediation and plurilingualism and providing scales for these communicative activities. On the one hand, the CEFR-CV opens up new perspectives on the language classroom, the teacher's role and the test developer's task. On the other hand, it has brought about new challenges for all stakeholders that can only be overcome by mediating the CEFR-CV to others, revising the existing CEFR resource documents, and providing training to teachers, testers and curriculum designers. Specifically, the manual for relating examinations to the CEFR needs to be revised in accordance with the new information presented in the CEFR-CV. Content Analysis Grids, used by testers to define and relate tasks to the CEFR, should be modified to reflect modes of communication rather than the four skills. A grid for mediation could be designed, contributing to a common understanding of mediation. Further research should be carried out into the construct validation of mediation tasks, which would help to resolve the confusion over the categorization of activities into modes of communication. Institutions and individuals should be encouraged to collaborate more so that everyone can learn from one another, and there should be more forums to share experiences of how the CEFR and the CEFR-CV are used around the globe.

References

Bachman, L.F. and Palmer, A.S. (1996) *Language Testing in Practice*. Oxford: Oxford University Press.

Bejar, I.I. (2008) Standard setting: What is it? Why is it important? *R&D Connections* 7 (October 2008). Princeton, NJ: ETS Research and Development. https://www.ets.org/Media/Research/pdf/RD_Connections7.pdf (accessed 23 November 2020).

Bocchino, R. (1999) *Emotional Literacy: To Be a Different Kind of Smart*. Thousand Oaks, CA: Corwin.

Brindley, G. and Slayter, H. (2002) Exploring task difficulty in ESL listening assessment. *Language Testing* 19 (4), 369–394.

Celce-Murcia, M., Dörnyei, Z. and Thurrell, S. (1995) Communicative competence: A pedagogically motivated model with content specifications. *Issues in Applied Linguistics* 6 (2), 5–35.

Cizek, G.J. (1993) Reconsidering standards and criteria. *Journal of Educational Measurement* 30 (2), 93–106.

Council of Europe (2001) *Common European Framework of Reference for Languages: Learning, Teaching, Assessment*. Cambridge: Cambridge University Press.

Council of Europe (2009) *Relating Language Examinations to the Common European Framework of Reference for Languages: Learning, Teaching, Assessment (CEFR). A Manual*. Strasbourg: Council of Europe.

Council of Europe (2020) *Common European Framework of Reference for Languages: Learning, Teaching, Assessment. Companion Volume*. Strasbourg: Council of Europe.

Leung, C. and Jenkins, J. (2020) Mediating communication – ELF and flexible multilingualism perspectives on the Common European Framework of Reference for Languages. *Australian Journal of Applied Linguistics* 3 (1), 26–41.

Little, D. (ed.) (2018) *The CEFR Companion Volume with New Descriptors: Uses and Implications for Language Testing and Assessment*. Report on VIth EALTA CEFR SIG, Trinity College Dublin, 27 January. http://www.ealta.eu.org/events/Report%20on%20VIth%20EALTA%20CEFR%20SIG%20rev%2023.02.18.pdf (accessed 23 November 2020).

North, B. and Piccardo, E. (2016) Developing illustrative descriptors of aspects of mediation for the Common European Framework of Reference (CEFR): A Council of Europe Project. *Language Teaching* 49 (3), 455–459.

O'Sullivan, B. (2011) Language testing. In J. Simpson (ed.) *Routledge Handbook of Applied Linguistics* (pp. 259–273). Abingdon: Routledge.

Petrides, K.V. (2009) Psychometric properties of the trait emotional intelligence questionnaire (TEIQue). In C. Stough, D.H. Saklofske and J.D.A. Parker (eds) *Asssessing Emotional Intelligence* (pp. 85–102). Englewood Cliffs, NJ: Prentice Hall.

Piccardo, E., North, B. and Goodier, T. (2019) Broadening the scope of language education: Mediation, plurilingualism, and collaborative learning: The CEFR Companion Volume. *Journal of e-Learning and Knowledge Society* 15 (1), 17–36.

Tsagari, D. (2018) Situating mediation within the classroom. In D. Little (ed.) *The CEFR Companion Volume with New Descriptors: Uses and Implications for Language Testing and Assessment* (pp. 15–17). Report on VIth EALTA CEFR SIG, Trinity College Dublin, 27 January. European Association for Language Testing and Assessment. http://www.ealta.eu.org/events/Report%20on%20VIth%20EALTA%20CEFR%20SIG%20rev%2023.02.18.pdf (accessed 23 November 2020).

Part 5: Afterword

13 Making the CEFR Work: Considerations for a Future Roadmap

Barry O'Sullivan

Like other areas of education, language learning programmes have long suffered from the tendency to silo their components. Specialists in testing, specialists in curriculum development, teacher educators and textbook writers often fail to communicate with one another and may well not share the same philosophy of education or view of learning. This easily leads to systemic incoherence and failure. The solution is to view areas of education not as a series of disparate specializations but as a comprehensive learning system (O'Sullivan, 2020) in which all elements combine to set a platform for success. In this chapter, I will argue that the adoption of the comprehensive learning system approach and the underlying philosophy of language learning and use provided by the Common European Framework of Reference for Languages *(CEFR; Council of Europe, 2001) and its* Companion Volume *(CEFR-CV; Council of Europe, 2020) offer a unique opportunity for education policymakers around the world. Consideration of how this opportunity can be converted into practice will draw on the practical and theoretical considerations raised by the contributors to this volume.*

Introduction

In this afterword, I will consider many of the main points made in the chapters presented in this volume. I will do this within the context of a perspective on how learning systems should be developed, which I have referred to over the years as the comprehensive learning system (CLS). I will also reflect on the existence of two CEFR documents (the original CEFR from 2001 and the CEFR-CV from 2020), in addition to why I see the CEFR and its variants playing a central role in learning system development in the coming years. Before moving on to these points, however, it may first be useful to quickly review the concept of the CLS.

The Comprehensive Learning System

The comprehensive learning system (CLS) is a model designed to demonstrate to programme developers, policymakers and other key stakeholders the need to fully integrate the different elements that comprise the system. This integration can be summarized in the form of a triangle (see Figure 13.1; though this figure is taken from a very recent publication, I have been using it in presentations for more than 15 years). The three elements are considered with equal focus *ab initio*: in other words, we consider all aspects of the system as being connected from the very beginning of the development or programme reform project. The central argument for such a system is quite basic: if the different elements are not fully aligned, then the system is likely to fail.

There has, over the decades, been a general failure across the language profession (and I include all players here) to fully appreciate the systemic nature of programme design, development and implementation. While I have no real issue with individuals claiming a specific expertise (I see myself as a specialist in testing and assessment), I have always argued against the imposition of silos, with curriculum developers, materials developers, teacher educators, testers, and so on, all positioning themselves in what must seem to the non-initiated as a 'them and us' context of work.

Looking at the situation purely from an assessment perspective, I can only agree with the argument put forward by Norris (2006: 580) that 'without a system for integrating assessment into program practice, FL [foreign language] educators will continue to do assessment where they must, though few will come to understand the value of using it'. If we are prepared to see the learning context as an integrated system then we could simply replace the word assessment with any other relevant term – curriculum design, teaching, or materials development for example.

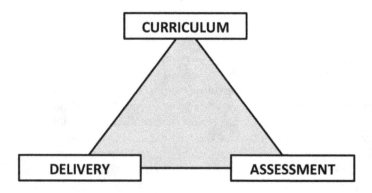

Figure 13.1 Modelling a comprehensive learning system (CLS) (O'Sullivan, 2020: 4)

The Comprehensive Learning System in Context

Comprehensive learning systems do not exist in a vacuum. Instead, they are clearly context-bound, so the idea of building a system without taking this context into consideration is equally clearly problematic. The context is situated within a specific educational and social background, which itself is defined by the stakeholder groups that comprise it. For the CLS to work, it must therefore *fit* with the educational and social philosophy of these stakeholder groups. Of course, this is unlikely to occur without some pre-determined actions from the developer or policymaker.

Figure 13.2 is informed by the work of O'Sullivan (2016) and Chalhoub-Deville and O'Sullivan (2020). It is based on a concept first devised to offer a perspective on test development and validation (the sociocognitive model) and suggests that a CLS can be viewed as an educational innovation the success of which should be evaluated (or validated) in much the same way as we would look at the appropriateness of interpretations of a test score when used in a particular context.

As stated above, the context-of-use refers to the educational and social context for which the CLS is to be developed. The consequences of introducing the CLS will be felt by those individuals who make up the main stakeholder groups. It is possible that an individual may legitimately claim membership of different groups (e.g. a teacher or policymaker who is also a parent), so the likelihood is they will be affected in a number of different ways. The theory of action that drives

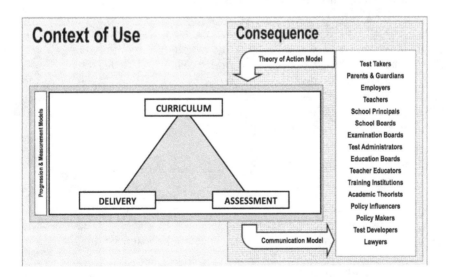

Figure 13.2 The CLS in context (based on Chalhoub-Deville & O'Sullivan, 2020)

the development and implementation of the system should itself be guided by the needs, expectations and hopes of the stakeholders. This is, in fact, a declaration of the intended outcomes of the introduction of the CLS: a public document (e.g. we may state that the innovation to the system will bring about a meaningful improvement in language learning). In addition, the theory of action sets out the pathway to the introduction and evaluation of the CLS.

The communication model refers to the plans set out by the team introducing the innovation to communicate with the different stakeholder groups throughout the process. Without this plan it is possible that there will be a communication breakdown during the development and implementation process that will threaten the perceptions of the whole project in the eyes of all or some stakeholders. Any such threat must be taken seriously as it could easily lead to the failure of the project. Lack of a communication model has led to the failure of innumerable educational innovation projects in the past.

With regard to the central section of the model, 'it is important to ensure that the theoretical approach to learning adopted by the developer has a sound empirical basis and is context-appropriate' (O'Sullivan, 2020: 4). The way in which the CEFR-CV has been conceptualized means that it offers the basis for the model of language progression that underpins the system. In addition, 'a sound empirical approach' demands that the system will be underpinned by a measurement model, which the CEFR-CV clearly is (see, for example, North & Piccardo, 2019; North & Schneider, 1998).

The core elements of the CLS itself are overviewed in Table 13.1, from which the most important messages to take away are:

- The system is dependent on having an operationalized model of language progression. Without this it cannot work effectively.
- The model selected must drive all three elements of the system.
- A full operationalization of the model is dependent on as complete and accurate an understanding of the learner as is possible, coupled with the astute selection of input for the tasks or activities to be included as part of the action-based approach.

Making a Comprehensive Learning System Work

As mentioned above, the educational philosophy underpinning the CLS must *fit* with the context of use and all elements must work together to form a symbiotic system, in which any decisions or changes around one element will have significant consequences across the model. In addition, the elements cannot be context-agnostic.

From the examples and comments in Table 13.1, it should be obvious that the starting point for any successful CLS will be to identify

Table 13.1 Operationalizing a CLS (broad outline) – Assessment System

CLS Element	Description
Curriculum	Clearly stated models of language progression and the action-oriented approach are adopted. Exactly how these are operationalized must be exemplified in the curriculum
Delivery	Teacher education
	Teaching – teachers are trained on the same underlying model; indicators of successful learning are clearly stated
	Materials – suitable input and tasks are set to encourage the learning and practice of appropriate language skills
	Physical – the physical space is suitable for the various activities proposed
Assessment	Input and tasks are suitable for the learning activities and for the learners and are based on the same language progression model as above
	Success is identifiable and accurately measured
	Score/grade is meaningful and of value

a comprehensive model of the target language. In an expanded version of Table 13.1, O'Sullivan (2020: 12–13) exemplifies this point with an example of the testing of reading comprehension. In that table, O'Sullivan refers to the Khalifa and Weir (2009) model of reading progression, which fits perfectly with the descriptors contained in the Processing Text scale from the CEFR.

Unfortunately, that scale has been so radically changed in the CEFR-CV that, in my opinion, its value to the developer is significantly reduced. In the original, the progression in terms of text complexity is very clear, and hence quite easy to operationalize in a set of classroom materials or tests (it was particularly useful when designing the Aptis reading test, for example). While the CEFR-CV version of the scale includes many of the original descriptors (see the elements printed in boldface in Table 13.2), I see two problems:

(1) The inclusion of additional descriptors that take an *action-oriented* rather than a *cognitive* perspective is likely to confuse the task developer (whether in a learning or assessment context).
(2) The change in the description of texts from 'demanding' to 'complex' at level B2 (marked by asterisks in Table 13.2). I see the former as relating to the writer in interaction with the text and the latter as relating to the text alone. That single word changes the focus of the descriptors.

It may be that the creators of the CEFR-CV believe that the decision to move towards a stronger action-oriented approach means that it is no longer appropriate to talk explicitly about reading progression from a purely cognitive perspective, and the replacing of the Processing Text scale may be a reflection of this position. However, from an

Table 13.2 Processing Text scales compared

	CEFR – Processing text (p. 96)	CEFR-CV – Processing text in writing (p. 99–101)
C2	**Can summarise information from different sources, reconstructing arguments and accounts in a coherent presentation of the overall result.**	Can explain in writing (in Language B) the way facts and arguments are presented in a text (in Language A), particularly when someone else's position is being reported, drawing attention to the writer's use of understatement, veiled criticism, irony, and sarcasm.
		Can summarise information from different sources, reconstructing arguments and accounts in a coherent presentation of the overall result.
C1	**Can summarise in writing long, demanding* texts.**	**Can summarise in writing** (in Language B) **long,** complex* **texts** (written in Language A), interpreting the content appropriately, provided that he/she can occasionally check the precise meaning of unusual, technical terms.
		Can summarise in writing a long and complex* **text** (in Language A) (e.g., academic or political analysis article, novel extract, editorial, literary review, report, or extract from a scientific book) for a specific audience, respecting the style and register of the original.
B2+/B2	**Can summarise** a wide range of factual and imaginative texts, commenting on and discussing contrasting points of view and the main themes.	**Can summarise** in writing (in Language B) the main content of well-structured but propositionally complex spoken and written texts (in Language A) on subjects within his/her fields of professional, academic and personal interest.
	Can summarise extracts from news items, interviews or documentaries containing opinions, argument and discussion.	Can compare, contrast and synthesise in writing (in Language B) the information and viewpoints contained in academic and professional publications (in Language A) in his/her fields of special interest.
	Can summarise the plot and sequences of events in a film or play.	Can explain in writing (in Language B) the viewpoint articulated in a complex text (in Language A), supporting inferences he/she makes with reference to specific information in the original.
		Can summarise in writing (in Language B) the main content of complex spoken and written texts (in Language A) on subjects related to his/her fields of interest and specialisation.
B1+/B1	Can collate short pieces of information from several sources and summarise them for somebody else.	Can summarise in writing (in Language B) the information and arguments contained in texts (in Language A) on subjects of general or personal interest.
	Can paraphrase short written passages in a simple fashion, using the original text wording and ordering	Can summarise in writing (in Language B) the main points made in straightforward informational spoken and written texts (in Language A) on subjects that are of personal or current interest, provided oral texts are clearly articulated.
		Can paraphrase short written passages in a simple fashion, using the original text wording and ordering.

(Continued)

Table 13.2 Processing Text scales compared (Continued)

	CEFR – Processing text (p. 96)	CEFR-CV – Processing text in writing (p. 99–101)
A2	**Can pick out and reproduce key words and phrases or short sentences from a short text within the learner's limited competence and experience.** **Can copy out short texts in printed or clearly hand-written format.**	Can list as a series of bullet points (in Language B) the relevant information contained in short simple texts (in Language A), provided that the texts concern concrete, familiar subjects and are written in simple everyday language. **Can pick out and reproduce key words and phrases or short sentences from a short text within the learner's limited competence and experience.** Can use simple language to render in (Language B) very short texts written in (Language A) on familiar and everyday themes that contain the highest frequency vocabulary; despite errors, the text remains comprehensible. **Can copy out short texts in printed or clearly hand-written format.**
A1	**Can copy out single words and short texts presented in standard printed format.**	Can, with the help of a dictionary, render in (Language B) simple phrases written in (Language A), but may not always select the appropriate meaning. **Can copy out single words and short texts presented in standard printed format.**
A0		No descriptors available

operational perspective, it seems to me that this presents materials and test developers with a real problem when it comes to devising a series of text-related activities for the emerging reader that are increasingly and systematically more difficult or complex. I would like to see the original Processing Text scale included in the CEFR-CV, with an additional set of scales covering the new descriptors.

Aside from the issue of changes across the two versions of the CEFR, it is clear that the concept of the CLS goes hand in hand with the philosophy that underpins the CEFR-CV. The advantage to using the CEFR as the driver for such a system is clear from the early chapters in this book. Unlike the ACTFL Proficiency Guidelines, which were designed purely with assessment in mind, the CEFR-CV was originally designed with all elements in mind, though it is interesting to see that North (Chapter 3) suggests that the CEFR-CV is primarily teaching and learning orientated. As we saw in her chapter, Malone (Chapter 2) reminds us that it is for this precise reason that it has been incredibly difficult to formulate a link (or crosswalk) between the ACTFL Proficiency Guidelines and the CEFR. It is entirely possible that the lack of flexibility in the former, necessitated by the requirement of the specific details required for test development and administration, means that its operational value across curriculum development and delivery is likely to be limited by the greater flexibility required of the system within these elements. After all, it is clearly unwise and impractical to build a system that does not allow for some significant localization across different use-contexts (countries, regions, schools, classrooms).

Why Learning Systems Fail

Educational reform initiatives fail for many different reasons. These are typically related to insufficient resourcing, planning or political will to see them through; see, for example, Lee and Lee (2016) who discuss the factors behind the failure of a major language testing programme in Korea. Initiatives also fail because they are not adequately thought through from a systems perspective. Failure to fully appreciate their systemic nature means that vital connections that underpin educational systems are often lost or ignored. One such connection, the link between the successful rollout of a curriculum and what happens in the classroom, has long been recognized. For example, Hargreaves (1994: 11) argues that 'the involvement of teachers in educational change is vital to its success, especially if the change is complex and is to affect many settings over long periods of time'. He goes on to suggest:

> if this involvement is to be meaningful and productive, it means more than teachers acquiring new knowledge of curriculum content or new techniques of teaching. Teachers are not just technical learners. They are social learners too. (Hargreaves, 1994: 11)

Hargreaves' position highlights both the importance of the teacher in interpreting and delivering the intended aims of the curriculum, and the recognition of the teacher as a dynamic learner – learning from their experiences and applying this learning to their classroom practice. Of course, this is not the only part of the system where the different elements need to be explicitly connected. Another example is highlighted by Graves (2008), who stresses:

> [the] need for teacher educators to work collaboratively with teachers to introduce innovation into the curriculum. Teacher educators have much to learn from teachers by spending time in their classrooms and teachers have much to learn from teacher educators by 'thinking together' about curriculum practice. (Graves, 2008: 176)

On reflection, the failure of the attempts to forge a link between the ACTFL Proficiency Guidelines and the CEFR referred to above reminds us that initiatives to introduce significant educational change that are based on changes to one part of the learning system alone tend to end in failure. In terms of the CEFR, an example of this comes from Little's introduction to Part 1, where he suggests that a likely reason for the failure of European Language Portfolio (ELP) to 'take root in Europe's education systems ... is the fact that the ELP was rarely part of an integrated and coherent reform of curricula, teaching/learning and assessment'. Of course, failure is not only due to this lack of strategic oversight (see, for example, Little, 2016: 166–167). We know from experience that change in educational systems is often slow and that rejection is common. Negishi (Chapter 1) points to the difficulty in establishing less focused-on elements of the CEFR (action-oriented approach, the social agency of language user/learners, plurilingualism and pluriculturalism, and mediation) in an education system dominated by what until recently has been a very dated approach to language testing.

My experience of working in an education faculty at a Japanese national university at the time of Hargreaves' (1994) observation reflects his message. The introduction by the Ministry of Education of a new curriculum that stressed communicating in English, was more or less totally ignored by the teaching community due to a lack of buy-in from the Ministry of Education itself (the 'course of study' didn't change), and from the major national examinations (the all-important University Entrance 'Centre' Test didn't change at all), teacher educators (student teachers were subjected to the same programme as usual), and materials developers (textbooks didn't change – not surprising as they were often written by teacher educators!).

Driving Standards and Practice

One of the great strengths of the CEFR project has been the recognition that the original and the CEFR-CV frameworks were not meant to be seen as a set of die-cast standards. Instead, it was always expected that they would be localized to fit with specific local needs. For many years now, test developers have addressed this feature of the CEFR in the way in which they identify elements of the CEFR to drive their test production or offer a post hoc rationalization for decisions made in the development of an existing test. Study of the chapters included in Martyniuk's (2010) edited volume of case studies involving the linking of tests to the CEFR attests to the varied quality of the claims made by these test developers.

The present volume reminds us of other ways in which the CEFR has been adapted for use in a particular context and for a specific purpose. Negishi (Chapter 1) describes the CEFR-J project, in which the original frameworks were reviewed and added to in terms of the subdivision of the A1 level in response to the reality of English language proficiency levels across Japan, where the vast majority of learners are to be found somewhere within this level. This project involved the development, scaling and validation of additional can-do descriptors that were locally appropriate to Japan's learning context. The success of the work undertaken by the CEFR-J team saw Negishi argue for the principled localization of the CEFR – a concept very much in line with the philosophy of the CEFR's developers.

The CEFR-CV explicitly sets out to refocus the application of the CEFR away from the area of assessment and on to those of curriculum and delivery as these terms are used within the CLS (CEFR-CV, 2020; North, Chapter 3, this volume). While I am very much in agreement with North that messaging around the application of the CEFR across the assessment world has dominated the past two decades, I do not believe that refocusing the CEFR-CV more towards teaching and learning will meet with a lot of success unless it is accompanied by a radical change in how policymakers and education professionals at all levels view the learning system. The concept of the learning system itself is, in my view, critical to the future adoption of all aspects of the CEFR-CV. I suggest this because I also agree with North that the CEFR-CV can offer theoretical and operationalizable support for curriculum, delivery and assessment.

However, it should not be forgotten that the proposal in the original CEFR for the categorization of the elements of language (reception, production, interaction and mediation) has largely fallen on deaf ears. Little (Introduction to Part 2), Levy and Figueras (Chapter 5) and de Jong (Chapter 4) all point to this rejection of the categorization. This is the case even within the language testing world, where there is no current example of the use of this categorization. This reluctance may be due to the traditional tendency of the whole industry towards caution and a reluctance to embrace change. However, it may also be due to the continuing fragmentation of the learning system into a whole series of siloed 'specialities'.

This suggests that, for the CEFR-CV to influence positive change, it must:

- be shown to be operationalized across all aspects of the education system. In other words, it must be shown to support a comprehensive learning system approach. This may simply mean that exemplifications of systems in which this has been successfully implemented are made freely available to key stakeholders. If these do not exist, then efforts should be made to implement and document such innovations;
- stress that those who intend to implement a CEFR-CV based learning system clearly think through the intended and potential unintended impact of the various decisions they make and set out a clear theory of action, or delivery plan, to ensure that the system itself is properly developed and evaluated;
- stress equally the need for these same people to apply an appropriate communication model to ensure that all relevant stakeholder groups are treated with the respect they deserve when it comes to the dissemination of information about the roll out and evaluation of the new system.

Ultimately, for any CEFR-CV based learning system to work there must be a realization at the classroom level that the categorization approach is appropriate and good for learners. For this to happen, the CEFR must be shown to be appropriate across all elements of the learning system. Hence the suggestion in this chapter that the CEFR-CV be incorporated as the basis for a true CLS, allowing it to fulfil the expectations of its original purpose (and title).

Some Observations

Plurilingualism

Despite the criticism of the concept of plurilingual communication (Leung, Chapter 6), we saw in Kirwan and Little (Chapter 9) the benefits of adopting a plurilingual action-oriented approach to learning in early years education. The approach clearly has a positive impact on the cognitive development of the children involved. However, the chapter also implies a need to reconsider how and what we formally test within a learning system. In the examples we see here there is no correct or incorrect output. Instead, we see confident children evidencing their creative and positive manipulation of proficiency in languages to communicate. An informal or formative assessment of learning is clearly appropriate here, while a more summative, judgemental approach is highly likely to undo any positive effects. On reflection, it seems to me that another important point should be stressed here. It is clear from the examples shared by Kirwan and Little that not all language learning takes place within the confines of the classroom. Learners don't necessarily switch off the 'learning' brain when they leave school, particularly when they have been given the freedom to think about and experiment with languages. There is clear evidence here that, given the stimulus provided by the particular adaptation of the plurilingual approach described by Kirwan and Little, they continue to adapt their formal learning to other learning – in this case languages, but quite possibly to other areas of learning as well.

It may well be that the application of the concept of plurilingualism is limited to the classroom and to the area of non-judgemental assessment. As de Jong points out (in Chapter 4), there does not appear to be an appetite for summative tests of plurilingualism. It may also be the case that this type of test is unlikely to emerge on a global or even regional level due to the interlanguaging nature of plurilingual communication. This suggests that local, more context-specific assessments of plurilingual competence are both more likely and more appropriate. Dendrinos (Chapter 7) exemplifies a local approach to plurilingual assessment that is context-specific. However, while the more traditional intralanguaging tasks were described in her chapter, we are left to wonder how the interlanguaging tasks might have looked.

Mediation

Both Lenz (Chapter 8) and Kantarcıoğlu (Chapter 12) point to the issues around the operationalization of mediation. While Lenz is quite sceptical of the scalability of mediation, in particular where learners are engaged in particular communication events (typically at a lower level), Kantarcıoğlu takes a different position. She points to the publication of the CEFR-CV as offering an invaluable broadening of our understanding of the constructs that underpin the CEFR and, through this, its application in our tests (and, I would expect, other CLS elements). She accepts that this brings challenges, both conceptual (in terms of how we operationalize the recently expanded descriptions) and practical (in terms of how we update the key documents that have, until now, supported the rolling out of the CEFR).

Localization

The very nature of the CEFR and CEFR-CV supports the concept of localization, and a number of chapters in this book offer concrete examples of localization of elements of the CEFR-CV in action. These include:

- the development of a test involving the evaluation of plurilingual competence in Greece, by Dendrinos (Chapter 7);
- the refining of the CEFR's vertical axis using 'local reference points' in Austria, by Berger (Chapter 10) – a solution also reported by Negishi in Chapter 1 in the context of the CEFR-J project;
- the operationalization of the mediation scales in a Turkish university context, by Kantarcıoğlu (Chapter 12).

The concept of localization is not actually referred to directly in the CEFR, at least by name. However, the implication of the uses of the framework have always been clear. The CEFR-CV was never meant to be interpreted literally and unquestioningly. In fact, the Council of Europe website related to the use of the CEFR at the time of writing this chapter (January 2021) included the following advice:

> There is a particular need for careful interpretation and adaptation when the CEFR's descriptive scheme and proficiency levels are for example used to explore the communicative needs of adult migrants and to guide the assessment of their proficiency in the language of their host community.

The two volumes

In his introduction to Part 1, Little warns against the rejection of the original CEFR in favour of the CEFR-CV as he sees this as potentially leading to users failing to take into account the human rights basis of the original – a reflection echoed by Negishi in Chapter 1. In this chapter,

I have noted an additional, perhaps more practical but nevertheless important consideration. The changes to the scales across the two CEFR volumes brings with it some significant issues for users. Examples of the changes I mean are:

- New scales (and descriptors) to be explored, understood and operationalized. This is not made easy in the CEFR-CV, where the new scales and the old scales cannot be distinguished.
- Changes to existing scales require first-hand research as no comparison of the CEFR and CEFR-CV currently exists. This may undermine trust in the CEFR-CV as it is time-consuming and the reasons for the changes may not always be transparent without research.
- Some scales have been either deleted or significantly changed, for example, the Processing Text scale mentioned earlier. It previously referred to the cognitive processing of text and how it changed over the levels, reflecting the Khalifa and Weir (2009) model. Now it primarily refers to interlanguaging and integration (reading or listening into writing or speaking).

This situation means that, for users who are fully familiar with the original CEFR, there is a significant amount of new learning required to get up to date with the various changes. For new users, and for the many current users who are less familiar with the background to the CEFR (i.e. in terms of its relationship to the Council of Europe human rights platform) and/or with the discussions in the CEFR around the concepts of plurilingualism, mediation and the action-oriented approach, the situation becomes even more complex. Clearly, a programme of education aimed directly at key stakeholders is critical to the ongoing adaptation of the CEFR-CV. This programme should reflect the knowledge gaps, of course, but unless the issue of having two volumes in circulation is adequately dealt with, any programme runs the risk that different individuals may be directed to different versions of the CEFR when searching online. Not an issue for the experienced user, perhaps, but clearly confusing for the novice or the uninitiated. When we also consider the fact that there are two different versions of the CEFR-CV available (Council of Europe 2018, 2020), which include slightly different descriptors and descriptor wording, the situation becomes even more confusing.

In Chapter 3 of this volume, North refers to a series of articles that will support those with an academic or policy-influencing interest in the CEFR-CV. While this should be seen as a positive development, the fact that there does not seem to be a similar focus on other key stakeholders (in particular teachers but also other non-expert users such as parents and school directors, for example) may mean that the relative failure of the CEFR to impact on curricular and classroom practice is set to continue. If the CEFR is to offer a meaningful basis for a CLS, then this issue must be targeted.

Final Words

The CEFR is not without its critics (see, for example, Figueras, 2012), and the same can already be said of the CEFR-CV. In this volume we have seen criticism of the concept of plurilingual communication (Leung, Chapter 6), the immense complexity of operationalizing mediation-in-context (Lenz, Chapter 8), and the danger of the unregulated inclusion of the vast array of descriptors in a curriculum (Dendrinos, Chapter 7), though it should be noted that it was never the intention for the CEFR or the CEFR-CV to be used in the ways described by Dendrinos. In fact, North is quite clear on the need for judicious and transparent selection of descriptors as a key stage in the application of the approach, a point also implied by Boyd (Chapter 11) when she argues for the development of a set of procedures for aligning curricula to the CEFR-CV that will gain support through being transparent and easily followed by non-expert stakeholders (though again I'd suggest that this should relate to all CLS elements).

In addition to the above, it is difficult to disagree with de Jong when he states (Chapter 4, this volume: 61):

> The CEFR-CV by itself does not represent a paradigm shift but, by offering the necessary and much called-for elaboration of descriptors for notions such as mediation and plurilingualism that were clearly signalled in the CEFR (2001), it enhances the paradigm shifting potential of the CEFR.

The closest thing to a paradigm shift in the CEFR-CV seems to be the refocusing away from assessment to other aspects of the learning system discussed above. I have suggested in this chapter that this shift is unlikely to be enough to guarantee adaptation in the future, arguing that for this to happen we need to view the CEFR-CV within the context of a comprehensive learning system. This is very much in line with the suggestion by Little (Introduction to Part 1) with regard to the relative failure of the European Language Portfolio referred to above.

Over the past two decades, the CEFR has had a significant influence in the area of language teaching, learning and assessment. It has offered stakeholders, both expert and non-expert, the means to communicate in a mutually intelligible way about language and how it is taught, learnt and assessed. The challenge now is to understand the role of the original CEFR in the context of the CEFR-CV and how the two can contribute to the creation of truly comprehensive learning systems. On the policy level, the situation is complicated by the failure of many decision makers to recognise the importance of alignment in whole system reform. The long-term impact of language educators working in silos, with myriad specialisms (curriculum development, materials writing, teacher education, language testing etc.) and associated agendas, only adds to the challenge. There is hope, however, when it comes to classroom practice, and here again I refer to Little, this time to his Introduction to Part 4. There, he describes how the CEFR-CV can facilitate constructive alignment by underpinning each stage of the learning system, from the curriculum document itself to how it is operationalised in the classroom, for example through directed teaching and learning activities. When combined with an expectation that teachers will align their assessment practices with these activities, we see a comprehensive learning system in the making.

References

Chalhoub-Deville, M. and O'Sullivan, B. (2020) *Validity: Theoretical Development and Integrated Arguments*. British Council Monograph Series. London: British Council and Equinox Publishing.

Council of Europe (2001) *Common European Framework of Reference for Languages: Learning, Teaching, Assessment*. Cambridge: Cambridge University Press.

Council of Europe (2018) *Common European Framework of Reference for Languages: Learning, Teaching, Assessment. Companion Volume*. Strasbourg: Council of Europe. https://rm.coe.int/cefr-companion-volume-with-new-descriptors-2018/1680787989 (accessed 28 January 2021).

Council of Europe (2020) *Common European Framework of Reference for Languages: Learning, Teaching, Assessment. Companion Volume*. Strasbourg: Council of Europe. https://book.coe.int/en/education-and-modern-languages/8150-common-european-framework-of-reference-for-languages-learning-teaching-assessment-companion-volume.html (accessed 2 December 2020).

Figueras, N. (2012) The impact of the CEFR. *ELT Journal* 66 (4), 477–485. https://doi.org/10.1093/elt/ccs037 (accessed 22 January 2021).

Graves, K. (2008) The language curriculum: A social contextual perspective. *Language Teaching* 41 (2), 147–181. https://doi.org/10.1017/S0261444807004867 (accessed 26 January 2021).

Hargreaves, A. (1994) *Changing Teachers, Changing Times: Teachers' Work and Culture in the Postmodern Age*. New York: Teachers College Press.

Khalifa, H. and Weir, C.J. (2009) *Examining Reading*. Cambridge: Cambridge University Press.

Lee, H. and Lee, K. (2016) An analysis of the failure(s) of South Korea's National English Ability Test. *Asia-Pacific Education Researcher* 25 (5–6), 827–834.

Little, D. (2016) The European Language Portfolio: Time for a fresh start? *International Online Journal of Education and Teaching* 3 (3), 162–172. http://iojet.org/index.php/IOJET/article/view/146/139 (accessed 26 January 2021).

Martyniuk, W. (ed.) (2010) *Aligning Tests with the CEFR: Reflections on Using the Council of Europe's Draft Manual*. Cambridge: Cambridge University Press.

Norris, J.M. (2006) The issue: The why (and how) of assessing student learning outcomes in college foreign language programs. *Modern Language Journal* 90 (4), 576–583.

North, B. and Schneider, G. (1998) Scaling descriptors for language proficiency scales. *Language Testing* 15 (2), 217–262.

North, B. and Piccardo, E. (2019) Developing new CEFR descriptor scales and expanding the existing ones: Constructs, approaches and methodologies. *Zeitschrift für Fremdsprachenforschung* (Special Issue: The Common European Framework of Reference, Illustrative Descriptors, Extended Version 2017, edited by J. Quetz and H. Rossa) 30 (2), 142–160.

O'Sullivan, B. (2016) Validity: What is it and who is it for? In Y.N. Leung (ed.) *Epoch Making in English Teaching and Learning: Evolution, Innovation, and Revolution* (pp. 157–175). Taipei: Crane Publishing Company.

O'Sullivan, B. (2020) *Comprehensive Learning Systems*. British Council Perspectives on English Language Education and Policy series. London: British Council. https://www.britishcouncil.org/sites/default/files/cls_bcps1_bos_30-09-2020_final.pdf (accessed 24 January 2021).

Index

CPSIA information can be obtained
at www.ICGtesting.com
Printed in the USA
JSHW021406110422
24809JS00004B/154